The discovery of Images
page 17

The kingston Page 62

W9-CBG-275

THE THEOLOGY OF ROMANTIC LOVE

THE
THEOLOGY
OF
ROMANTIC
LOVE

a study in the writings of
Charles Williams

MARY McDERMOTT SHIDELER

A romantic theologian does not mean one who is romantic about theology, but one who is theological about romance, one who considers the theological implications of those experiences which are called romantic.

—C. S. Lewis, ESSAYS PRESENTED TO CHARLES WILLIAMS, vi

HARPER & BROTHERS

Grateful acknowledgment is made to the following
for permission to quote from the works indicated:

A. Watkins, Inc.: Dorothy L. Sayers, *Introductory
Papers on Dante* (London: Methuen and Company, Ltd.,
1954), copyright © 1954 by Dorothy L. Sayers; and
Dorothy L. Sayers, *Further Papers on Dante* (London:
Methuen and Company, Ltd., 1957), copyright © 1957
by Dorothy L. Sayers.

The Macmillan Company: C. S. Lewis, *That Hideous
Strength* (New York: The Macmillan Company, 1946),
copyright 1946 by C. S. Lewis.

Library of Congress catalog card number: 62–7300

To
my mother
KATHARINE S. McDERMOTT
and
my husband
EMERSON W. SHIDELER

I thank God for you both

CONTENTS

PART III

The Co-Inherent Life

THE THEOLOGY OF ROMANTIC LOVE

CHARLES WALTER STANSBY WILLIAMS

Born September 20, 1886, in London, England.

Educated at St. Albans Abbey School, St. Albans Grammar School, and University College, London. Honorary M.A. (Oxon.), 1943.

Married Josephine Conway, whom he renamed Michal, in 1917. One son, Michael, born 1922.

Employed 1904–1908, New Connexion Publishing Office and Book Room; 1908–1945, the editorial staff of the Oxford University Press, Amen House, London.

Lectured at the City Literary Institute of the London Day Training College, the Balham Commercial Institute, the New Park Road Evening Institute, the British Institute of the University of Paris, Oxford University.

Author of approximately 40 books, and more than 200 shorter pieces. See Bibliography.

Died May 15, 1945, in Oxford.

INTRODUCTION

Bottom: . . . to say the truth, reason and love keep little company together now-a-days. The more the pity, that some honest neighbours will not make them friends.

—A MIDSUMMER NIGHT'S DREAM, III, i

Charles Williams' development of the theology of romantic love grew out of his discovery of the unexpected but precise analogy between the Christian doctrines which he had been taught since childhood, and the vivid personal experience of falling in love. He dedicated one of his theological studies to his wife, with the words "To Michal, by whom I began to study the doctrine of glory";[1] and a critic of his early work, in discussing the place Williams gave to romantic love, reported that "he was 'startled to find it' (the poet himself is quoted) 'an exact correlation and parallel of Christianity.' "[2]

Williams was not the first Christian romantic—Dante and Kierkegaard are among his great predecessors—but he stands alone for the lucidity and rigor with which he analyzed that position and traced its logical and practical implications. His pattern of thought and interpretation of the Christian faith can hold their own in the high places where the doctors debate these matters. His manner of presenting that pattern ranged from astute literary criticism and "a History of the Holy Spirit in the Church,"[3] to novels in which the most absorbing qualities of the adventure tale, the detective story, and science fiction are blended with tremendously exciting vistas of other worlds and of sanctity.

None of his work is widely known. But where it is read and discussed, it provokes reactions of such astonishing violence that no student of his work can avoid inquiring into the phenomenon. As Dorothy Sayers de-

1

scribed the situation, Williams' writing is "so individual as at a first encounter to disconcert, perplex, or even antagonise those on whom it did not, on the contrary, break as a sudden light to them that had sat in darkness."[4] This abrupt cleavage among his readers cannot be attributed to simple agreement or disagreement with his views, because along the axis between those poles is ample room for partial concurrence or for neutrality, and because among those who share his general position are many who reject his formulation of it.

Part of the answer certainly lies in his literary style, which annoys some people as heartily as it delights others. Part lies in his illustrative material, which sometimes gives offense—for example, his references to unfamiliar legends and to unpleasant subjects such as the uglier procedures of witchcraft. Further, he redefined important words like "romantic" and "love" and "good," which is legitimate but which has a tendency to confuse, if not to irritate, those who are wedded to other definitions.

C. S. Lewis specifies another source of difficulty in his comment that Williams

starts from the very depth of the romantic tradition and, without ceasing to be romantic, advances to the acceptance of all that is at first sight furthest from romanticism. In him the poetic tradition which had begun in Pantheism, antinomianism, and revolt, ends in Nicene theology, moral severity, and the celebration of order.[5]

We do not expect to find reason conjoined with romanticism; especially, we do not expect to find an extreme romantic insisting upon disciplined intellectual analysis of the romantic experience itself and of its implications. Consequently, we tend not to take that demand seriously, and find ourselves baffled by Williams' treatment of the subject.

Beyond these, however, lies another element of his presentation that has created more trouble than all the rest of the difficulties put together: Williams wrote in images, during a time when the art of comprehending imagery was almost unknown. As a result, those people to whom imagery is a natural process recognize instantly what he is saying, although they may well disagree with it, while non-imagists not only fail to grasp his meaning, but often are actively repelled by this confrontation with a type of mind that differs radically from their own.

Whether Williams himself realized the extent to which the use of imagery hindered the understanding of his work, I do not know. I think it probable that he did not, that like most of the rest of us, he universalized the style of thought that was completely self-evident to him. This ought not to be surprising: one learns of this variation in the very process of thinking only by prolonged intercourse with dissimilar minds, and few imagists are forced by circumstance to come to terms with those who employ other kinds of symbols, just as few non-imagists (let us anticipate and call them allegorists[6]) find themselves constantly in the company of imagists. Usually life permits each to immerse himself among the persons and within the fields of discourse where his natural predilections will be shared. For instance, a naturally strong allegorist is more likely to concentrate his studies upon the *Summa Theologica* than upon *Either-Or,* while the imagist will choose to examine the theology of Kierkegaard rather than that of Aquinas. In a very real sense, Aquinas and Kierkegaard use different languages—languages which differ not so much in their words as in their structures. One cannot follow the movement of Aquinas' argument without submitting to his logic, but one cannot follow Kierkegaard—or Dante or Wordsworth or Charles Williams—by limiting himself to the kind of logical thought which is a prerequisite for the study of Aquinas. And this is fundamentally not a matter of doctrine but of types of mind.

My writing about Williams started with the recognition of this divergence between minds, and with the conviction that his basic concepts can, and ought to be, translated into language that allegorists can easily grasp. But before proceeding further with this project, my own position needs to be stated. For the most part, I have found Williams' work neither difficult nor obscure, but clear and compelling. This does not mean that I claim a special revelation of his meaning, or a special authority in presenting it, but only that, in George Fox's phrase, he "speaks to my condition." My native bent is toward the Ways of Imagery, specifically the Way of the Rejection of Images, but my life has been intimately bound with dyed-in-the-wool allegorists, so that it has been necessary for me to learn allegory the hard—very hard—way. And I have learned also to respect it profoundly. The attempt to explain Williams' imagery to these allegorists, however, has involved so

many step-by-step demonstrations over such a long period of time that
the difference, even the opposition, of allegory and imagery has become, for me, unmistakably clear. There are, of course, individuals
who are more or less at ease in both processes, and a few who are
equally skilled in both. But the trend is readily observable, and the
extremes clash—or ostentatiously avoid each other—frequently enough
to intimate that the phrase "different points of view" sometimes refers
to a deeper division than is usually recognized.

Williams' imagery has created two kinds of problems. It has be-
wildered some of those who have read single books, and it has obscured
the fact that his entire work is undergirded by a complex, but ex-
ceptionally coherent, pattern of ideas. Beneath his images, his laughter,
and his passion lies a theological structure which is as astonishing for
its scope and consistency as for its originality, and which gives to his
separate books and ideas their enduring strength. The design may not
be immediately apparent, but it exists in his first sonnets and his unfinished saga of the Holy Grail, in the reviews that he wrote because he
needed the money and in the fiction which sprang from his exuberance
in living. Many of the concepts which make up this pattern are
familiar; a few are startling in their freshness; not one is esoteric. But
the manner in which he related those concepts with each other is
frequently obscure, and demonstration of the links among them may
require information gleaned from a number of sources. A question pro-
pounded in one book may be fully answered only in another, and the
steps in developing a chain of argument may be scattered among an
article, a novel, a biography, a theological study, a work of literary criticism, and two or three book reviews.[7]

Therefore, while Part I of this book deals with certain necessary
preliminaries—the method of imagery, and one of Williams' key images,
the figure of the young girl Beatrice whom Dante loved—the major
portion of the analysis is devoted to laying out the structure of his ideas,
stating it, so far as possible, in systematic form and propositional terms.
Part II presents Williams' formulation of the theology of romantic love
with respect to the Christian doctrines of man, sin, salvation, God, and
the world. Part III carries this systematic theology into its implications

for practical living; it is an exposition of Williams' system of personal and social ethics.

"Patterns are baleful things," Williams wrote with reference to his own work, "and more so because the irony of the universe has ensured that any pattern invented by man shall find an infinite number of facts to support it."[8] Yet intellectual patterns are necessary for ordering experience, and we create them whether we will or no. Facing that irony, we may apply to Williams' theology the words that he wrote of his other great love: "Poetry is a good game—let us take it lightly. But it is also 'liberty and power'—let us take it seriously."[9]

The warning against rigid clinging to our patterns needs to be supplemented by two others. Williams' thesis that romantic love and Christianity supplement each other does not imply a necessary interdependence between them, any more than between Christianity and politics, scholarship, art, business, or housekeeping. All such activities can be followed independently of the Christian orientation, or within it, and each has its proper techniques, standards, and goals that are profoundly not those of Christianity or of any other religion. However, non-Christian romanticism, and non-romantic Christianity, are other problems; for all their importance in their own right and for Williams, they cannot be dealt with here except in passing.

Nor does the juxtaposition of Christianity with romanticism prove anything about either. All that it does or can do is to clarify certain Christian doctrines that are sometimes considered unimportant, unintelligible, or merely stupid, and to place romantic love in a frame of reference that gives it dignity and meaning. But Christian romanticism does not establish any truth or verify any conclusions; it does not relieve its adherents from the duty of being perceptive, intelligent, and skeptical, nor from the need to make decisions about both Christianity and romanticism.

Finally, this study is an introduction to Charles Williams' principal themes, not a full analysis of his entire thought. In order to keep clear the main outlines of his theology, certain areas of his work have had to be omitted. Two of them, in particular, will be missed by those who are already familiar with his writings: his discussion of the nature and function of poetry, and his development of the relationships between the Way of the Affirmation of Images and the Way of the Rejection of Images. The former is not directly relevant here; the latter was omitted, after long consideration, on the ground that Williams' treatment of the Negative Way could not be adequately handled until the nature of the Affirmative Way was thoroughly understood. And his major contribution to the great stream of Christian thought was, I believe, in his exposition of the Affirmative Way.

First and last, I offer my gratitude to those to whom this book is dedicated, as much for their exacting criticisms as for their loving encouragement.

Second only to them in my gratitude is Mr. Raymond C. Goffin, who originally suggested that I write a study of Charles Williams' thought, and who has actively supported my project.

Many others also have given generously of their time and knowledge in reading the manuscript and in making invaluable suggestions. I cannot name them all here, but these few must be included: Anne Ridler; Dr. Joseph Sittler; Br. George Every, S.S.M.; Prof. C. S. Lewis; the Rt. Rev. Goodrich R. Fenner; Dr. Robert McAfee Brown; Maryal Stone Dale. My enduring thanks to each, individually.

A special word must go to Mrs. Charles Williams. Her graciousness, her swiftness in encouraging me, her warmth of response, have placed me deeply—and happily—in debt to her.

Anne Ridler, and through her Linden Huddlestone, enabled me to locate a great deal of material by Charles Williams which would have been exceedingly difficult to find without their help. The Bibliography owes much to their generous sharing of their research. I did not learn of the bibliographical triumphs of Prof. Lawrence R. Dawson, Jr., until too late to include in my Bibliography more than half a dozen items from his list of reviews by Charles Williams. I hope that he will soon publish in full the results of his labors.

Elizabeth Windsor, Reference Librarian at Iowa State University, and her staff, have worked miracles on my behalf. This book could not have been written without their wonderfully able, patient, and friendly help. I must add, too, that the Export Department of Blackwell's, in Oxford, has aided me immeasurably, in finding books and articles and in a dozen less direct ways.

The following publishers have granted me permission to quote from books and articles originally published by them; I acknowledge gladly their part in making this book possible:

The Canterbury Press, for a quotation from Williams' *Flecker of Dean Close*.

The Dacre Press: A. and C. Black Ltd., for quotations from Williams' *Religion and Love in Dante*.

The Dublin Review for material from Williams' articles "Blake and Wordsworth," "The Image of the City," "The Index of the Body," and a review of Middleton Murry's "The Betrayal of Christ by the Churches."

Edinburgh House, for quotations from *The House of the Octopus*, by Charles Williams, which they published.

James Clarke and Co., Ltd., for material from *The Way of Exchange* and *What the Cross Means to Me*.

Messrs. Longmans Green and Co. Ltd. London, for an extract from the Introduction by Charles Williams to *The Letters of Evelyn Underhill*.

The Macmillan Company, for a quotation from C. S. Lewis' *That Hideous Strength*, copyright 1946, and used with the permission of the Macmillan Company.

The Oxford University Press, for extensive quotations from Williams' *Divorce, The English Poetic Mind, Judgement at Chelmsford, Reason and Beauty in the Poetic Mind, The Region of the Summer Stars, Seed of Adam, Taliessin through Logres, Thomas Cranmer of Canterbury, Three Plays, Arthurian Torso* (with C. S. Lewis), and *Essays Presented to Charles Williams* (C. S. Lewis, ed.).

A quotation from Williams' "The Church Looks Forward" is reprinted by permission from *St. Martin's Review*.

Time and Tide has permitted me to quote from Charles Williams' "Church and State," "Dialogue on Hierarchy," "The Divine Realm,"

"Dr. Joad and Sin," "The Doctrine of Largesse," "The Free Act,"
"Men and Books," "St. Anselm's Rabbit," "St. John and Dr. Singer,"
and "The Theology of Crisis."

A. Watkins, Inc., for permission to quote from *Introductory Papers
on Dante,* © 1954 Dorothy L. Sayers, and from *Further Papers on
Dante,* © 1957 Dorothy L. Sayers.

David Higham Associates, London, and A. Watkins, Inc., have
granted me permission to quote from the following works of Charles
Williams: *All Hallows' Eve,* © 1945 Charles Williams; *Descent
Into Hell,* © 1937 Charles Williams; *The Descent of the Dove,* ©
1939 Charles Williams; *The Figure of Beatrice,* © 1943 Charles Williams; *The Forgiveness of Sins,* © 1950 Charles Williams; *The Greater
Trumps,* © 1950 Charles Williams; *He Came Down From Heaven,* ©
1938 Charles Williams; *The Place of the Lion,* © 1951 Charles Williams; *Shadows of Ecstacy,* © 1950 Charles Williams; *War in Heaven,*
© 1949 Charles Williams; *Witchcraft,* © 1941 Charles Williams.

Last, I again offer my gratitude to Mrs. Charles Williams for allowing me to quote from published material which is out of print or not
covered by publishers' copyrights.

PART I

The Imagery of Love

This also is Thou; neither is this Thou.
            —*The Descent of the Dove*, viii,
            and elsewhere

1
THE WAYS OF THE IMAGES

O Thou Mercy, is this the secret of Thy might?
When Thou showest Thyself, that Thou art not there
to be found? we find Thee where Thou art not shown.
. . . .
O Thou Mercy, is this the thing to know?
—SEED OF ADAM, 12

The theology of romantic love is grounded in the declaration that that which is loved romantically is, for the lover, an image of God. Therefore the nature and techniques of imagery must be made clear at the outset. And because images are special types of symbols, they must be distinguished from other types. The drawing of three boundary lines across the field of symbolism will provide the requisite background for understanding imagery as Charles Williams used that word. The first line separates arbitrary from natural symbols; the second divides natural symbols into allegories and images; and the third differentiates the principal ways of handling images: their affirmation, rejection, and perversion.

ARBITRARY AND NATURAL SYMBOLS

The difference between arbitrary and natural symbols can be quickly stated by means of one illustration. A horizontal line bisected by a vertical line thus, $+$, signifies in mathematics the process of addition. Nothing in the design corresponds to, or suggests, the operation of adding, but certain people have agreed to assign this meaning to this figure, and it is so for them. It is an arbitrary symbol.

However, these same two lines can be used as a natural symbol. They can be painted on a board and placed beside a highway to indicate a

11

crossroads. Here the intersection of the lines corresponds to the essential character of these roads at this place, i.e., they intersect, and, as Dorothy Sayers says, "that, precisely, is the distinctive mark of the natural symbol; it is itself an instance of what it symbolises; and therefore, by simply being what it is, it tells us something of the nature of that greater thing for which it stands."[1]

For the purposes of this study, arbitrary symbolism is not important except for its part in defining what natural symbols are not, and for emphasizing that always the natural symbol resembles its referent in some manner, close or remote. The $+$ is like the crossroads, and because a crossroads requires of the traveler a choice among directions, it is also like any point of decision. Thus Williams was using an easily recognized natural symbol when he wrote of one of his characters, "At the junction of roads, as at a junction of his mind, he stopped and waited."[2] On the other hand, none of these—the highway sign, the crossroads, or the decision—symbolizes naturally the process of steady development. For that other symbols would be appropriate: the mathematical sign $>$ meaning greater than, or the growth of a tree, or the rising of bread.

ALLEGORIES AND IMAGES

Natural symbols are divided into allegories and images on the basis of the ways in which the symbols are related to their respective referents. Taking allegory first, and following Williams' terminology, the allegorical symbol is "suggestively similar"[3] to its referent, or basis. In that masterpiece of allegory, *The Pilgrim's Progress,* despair is symbolized by a giant, doubt by a castle, and probably anyone who has been assailed by despair or trapped in doubt will agree that these figures are indeed suggestively similar to those states, although nobody—least of all Bunyan—pretends that this particular person and building have ever existed outside the narrative in which they appear.

The allegorist constructs his symbols in order to make his basic idea clearer or more engaging, and he can alter that symbol at will. He can make Giant Despair the proprietor of a cave instead of a castle. Or he can portray despair not as a giant but as a dragon or an angel, or even as a seductive woman. He already knows the nature of his referent, so he can picture it in any way that suits his convenience. It is the same process of construction as that used by the physicist when he builds a model of an atom out of wires and corks to demonstrate graphically the thing he is talking about, or draws a diagram, or works out an equation. And the physicist, like the storytelling allegorist, is perfectly free to change his symbols when he pleases or to abandon them when their usefulness ends.

In imagery, however, the symbol is not constructed but discovered. While the allegorist imagines a decision situation that will convey his precise meaning, the imagist begins with the actual world of his experience and finds that the persons, events, and things that confront him do in fact suggest meanings beyond themselves. He sees a man in Piccadilly Circus looking at street signs, obviously uncertain as to which way to go, and recognizes this as an example of decision; that is, it becomes for him an image of decision. Or like Dante, he falls in love and finds that his beloved reveals to him the very nature of love: she is his image of love. Or he realizes that the legend of the Holy Grail is for him an image of man's quest for salvation.

An imaging thing, person, or event exists independently of its imaging function. The gentleman in Piccadilly heads toward Waterloo Place, ignorant that in his quandary he has served to illustrate a general concept for a bystander. Whatever his immediate business, it can scarcely have been to provide this discussion with a pertinent instance. Similarly, no doubt Beatrice's personal life was influenced by Dante's love for her, in so far as she and others around her were aware of it, but there is no evidence to indicate that she recognized her position as an image for Dante. And the Grail legend exists as a good story, whether or not one imputes to it any factual basis or personal meaning at all. All images have their own existence and identity as individual things, and the imagist cannot change them without violating the integrity of the thing or of his method. An image exists in its own right, not for the sake of its referent, and not for the sake of the imagist.

The importance of the image's integrity is derived from its function as a means for discovering the character of its basis. The imagist does not know, or knows only partially, that thing to which the image refers, and the image itself is his key to the unknown. Therefore, he cannot modify the imaging thing, person, or event without destroying its usefulness as a key. For example, if the Grail story becomes for someone an image of a way to God, then any alteration in the story will change the meaning that it conveys to him. Anyone may, of course, retell the story, as Malory, Tennyson, Williams, and many others have done, to shape it more to his liking. But this process treats the legend as an allegory, a form for expressing what the redactor already knows or believes. To the degree that he changes it, it ceases to be an image for him—although his work may turn it into a more vital image for others. Both ways of handling the legend are valuable, and equally valuable, but they serve different purposes.

Williams gave the name "identity"[4] to the relationship between the image and its basis, intending two meanings of the word which must be separated in order that later they may be reunited with full comprehension of the implications that are involved. First: a thing has identity when it is itself and not some other thing. Second: two or more individual identities may be identical with each other in respect to some feature that they share. The + drawing consists of intersecting lines; roads also intersect; therefore the two separate and specific identities, + and crossroads, have identity with respect to intersection. In Williams' phrase, they are "categories of identity." This goes far beyond suggestive similarity, because the two identities are not merely like each other, but are partakers of the same nature. Being instances of the one reality "intersection," they are to a degree identical with it, and through it with each other.

The example of intersection was chosen for its simplicity, and will not carry the full weight of the concept of identity as Williams applied it. Most of the more subtle implications must wait for examination until complex images have been introduced, but two of them need to be mentioned here in order to forestall misunderstanding. (1) In all imagery, the differences between categories of identity are at least as important as the similarities. Lines are not roads, nor roads lines, and woe to the map reader who forgets it or who ignores the scale. The image is, but also it is not, identical with its basis, an ambivalence that generates both the strength and the weakness of the method. (2) Although any symbol's referent is greater than the symbol itself, the meaning of "greatness" will depend upon the particular case. Obviously, God himself is greater in power and significance than any image of him, but the basis "intersection" is greater than lines or roads only in the sense that it is more widely inclusive. It denotes a general concept under which a multitude of examples can be subsumed. Whether the convenient abstraction implies an archetypal reality is not at issue here: whatever way one resolves the ancient question of Platonic ideas does not affect the analysis or techniques of imagery.

The distinction between allegory and imagery goes far deeper than literary artifice. They do not have the same history,[5] nor the same philosophical presuppositions. Allegory assumes sufficient similarity between ideas and things that the ideas can be described in terms of things, but in the process of communicating these ideas—or of thinking—the allegorical symbols themselves have no significance apart from their function as illustrations. Always, in allegory, the symbol is introduced solely for the sake of its basis. The logician draws a circle on the blackboard to indicate a class of objects; the chemist devises a formula; Bunyan tells a story. But the logician is not talking about circles, nor the chemist about letters and numbers, nor Bunyan about dungeons and mountains and local fairs. However, until and unless man develops telepathy, the only way that ideas can be transmitted or preserved is by their transformation into pictures, models, words (most of which are arbitrary symbols), or other symbols.

So far as the allegorical method is concerned, it makes no difference whether arbitrary or natural symbols are employed. What is at stake is the movement of thought from general to particular—from ideas to symbols, from heaven to earth—which is always the same, and always opposite to the imaging movement from particular to general—image to idea, earth to heaven. Logical deduction and induction reflect these motions, but in miniature: they are instances and images of relationships that are more fundamental and more pervasive than purely intellectual operations.

The great virtue of allegory lies in its precision. Although no symbols can exactly reproduce their referents, they can be maneuvered so as to achieve a striking degree of accuracy. The discipline of philosophy provides a superlative case in point, by its consistent demand for precise

definitions, clear and objective propositions, and strict logical relationships. Neither the historical importance nor the enduring accomplishments of allegorical thought can easily be overstressed. It is one of the
great ways of intellectual and spiritual life.

In contrast with this acuity, imagery appears vague, erratic, and
apocryphal. And so it sometimes is, even in the hands of such masters
as Dante and Williams, because the imagist works from subjective
impression: "cedars and junipers suggested women to Lord Rochester
as naturally and inevitably as the fallen yew suggested religion to
Francis Thompson, or the storm-swept oak the grand scope of the
human heart to Wordsworth."[6] But to the allegorist, no tree suggests
anything at all. Trees are trees, conceivably useful as illustrations, but
not of themselves pointing to anything other or greater. The allegorist
may have been taught that the heavens declare the glory of God, so
when he gazes at the one he dutifully recalls the other, but so doing he
only echoes the conclusions of the method of imagery; he does not
use it.

It is a limitation for the allegorist not to use imagery, but it is not a
fault, just as it is a limitation but not a fault when a philosopher does
not also paint pictures, or a poet admits his incompetence as an engi-
neer. What is a fault is for the allegorist to succumb to the sins of
narrowness which threaten the glories of precision. One such sin is the
insistence upon the exclusive validity of his own way, the refusal to
allow the legitimacy and importance of what Wordsworth named "the
feeling intellect," and what Williams described as "the logic of the intellectual heart . . . of those terrifying syllogisms . . . which are as
much of the blood as of the brain."[7] To follow one's own way is one
thing; to exclude other ways as being inept or unproductive is another.

The imagist is not so much inclined to exclude the Way of Allegory
as he is to include allegory as a variant upon imagery. As might be expected, often his definitions and analyses are not precise enough. His
glory lies in the wealth of relationships that he discovers, and in his
passionate insistence upon including in his examination all the phenomena that reach his attention—emotions, evaluations, and impulses
as well as ideas and logical relationships. In imagery, Miss Sayers
writes,

there is simply the showing of a picture, or the telling of a story, in which the truth is shown in action, and the universal structure of reality is laid bare. Because it is an image, and not an argument, it speaks directly to the senses and the intuition of those to whom it is shown; and because it springs out of personal—if you like, out of existential—experience, it appeals to the personal and historical experience of men, and gathers into itself all the experience which they themselves are able to bring to it. And because it is rooted in the fleshly and the visible, it remains an expression of the *whole* of human experience: it does not encourage what is so often (rather tiresomely and unchristianly) called "a more spiritual attitude to life," but rather, one might say, calls for a much more living attitude to the spiritual.[8]

Imagery has its limits, and its critical danger of nebulousness; the next section will elaborate on these. But then, all ways are limited, all ways are dangerous, and all are difficult. Almost the only easement comes by recognizing the differences with sufficient clarity that we do not waste our energies nor distract our minds by applying to either allegory or imagery the processes and criticisms that are appropriate only for the other. The sign language of mathematics and the sign language of liturgy are both valid, but they have their own disciplines, techniques, potentialities, and restrictions, and no good comes from confusing them.

THE DISCOVERY OF IMAGES

The discovery of identities between images and their bases is the function of imagination. The limitation and definition of identities is the function of reason. So far as imagery is concerned, neither imagination nor reason has any power except in conjunction with the other.

Let us for the last time return to the extremely simple example of the figure $+$. As an arbitrary symbol, imagination has nothing whatsoever to do with it; one is told the significance and memorizes it. But when the $+$ is taken as a natural symbol, the active imagination discovers that it can have a multitude of bases, such as crossroads, decisions, the meetings of persons, minds, ideas, or cultures, the crossing of purposes, and so on indefinitely. Further, when certain historical data are available to the imagist, by imagination he can recognize the $+$ as a crude picture of a Roman instrument for executing criminals,

and thus it can become an image of torment and death, and beyond
that an image of a specific man who died on one of those crosses and
of the faith that bears his name.

The straightforward collection of many bases for a single image is an
elementary procedure in imagery. More advanced is the operation of
weaving intermediary relationships among the various categories of the
identity. Our friend in Piccadilly can be seen as imaging the crucifixion of Christ, because both have identity with decision. The Roman
cross carries the sense of the decisive meeting point of life and death.
The cross of Christ's crucifixion can be taken as an image of the cross-
purposes that led to that event, and that lead always to some form of
anguish. It suggests the separation, union, and again separation of the
two natures in Christ, and diagrams the identity-in-diversity of the
Incarnation with respect to time and eternity.

The technique of imagery is capable of producing a richness of
interplay among ideas such as is hardly possible with any other style of
thought. Three illustrations from Williams will exhibit this, the first
being from his biography of Sir Francis Bacon.

Nature treads her prints upon several subjects, and her footsteps are
not similitudes but identities. So the principles of nature correspond to
the rules of government; the practice of music to the habit of affection,
the delight of quavering music with the playing of light upon water;
commutative and distributing justice with arithmetical and geometrical
proportion.[9]

This is a startling concatenation of identities—nature and social organization, sound and light, justice and mathematics—but let us not
linger over the details; they will be filled in elsewhere. Here it is only
the general effect which is important.

The second example comes from Williams' Arthurian cycle of poems,
where he describes the unswerving devotion of the Princess Dindrane*
in following her religious vocation:

> The hazel of the cattle-goad, of the measuring-rod,
> of the slaves' discipline, of Logres' highway, of Merlin's
> wand of magic, of her lord's line of verse,

* The pronunciation of Dindrane, and of other unfamiliar names from the
Arthurian legend, will be found in the Index.

of the octave of song, of the footpace under the altar,
straight and strong, was in Dindrane's bare arm,
fair measure in the body of the body's deeds.[10]

All these images, from the hazel bush to Dindrane's physical journey to the convent ("the body's deeds"), are categories of an identity which may, for convenience, be called straightness. All contain a quality of directness in line or in movement, and an implicit refusal of delay or deviation. By bringing these images together, Williams not only strengthens the mood of purposefulness in the poem, but also conveys the idea of a universal pattern of interrelationships, presents evidence for it, and evaluates it—in six lines. The novice in imagery probably will not comprehend all this at first glance: this is the subtlety and profundity of a genius with imagery when he was at the height of his powers. But the pattern is there.

Third, the multiplicity of possible relationships in imagery enables the skilled imagist to work with several referents at once, without repetition or confusion. From Williams' novel *Many Dimensions* comes an especially vivid instance of this, the image being the stone from King Solomon's crown which was "the First Matter . . . from which all things are made,"[11] and which—among other powers—gave its possessor the ability to move at will from one place or time to another. There is no doubt but that the Stone is intended as an image; it is less clear what the image is supposed to signify. No "right answer" can be established, because the Stone properly communicates different meanings to different readers, and also because it refers simultaneously to several levels of meaning. Five of these can be differentiated briefly to suggest the potential scope of this image, and to demonstrate the effect of each interpretation upon the understanding of the novel as a whole. (1) The first reading of the image contains and is the medium of expression for all the others: taking the figure literally, the Stone is a magical talisman, and the story consists of a gripping adventure tale based on the conflicts among a number of persons who want exclusive possession of it. (2) Since the Stone is by definition "first matter," it images the entire material universe, and the problem of the novel becomes: what happens when man relates himself to the physical world in various ways? (3) Another referent for the Stone is suggested by a remark that Williams makes in a different context, where he refers to money as "not so much gold or even riches but, the medium of man's relation to man, the material symbol of the world's activities, the 'first matter' containing the flow and ebb of created things."[12] How, then, ought money to be acquired and spent? (4) Because the Stone possesses powers, it likewise images all energies of matter, spirit, and God, and raises all the questions involved in the use and misuse of power. (5) The Stone, being an image, is an example of imagery and its possibilities. This identification opens into the depths of spiritual life and knowledge, and on this basis the book explores the ways in which man can use imagery to relate himself to uttermost realities, and the kinds of life and death to which these ways lead.

THE DISCIPLINE OF IMAGERY

As these examples from Williams' biography, poetry, and fiction indicate, the multiplication of meanings for an image can spread so widely and in so many directions at once as to raise serious problems for the interpreter. How can interpretation of an image be disciplined? Which, and how many, of the possible interpretations does the imagist intend? How can it be determined whether the reader's interpretation is consonant with the nature of the image itself and with the author's intention? What are the standards by which one can distinguish the proper use of images from the far-fetched elaborations of an imagination gone wild?

The answer is: by intelligence, reason, under any name the faculty of the mind which discriminates and questions and orders and defines, which rejects contradictions, demands evidence, examines assumptions, and tests implications. Williams named accuracy as the norm of reason, meaning a rigorous intellectual precision of such significance in his theology that he wrote of accuracy as "the first law of the spiritual life,"[13] and, in a remarkable pair of statements, declared that "hell is always inaccurate,"[14] and "heaven is always exact."[15]

Reason, applied to the problem of interpreting images, attends first to the definition of imagery: an image exists in its own right; it points to something greater than itself; and it represents in itself that great-

ness to which it refers.[16] The last of these points provides the first major
check upon aberration: any image has some intrinsic limits, since it is
its own proper nature that represents the greater thing to which it
refers. Thus, the Stone can image nature, but it cannot image the City
of God; it can image power but not complexity. One can conceivably
take it as an image for substitution, but imagination (mine, at least)
refuses to identify it even remotely with purposeful action.

A second technique for controlling interpretation makes use of the
frame of reference within which the image and its basis occur. It is
reasonable to expect that a particular author's images will be consistent
with the pattern of thought manifested in the respective books where
they appear, and probably with the wider context of his basic philosophy as revealed in his entire body of work. If an interpretation for
a given image appears to be consonant with, and to illuminate, the
whole of a man's writings, while intensifying its detailed consistency, it
is probably sound. This leaves a good deal of latitude for further
interpretation and for contradictory judgments,[17] but part of the value
of imagery lies precisely in the flexibility that reason disciplines but
never destroys.

Third, reason studies with meticulous care the differences between
images and their referents. In "The Sister of Percivale," the king's poet
Taliessin watches a slave girl at work and sees the City of God in her
eyes: "The horizon in her eyes was breaking with distant Byzantium."[18]
He discovers an identity. But he most emphatically does not confuse
the image "eyes" with its basis "Byzantium," nor suppose that the
whole is comprehended fully in any of its parts, nor leap into the mind-
lessness of believing that the image is, without qualification, the referent.
Eyes and Byzantium are two very different things, and the difference
is necessary to the imaging function. It is possible for the image to
point beyond itself only because it is distinct from that to which it
points. It can serve as a representative only because it is separate from
that which it represents.

This fact creates an ambivalence in the nature and operation of
images. They are identical with, and different from, their bases, and
they at once reveal and conceal their bases. Williams' epigram, "This
also is Thou; neither is this Thou,"[19] while referring specifically to

images of God, is equally pertinent to all images without exception. The identities reveal and the differences conceal the greater things. Thus, the hurricane reveals God's power in nature, while it conceals his power in the still small voice. Or, the mildness of an April day that speaks of his loving care, hides the majesty of his judgment. More subtly, the identities themselves sometimes conceal the basis, and the differences bring revelation. The very exquisiteness of the spring morning that images the freshness of life in God may by its immediacy persuade one to forget its source in him. The passionate embraces that are categories of identity with immutable charity can deflect lovers from that nobler end. So also, the mathematical norm of straightness is demonstrated in the failure of any actual straight edge to fulfill that specification, and man's finiteness provides one of his few ways for apprehending infinity.

Reason's principal task with images is to clarify these identities and differences, and to maintain the precarious balance between "is" and "is not." Without this clarification, fact and meaning alike are abandoned, and thought disintegrates into a maundering among slipshod impressions. Soaring flights of fancy do not by themselves constitute imagery. Honesty and sincerity are no more adequate substitutes for intellect in poetry, theology, and worship than in mathematics. An honest mistake remains a mistake, and no degree of sincere good will, by itself, can redeem imprecision. Ignorance, which is the absence of accuracy, wreaks as much havoc as intellectual error resulting from inaccuracy, and where either prevails, imagination and reason perish together.

Yet even in the full flower of their disciplined interaction, reason and imagination cannot produce the certainty of truth, but only a reasonable probability. The limitation that is intrinsic to all finite things precludes complete intellectual finality, and the very abundance of the alternatives supplied by imagination makes it an unstable foundation for any claim of inerrancy. The well-known arguments do not need to be labored: the fallibility of the senses, the inevitable weighting of evidence, the gross uncertainty of the relationships between things and ideas about those things, all building up to the proof—as if proof were needed—that man is not omniscient. He cannot attain absolute truth at all, except within certain restricted frames of reference where principles are related to each other according to prearranged rules, as in various geometrical systems or in fictional worlds. So far as "knowing reality" is concerned, man may acquire a pleasant feeling of certitude, but this is all, and recognition of the fundamental unreliability of all human knowledge probably represents the nearest that he can come to absolute certainty of truth.

Although at best finite man can attain only approximations to ultimate reality and truth, beyond question some approximations are closer to reality than others. Ideas are no more equal in accuracy than they are identical in content. Some degree of knowledge is possible: we know in part, we see if only through a glass darkly. To deny this is to reject even the remote possibility of thought and to give ourselves to chaos. "The split in our brain, as Siger of Brabant is said to have felt, is very deep. That does not do away with our duty to our brain,"[20] either in its reasoning or its imaging capacity.

Faced with this uncertainty, some take to the quicksand of apathy. "If I cannot be certain, then what is the use of thinking or believing anything?"—which is an evasive way of saying, "Since I cannot be God, I refuse to be man." Others, desperate for the security of a rock to stand upon, resort to unreasonable but comforting dicta such as "This is self-evident . . . this was revealed . . . this can be proved." The assurance thus acquired, however, is illusory. "It is the old trouble which the wise Greek had seen so long ago: 'Give me an inch of earth to stand on and I will move the world.' But there is no inch of earth; there never has been; there never . . . can be."[21]

According to Williams, the only feasible alternative is to walk upon the water, or better, to run thereon. Man does not and cannot know reality finally and absolutely; therefore it is his duty, and may become his abiding joy, to be skeptical, to develop "the delicate incredulity which is the proper decency of the mind."[22] The skeptic (in this sense) grounds himself in the affirmation of uncertainty, and in the grand affirmation that things may or may not be what they appear to be, but that even an appearance has validity, if only as an appearance. In Williams' novel *Shadows of Ecstasy*, one of the characters meditates upon romantic love:

A thing that seemed had at least the truth of its seeming. Sir Bernard's mind refused to allow it more but it also refused to allow it less. It was for each man to determine how urgent the truth of each seeming was. . . . A thing might not be true because it appeared so to him, but it was no less likely to be true because everyone else denied it. The eyes of Rosamond might or might not hold the secret origin of day and night, but if they apparently did then they apparently did, and it would be silly to deny it and equally silly not to relish it.[23]

Williams here defines his own basic doctrine of knowledge, repudiating credulity and incredulity alike, and substituting for both the deliberate and joyous skepticism that "neither denies nor conceals; neither fears nor flies. It desires only accuracy; 'look, look; attend.' "[24] He wrote this of true romanticism; it is quoted here because it is the skepticism of the romantic which protects him from its perversions, and from "the last illusion of reason, that because man must desire and must even know the universe to be reasonable, therefore it is reasonable."[25]

There is obdurate irony in the fact that man desperately needs truth, and that his very humanity should cut him off from any such possibility. But in Williams, this is a "defeated irony," an "excellent absurdity," a source and occasion for joy, and the ground for any adequate faith. He built his theology—and from the reports, he lived—with the solemn delight of a child balancing along a curbing. Everything depends on it; nothing depends on it. "This also is Thou; neither is this Thou." Therefore rejoice.

THE AFFIRMATION, REJECTION, AND PERVERSION OF IMAGES

The precision that requires a tension between "This also is Thou" and "neither is this Thou" does not compel equal emphasis upon them. It does specify that neither shall completely exclude the other. In practice, most of those who use imagery tend to stress either the revealing or the concealing functions of the image: they find themselves in a world where nature and art and events and other persons do point beyond themselves to greater things, or they naturally feel themselves impelled to push aside these phenomena in their desire for a more direct knowledge. Williams named these the Way of the Affirmation of

Images, which accents the phrase "This also is Thou," and the Way of
the Rejection, or Negation, of Images, which accents the complementary "neither is this Thou."

Most of the notable expositions of these ways have come out of the
arguments and experiences where the basis in question was God. This
is the classic and extreme problem in imagery, because God—if he
exists at all—seems not to be directly knowable except in some forms
of the mystical vision. Therefore the indirect ways of knowing God by
means of images, either in their affirmation or in their rejection, become vitally significant.

Historically, the Way of Rejection has received more attention than
the Affirmative Way, partly no doubt because of its dramatic contrast
with ordinary life, and partly because its followers have usually described their position in specifically theological terms. Its themes reverberate in the mystics—Dionysius the Areopagite, St. Teresa of
Ávila, St. John of the Cross, *The Cloud of Unknowing,* and elsewhere:
the flesh hinders the spirit; sensed beauty hides ultimate beauty; human
love veils the divine love. All images, even the holiest, conceal God,
not because they are evil but because they are finite. Reason and imagination, as well as sensation, hamper "the flight of the alone to the
Alone." So Williams' character Richardson, the bookseller's assistant,

read in those books of the many ways which are always the Way. But
not by books or by phrases, not by images or symbols or myths, did he
himself follow it. He abstracted himself continually from sense and
from thought, attempting always a return to an interior nothingness
where that which is itself no thing might communicate its sole essential being.[26]

The Way of Rejection of Images makes way for the One who, in some
place or state or mode of being, is in Himself: unimaged, absolute, and
wholly other.

The Negative Way of the mystics is fulfilled and corrected by the
Affirmative Way, which is that of romanticism. To its adherents, the
heavens indeed declare the glory of God, and the firmament shows
clearly that it is his handiwork. They witness that he discloses himself
in all things. Human love manifests divine love; particular beauties
exhibit ultimate beauty; spirit requires flesh for its completion—they

are categories of one identity. Many, perhaps most, people require these affirmations for their spiritual and intellectual growth, although, as Miss Sayers writes,

it is essentially the way of the artist and the poet—of all those to whom the rejection of images would be the rejection of their very means to intellectual and emotional experience; and it would seem to follow from this that the great Masters of the Affirmative Way will tend to be secular, and that they will be more concerned to record their experience than to analyse it in the manner of the regular theologian.[27]

Even so, the Affirmative Way has sometimes been treated as merely a concession to human frailty, a second-best method provided for those who are incapable of the Way of Rejection or unwilling to accept its requirements. This Williams explicitly denies.

It is not to be rashly assumed that the Way of Affirmation is much easier than the Way of Rejection. To affirm the validity of an image one does not at the moment happen to like or want—such as that of one's next door neighbour—is as harsh as to reject an image—such as oneself as successful—which one does happen to like and want.[28]

The disciplines of poetry are as high and as demanding as those of asceticism; the affirmation of the body in marriage can be as laborious as its rejection in celibacy.

This equivalence of effort is further emphasized by the need for each way to include some portion of the other.

Neither of these two Ways indeed is, or can be, exclusive. The most vigorous ascetic, being forbidden formally to hasten his death, is bound to attend to the actualities of food, drink, and sleep which are also images, however brief his attention may be. The most indulgent of Christians is yet bound to hold his most cherished images—of food, drink, sleep, or anything else—negligible beside the final Image of God. And both are compelled to hold their particular Images of God negligible beside the universal Image of God which belongs to the Church, and even that less than the unimaged reality.[29]

This point is more important than may be immediately evident. The statement "neither is this Thou" has no meaning unless "this" has content: the Way of Negation is built upon the prior affirmation that there exists something to be rejected, and it seeks an affirmative culmination, the very presence of Very God. Conversely, the Affirmative Way is grounded in the rejection of complete identity between image and basis, and presses toward the God who, being beyond all imagery, is in the strict sense unimaginable. Each way requires for its very existence some element both of the conviction that is the mitre of Affirmation, and of the skepticism that is the crown of Rejection. Their functions differ, but their life is one.

The one Way was to affirm all things orderly until the universe throbbed with vitality; the other to reject all things until there was nothing anywhere but He. The Way of Affirmation was to develop great art and romantic love and marriage and philosophy and social justice; the Way of Rejection was to break out continually in the profound mystical documents of the soul, the records of the great psychological masters of Christendom.[30]

The choice between the Ways, the manner of choosing, and the kind of balance to be maintained between them, is an intensely personal business that cannot be regulated by another person, or possibly even by oneself. It does not matter very much, so long as they are held together. But it is not altogether easy to unite them. The perversions of both Ways are more comfortably sustained than the tension which imagery demands, and which the Christian faith traditionally has required.

Williams traced the multiform perversions of imagery back to a single root: the failure of reason. "The circles of hell contain what is left of the images after the good of intellect has been deliberately drawn away."[31] The most obvious loss of intellect occurs where images are split off from their bases: (1) by abandoning the basis entirely and concentrating upon the image, which is idolatry and leads to the sterile serenities of materialism; or (2) by denying that the imaging thing exists in any authentic sense, until the things which seem are refused even the truth of their seeming, and this becomes gnosticism or docetism; or (3) by identifying the image wholly with its basis, which turns into pantheism. An imbalance of imagination, reason, and skepticism can produce sentimentality, fanaticism, intellectual apathy, or "the surrender of intellect to the disordered sensualism of the moment."[32] Less obvious are the corruptions produced by denying to the image its proper integrity, notably when an imagist insists upon seeing in the image what he wishes to see, and desires to prevent it from changing when and if its proper life produces alteration in it. These all will be examined in succeeding chapters, in terms of Williams' doctrine of the nature of man. For the moment it is enough to indicate the source of the perversions of imagery in the failure of intellect.

One final point, and the preliminaries will be finished. As the Way of Affirmation and the Way of Rejection supplement each other, so the Way of Allegory supplements the Ways of the Images. Dante's *Comedy*, and Williams' poetry and novels, are allegories, written to convey ideas, but the ideas in question were discovered by means of images and are presented in images. The ascent from image to basis, and the descent from idea to allegorical symbol, are not mutually exclusive, but complementary. Thought includes many operations, and "on that golden ladder of exchange the angels of joy run ceaselessly up and down; would you deny them any of their heavenly occasions of movement?"[33] This book is primarily concerned with the angel of imagery; the momentary attention paid to the one implies no derogation of the others, but only that here it is desirable to discuss one thing at a time.

2

THE IMAGE OF BEATRICE

So lightened o'er my path thy face and form,
A law, a creed, a rapture, and a storm!
—POEMS OF CONFORMITY, 41

The experience called "falling in love" appears not to be universal, but in the contemporary Western world it is common enough that frequently it is regarded as normal, and sometimes as the criterion of love. Certainly, the fact of romantic love confronts us daily in the newspapers, hourly on television, with monotonous regularity at marriage license bureaus, and in divorce courts where a new love may serve as an acceptable excuse for discarding the old. Sociologists, psychologists, and biologists probe its symptoms; poets and versifiers expatiate upon its manifestations; cartoonists and preachers regard it as open territory. The event is described as ridiculous, sublime, a transitory episode appropriate only for adolescents, a form of temporary insanity, the sole justification for living at any age, normative, normal, abnormal, pathological, and good clean healthy fun. No doubt it is all these things.

"One way or another this state is normal," Williams writes; "what is not yet normal is the development of that state to its proper end."[1] In spite of the advertisements, entertainments, industries, and arts which, in our culture, focus upon romantic love, romanticism itself has not often been taken seriously. Neither lovers nor theologians are accustomed to ask, concerning either falling into or falling out of love, "Is it serious? is it capable of intellectual treatment? is it capable of belief, labour, fruition? is it (in some sense or other) *true*?"[2] Nor are they apt to take up the point that the romantic lover feels as if he had had a revelation, to inquire "what precisely is being revealed? what is the evidence? by what procedures can this be checked?" Even the term "romantic" has so seldom been closely defined, and so commonly been confused with the corruptions of romanticism, that Williams found it necessary to justify his use of it.

I keep the word Romantic for three reasons. The first is that there is no other word so convenient for describing that particular kind of sexual love. The second is that it includes other loves besides the sexual. The third is that in following the Dantean record of his love it may be possible to understand something more of Romanticism itself, and of its true and false modes of being. The word should not be too narrowly confined to a literary manner. It defines an attitude, a manner of receiving experience. . . . That there is a false Romanticism I willingly concede; . . . But the false does not abolish the true or the value of the true, any more than the cheap use of the word Romantic spoils the intellectual honour which properly accompanies it.[3]

Let us then investigate these experiences, in order to define the nature of romantic love as contrasted with other kinds of love, to examine in detail what it is that romantic love reveals and conceals, and to determine what the lover can and cannot, should and should not, do about these events.

DANTE AND BEATRICE

The intensely personal quality which is an essential mark of both romantic love and imagery prohibits us from beginning the analysis of romanticism with such diffuse words as "person," or "lover" and "beloved," although we shall return to them for convenience. These are general terms, but falling in love does not occur in general: it is highly specific. Therefore we must start from a concrete instance where a particular, unique individual falls in love with another particular, unique individual. Williams chose for his principal image of romantic love one of the great love stories of all time, that of Dante for Beatrice, and the choice has many advantages. Since the incidents actually happened to real people, they cannot be lightly dismissed as fantastic in the way that a fictional account could be. And because Dante was not only a romantic lover, but also one of the greatest of poets, he reported his reactions in language of surpassing precision, clarity, and beauty. Further, the historical events comprise almost the irreducible minimum for romantic love: Dante never became involved in the complications intrinsic to close friendship with his beloved, not to mention those of courtship or marriage. The facts of falling in love, and of being in love, stand here with elemental simplicity.

To review that story: Dante first met Beatrice when he was a child of nine; by the time he was eighteen he had fallen deeply in love with her. They were sufficiently well acquainted to speak to each other when they met on the street or at social gatherings, but no development of their relationship into intimacy is known. Once Beatrice deliberately snubbed Dante, because she had heard rumors about him that displeased her. We have no way of knowing whether this rejection—which hurt him profoundly—reflected anger at a personal affront or impersonal disapproval of his behavior, and it does not matter particularly. She married someone else and died when she was twenty-three. Dante also married, had children, and in one of the political crises of the time was exiled from his native city Florence. He died in 1321 at the age of fifty-six, thirty-one years after Beatrice's death, still in exile.

Dante's significance for the theology of romantic love lies in his explicit awareness of Beatrice as an image, and in the penetration with which he described himself (the imagist and lover), Beatrice (the image and the beloved), and the structure of the relationship between them. One part of that structure, the romantic moment of the actual falling in love, will be our first concern.

THE ROMANTIC MOMENT

One characteristic unites all the events that are properly termed romantic: *the shock of an intense personal experience.* Something is suddenly and shatteringly discovered, involving the whole of one's being in an integrated response. Dante described it as a " 'stupor' or astonishment of the mind";[4] modern philosophers speak of the "existential shock." It is essentially a moment—brief or prolonged—of violent change, after which nothing will ever be the same again, and it has two salient features: givenness, and passion.

To say that the romantic shock is "given" means simply that it is a gift, something bestowed upon the romantic by forces that he cannot control.

It seems that no one yet discovered that light of glory in any woman or any man by hunting for it; it seems that it may exist where it is not wanted. It has its own methods; "my ways are not your ways, saith the Lord." It is not of a nature certainly to rival the electric light, but whether that is due to its weakness or to the lover's imperfection is another matter. The schools are divided.[5]

Dante did not decide to fall in love with Beatrice, or to fall in love at all. The idiom is curiously exact: he fell. It seems to be typical if not invariable: the moment can be desired but it cannot be willed. Whatever its source in physiology, the unconscious, social patterns, God, or anything else, the lover can no more generate or arrest it than he can generate or arrest a given bolt of lightning in a summer thunderstorm. Once it has happened, to a large degree he can govern what he does with it, as lightning can be deflected by lightning rods, but so far as determining its occurrence is concerned, he is practically helpless. Some other loves and kinds of love are subject to man's will, but the romantic is not.

The word "passion" here signifies that emotional intensity which results when a whole person, functioning as a single, integrated entity, focuses all his powers upon a single object. Dante described the Beatrician moment of falling in love as having three effects upon him: "It moves the heart as the seat of spiritual emotions, the brain as the centre of perception, and the liver as the place of corporal emotions."[6] The awakening is of the complete person. Sexuality is stimulated and emotions are disturbed; these we take for granted in dealing with romanticism, and the theology of romantic love maintains their importance from start to finish.

The *New Life* of Dante does not begin to talk *only* of the spirit; no, that young and great doctor faints at the sight of his beloved; he cries when she cuts him; he is like any hysterical adolescent—that is, like anyone much in love. And the great surge of passion that immortally follows is precisely not a passion in which sensuality is refined away; at the close of the *Purgatory* she says to him: "You should have been faithful to my buried flesh," *mia carne sepolta,* and in her actual eyes he sees reflected the two-natured Gryphon of Christ.[7]

In the Beatrician form of the romantic moment, the physical response is specifically sexual, but the pre-eminent moment of romantic love is not, of course, confined to the moment of romantic sex love. There are other moments of intense experience combined with potentiality of further experience. Great art has it and politics and nature and (it is said) maturity. But few of these have had the same universality and few, owing to the chance of genius, have undergone the same analysis.[8]

Wordsworth felt a like passion for nature, Sir Francis Bacon for the universe,[9] St. Augustine of Hippo for God. These loves contain no patently sexual elements, but the body has other organs and activities than those of reproduction, and the physical aspects of the shock may be expressed by circulation, digestion, or respiration rather than by the sexual centers. "Romantic love between the sexes is but one kind of romantic love, which is but a particular habit of Romanticism as a whole, which is itself but a particular method of the Affirmation of Images."[10]

And the mind is shaken as well as the body. "The true Romantic, maintaining the importance of what Blake calls 'the visionary Fancy or Imagination,' admits and believes that the holy intellect is part of it."[11] Indeed, reason has so high a significance for romanticism that when it is not included in love's excitements, what results will not be romanticism at all, but some variety of pseudo-romanticism: lust, extravagant fervor, or sentimentality.

The effect of the romantic moment upon the lover's intellect is most clearly demonstrated in the contrast between the two major varieties of romanticism, the positive and the negative. The romantic moment produces a conversion in the lover's world view: he turns away from a former orientation, and toward something new which is usually an extreme either of order and delight or of chaos and horror. "She felt . . . the hint of a new organization of all things . . . an infinitely alien arrangement of infinitely familiar things. The bottom had dropped out of her universe, yet her astonished spirit floated and did not fall."[12] "He has lived in one world, and now he begins to live in another; this is change."[13] The positive romantic moment of love and the negative romantic moment of outrage are identical in structure; in content they are diametrically opposed.

Williams' summary of Dante's experience will serve to sketch the positive romantic moment:

He is, it seems, "satisfied" by Beatrice; his sensations, his emotions, his ideas, his faith, coalesce. Perfection in some strange sense exists, and walks down the street of Florence to meet him. She is "the youngest of the Angels"; her image in his thought "is an exultation of Love to subdue him," yet so perfect that Love never acts without "the faithful counsel of reason, wherever such counsel was useful to be heard"; she is "the destroyer of all evil and the queen of all good"; she is the equivalent of heaven itself. . . . He says that when she met him in the street and said good-morning, he was so highly moved that he was, for the moment, in a state of complete good-will, complete *caritas* towards everyone. If anyone had at that moment done him an injury, he would necessarily have forgiven him. He has not only fallen in love; he is, strictly, "in love." He is aware of that beyond everything; "if anyone had asked me a question I should have been able to answer only 'Love.' " . . . "I have been," he said soon after that description, "at that point of life beyond which he who passes cannot return"; and this indeed is the description of such a "falling in love"—it is a region from which no creature returns afterwards. One is never the same again.[14]

Dante was more articulate than most soap-opera heroes, movie queens, teenagers, and the rest of us in love, but the basic response is the same for all. At one stroke everything is changed; all proportions and balances shift into a fresh pattern; a new being inhabits a new world of ecstasy and beauty. The lover moves for a time in a universe which is strange to him, and where he is strange to himself.

The negative romantic moment bears many names. Kierkegaard called it "*angst*—dread," Tillich "the abyss," psychiatrists "anxiety," Williams "outrage." It is the shock experienced by Wordsworth when England attacked the French Revolution, by Dante when Beatrice died and much later when he woke in the dark wood, by Shakespeare's Troilus when he learned that his wife Cressida loved someone else.

The crisis which Troilus endured is one common to all men; it is in a sense the only interior crisis worth talking about. It is that in which every nerve of the body, every consciousness of the mind, shrieks that something cannot be. Only it is.

Cressida *cannot* be playing with Diomed. But she is. The Queen *cannot* have married Claudius. But she has. Desdemona *cannot* love Cassio. But she does. Daughters *cannot* hate their father and benefactor. But they do. The British Government *cannot* have declared war on the Revolution. But it has. The whole being of the victim denies the fact; the fact outrages his whole being. This is indeed change . . .[15]

Again, a new man moves in a new world, among new proportions and balances. Again, nothing will ever be the same afterward.

In so far as the romantic moment, whether positive or negative, is an experience, it is an irreducible fact, and although reason can attack its appropriateness, its importance, or the conclusions drawn from it, it cannot deny to the experience its existence. "A thing that seems has at least the truth of its seeming." And sooner or later, a question concerning such experiences must be asked and answered. It can be variously phrased. Are these experiences to be treated as more or less temporary aberrations of the mind, or as accurate perceptions of the nature of the world and of man? On what reasonable grounds can one appraise the relationships of the three experiences that are directly involved in romanticism—the life before the romantic moment, the vision of wholeness engendered by falling in love, and the nightmare encounter with outrage? What does one do when one experience flatly contradicts another?

One must do something. The romantic shock forces upon man the necessity to act. The lover cannot stand indefinitely on a street corner looking at a girl: she will depart or the police will move him on. The nature-poet cannot lie forever on a hill contemplating the sky: he will die of thirst, starvation, or exposure. The victim of dread cannot perpetually seclude himself in his room: he will be taken to a hospital. But even if these were possible, suspension of activity itself constitutes a form of acting and reflects, however obscurely, an act of choice. Likewise, any fresh idea must be acted upon, by dismissing it or by incorporating it into one's thought; and emotions require some kind of response from intellect and will, if only attention.

When confronted with any shock, "there are several things we may do about it—ignore it, explain it away, explore it, or lose ourselves in it."[16] (1) Ignoring it is implicitly a refusal to think, which may be legitimate: in the finite span of this life, we cannot study all the experiences that we undergo. But to ignore it may reflect intellectual sloth: we evade the labor of bringing the new and old experiences into a common frame of reference. To say "This happened and then that. Things simply happen. What difference does it make?" implies that intellect is irrelevant to romanticism, and that the shock has no meaning except for its momentary pleasures or terrors. (2) Explaining it away, one attributes the experience to a physical, psychological, sociological, or other source, and concludes that the source satisfactorily elucidates the full meaning of the event. We have been told, "By their fruits, and not by their roots, we shall know them"[17] but some reject that teaching. (3) Losing oneself in romantic love, one treats the experience as an end in itself, so that falling in love excuses any emotional or physical unions, and falling out of love—or in love with somebody else—excuses equally sudden separations, and the beginning of another repetition of a cycle that has no inherent end.

Each of these three alternatives in some fashion refuses the intellect full access to one or all of the experiences, and assumes (although the assumption may be hidden) that an experience can be nullified by other experiences. But neither logic nor any other discipline provides a ground upon which one experience can properly cancel out another. If any of them is to be taken seriously as an object for intellectual examination, all must be. If one predicates that love has meaning, then outrage has meaning as well, and so does the miasma of monotony, frustration, and aimlessness that envelops man during much of his life. This leaves us with the last of Williams' list of possibilities: exploration. In following that, we shall be occupied here almost exclusively with the Beatrician type of romanticism—that is, with falling into love, and not with falling into anxiety or outrage—but the limitation arises only from practical necessity. To trace in detail the parallels and divergences of outrage would require a book twice the length of this, and readers with four times the patience.

Before proceeding, one note is necessary. As sexual love is only one of the types of romanticism, so romantic love is only one of the kinds of love. Passion is not a requisite for loving, nor sudden onset a criterion for existential involvement. Sweetness and serenity, quiet affection and gradual development, belong as truly to the Kingdom of Love as do the tumults of the romantic encounter. The absence of the romantic response to experience implies no disparagement, because this can be a difference in style of loving, rather than a difference in degree or depth of love. Romanticism and non-romanticism cannot conceivably substitute for each other, any more than light can substitute for darkness or darkness for light. Each has its own function, and for all the useless wars that their partisans wage, they do not conflict.

THE IMAGE OF LOVE

The romantic shock occurs when a particular person, thing, or event is perceived as "a whole being significant of a greater whole,"[18] that is, when it becomes an image. Thus for Dante, Beatrice is a whole being existing in herself; she reveals something greater than herself; and she is an instance of that which she reveals. Let us take these elements in order.

First: Beatrice, the thirteenth-century Florentine girl, has a specific identity. She is herself and not some other thing, and no other person or thing can possibly take her place at the center of Dante's attention. It is *this* girl whom he loves, having *this* body and *this* smile and *this* mind and spirit. When she dies, it is an infinitely irreplaceable loss. Her uniqueness appears to Dante as a quality independent of his love for her, and cold reason confirms him. All scientific, philosophic, and poetic knowledge affirms that every separate thing is unique: blades of grass, and leaves on the same tree, measurably differ. But Dante knows this, of Beatrice, with his heart and his running blood as well as with his mind.

In addition, Beatrice is to Dante not only unique, but integrated. Her identity cannot be broken: her smile is intrinsic to her self, not an accident of her flesh; likewise, her self is intrinsic to her smile. For all Dante's analysis of Beatrice, he does not separate her "soul" or "self" or "spirit" from her body. "She is the substance of spirit":[19] her single, indivisible person combines into an organic unity things hitherto regarded as mutually exclusive, so that by her physical death Dante loses her entirely.

Second: Beatrice's whole being reveals to her lover a greater whole. "The experience—the sight, that is, of the beloved—arouses a sense of intense significance, a sense that an explanation of the whole universe is being offered, and indeed in some sense understood; only it cannot yet be defined."[20] Dante's attempts to define it led him to the words salvation, blessedness, love, God, and he meant them. She was for him the *theotokos,* the God-bearer, the means by which God communicated himself.

Dante was, of course, well informed on Christian doctrines and thoroughly convinced of their truth. The appearance of Beatrice did not introduce him to the Christian definition of God, or assure him of something that he had formerly doubted. Rather, it provided him with a new manner of knowing God and all the world besides. It would be correct to call this "existential knowledge," but that phrase does not ordinarily carry the feeling of burning clarity that is needed here, nor connote "the unity of all authorities of blood and brain, triply obedient" to each other and to fact "in the true equilateral ease."[21] Neither does it convey the sense that the image is observed to be the God-bearer, an identification which does not result from a chain of argument, but which is as immediate and unmistakable as the recognition that a storm cloud has a threatening aspect. Dante may have been deluded in his belief that God was being revealed in Beatrice, or that there is a God at all, but he is not alone in his declaration that "the Divine Glory is perceived and apprehended as immanent in some created person or thing"; and as Miss Sayers goes on to specify,

Traherne sees the corn as "orient and immortal wheat" and men and women as "immortal cherubims"; Wordsworth sees "meadows, grove, and stream . . . apparelled in celestial light"; Blake cries out " 'What!' it will be questioned, 'when the Sun rises, do you not see a round disk of fire somewhat like a guinea?' O no, no, I see an Innumerable company of the Heavenly host crying 'Holy, Holy, Holy, is the Lord God Almighty.' "[22]

Third: Beatrice is an example of that glory. "The superstitions make heaven and earth in the form of the beloved; the theology declares that the beloved is the first preparatory form of heaven and earth."[23] Dante sees the Creator in the creation, the Father in the child, the Basis in the image, and it is precisely because she is unique, personal, singular, that she performs this function for her lover. The key to romantic love lies in the individual; it is permeated throughout by what has been called, in another connection, "the scandal of particularity." Therefore she appears to be not only good but the visible norm of goodness. Therefore her beauty reflects and contains all beauty. Therefore no blessedness or joy is foreign to her, and no delight is possible apart from her. "This is the identity of the Image with that beyond the Image. Beatrice is the Image and the foretaste of salvation."[24] This identity justifies the lover when he speaks of his beloved as adorable; it vindicates his impulse to treat her with the reverential awe with which one is expected to approach the divine. She is emphatically not God, but as the God-bearing image "she is the Mother of Love—of *caritas,* and even of a *caritas* beyond any *caritas* we can imagine; she is the chosen Mother of the goodwill of God,"[25] so that reverence is her due.

Dante is in love. His friends laugh at him: they know that Beatrice is not actually the quasi-deity whom Dante worships, but a fallible and erring, perhaps even a commonplace girl, or petulant or unchaste or stupid, and subject to pain, illness, decay, and the corruptions of the many sorts of death. From their point of view, Dante's belief about her marks him as a fool. It is not only that no human being could attain the perfection which the lover attributes to his beloved, but that their friends know that in fact she does not. They testify from their own experience of her: here she was gross; there she lied; elsewhere she was rude.

The friends are many, and they know. The lover stands alone, but he also knows. It has been customary to allow the majority to rule between them, especially since sooner or later the lover almost invariably comes to share the general opinion. Romantic theology, however, claims that both witnesses are right: Beatrice is in fact what Dante perceives her to be, and she is also what the others see. The one indivisible girl has two natures.

Her, or his, humanity is an extremely maculate humanity, and all the worship under heaven ought not to prevent her lover from knowing (with reasonable accuracy and unreasonable love) when she is lazy, lewd, or malicious. She has a double nature, and he can have double sight.[26]

Here neither idolatry nor cynicism will serve. Beatrice is the God-bearer, and she is a woman. More exactly, she is the God-bearer because she is a woman:

she is a given fact which has in two categories of experience different names. But the fact itself is identical everywhere. Dante may have been merely insane when he believed this; as any other lover may who believes that the wrists of his lady are moral goodness, or her forehead aboriginal light, or her hands executive intelligence. He may; or he may be entirely sane. The important thing is that no one in that state of apprehension, false or true, has any belief in "suggestive similarity". . . . For identities of that kind we have to start with figures as intensely themselves as can be managed; the less themselves they are, the less identical with facts in another category they become. But the more themselves they are, the less "suggestively similar" of another kind of fact can they be. This is the law of symbolism—that the symbol must be utterly itself before it can properly be a symbol. But the more himself a man is the less is he likely to be *similar* to anything, even a virtue . . .[27]

Because of this duality in Beatrice's nature, she at once conceals and reveals the reality which she images. Being human, she cannot be completely identified with the Divine or any other perfection, nor perfectly transmit its nature. On the other hand, being an image she has identity with her basis; she repeats its actual nature. She is at once exclusive of all other glories, and yet as an image of God she includes them all.

Beatrice was, in her degree, an image of nobility, of virtue, of the Redeemed Life, and in some sense of Almighty God himself. But she also remained Beatrice right to the end; her derivation was not to obscure her identity any more than her identity should hide her derivation. Just as there is no point in Dante's thought at which the image of Beatrice in his mind was supposed to exclude the actual objective Beatrice, so there is no point at which the objective Beatrice is to exclude the Power which is expressed through her. But as the mental knowledge or image of her is the only way by which she herself can be known, so she herself is (for Dante) the only way by which that other Power can be known—since, in fact, it was known so. The maxim of his study, as regards the final Power, was: "This also is Thou, neither is this Thou."[28]

This paradox of "the exclusive-inclusive thing" comes close to the heart of reality and of knowledge. Keats hears the exclusive nightingale and his inclusive world is transformed. Israel is told that it shall be exclusively blessed, and inclusively a blessing. The Christian faith defines its Lord as fully man, the exclusive thing, and fully God, the inclusive

Thing. And in a manner that will later become evident, imagery, the exclusive mode of knowing, is an instance of the inclusive operation of exchange. In all this, however, "the vision of perfection does not at all exclude the sight of imperfection; the two can exist together; they can even, in a sense, co-inhere. To suppose anything else would be a false romanticism of the worst kind."[29]

Dante sees archetypal Love within its type, Beatrice, the two separate but inseparable realities mutually interpenetrating each other. The strands are woven together in a web of passionate delight, where nothing loses its individual identity, and where each sustains the identities of imagery. The unity of perfection shouts to him from every sound; he tastes it in food and drink; his hands take hold of it.

And then Beatrice dies.

THE DEATH OF THE IMAGE

It is not always physical death which intervenes between lover and beloved: death often comes instead as the loss of the Beatrician quality in the beloved, when the lover falls out of love as decisively, if not as swiftly, as he first fell into it.

. . . the fact need not be denied because it means a great deal more than itself. For nothing seems to be more certain than that the original glory, the *Beatricianness* of Beatrice, does either disappear or at least modify itself. In this also we have an exclusive-inclusive event. Beatrice dies; that is the exclusive. The light and beatitude disappear; that is the inclusive. In the imagination the two need not be hostile, nor in fact. "The City is widowed," says Dante, quoting Jeremiah. It is apt to be a blow.[30]

The romantic moment has an end as well as a beginning, and at its end the romantic lover confronts an imperative question, whether to abandon the principles which were demonstrated to him in the Beatrician vision, or to adhere to them now that it has gone. In its most direct form, it is the issue that Anthony, in *The Place of the Lion,* faced: "Moments of love were either reality or illusion; the instant knowledge required his similar decision."[31] The decision cannot be based upon any evidence as such, because the evidence remains the same either way. It is a question of how the evidence shall be organized and, specifically, of how much weight shall be assigned to the romantic moment. Reality or illusion? Both possibilities are intelligent; probably they are equally intelligent. But the lover cannot pursue both ways; he must choose one. And if he chooses that romantic love shall be to him a reality, these are the problems that he faces when his Beatrice dies, or her Beatrician quality fades:

Why must Beatrice die? What constrains the romantic moment to be, as it obviously is, a moment? What in the nature of the world and of man makes possible the luminous clarity of the Beatrician experience, and how can it be restored?

PART II

The Diagram of the Glory

The word glory, to English ears, usually means no more than a kind of mazy bright blur. But the maze should be, though it generally is not, exact, and the brightness should be that of a geometrical pattern.

—*He Came Down from Heaven*, 33

3
THE ADAM

All things were named—all but man himself; then the sleep fell upon the Adam, and in that first sleep he strove to utter his name, and as he strove he was divided and woke to find humanity doubled. The name of mankind was in neither voice but in both; the knowledge of the name and its utterance was in the perpetual interchange of love.
—THE PLACE OF THE LION, 191

The theology of romantic love answers the lover's great "Why?" at Beatrice's withdrawal, in death or in falling out of love, by referring him to the Christian analysis of the nature of the world and of man. "Life (experience suggests) is a good thing, and somehow unendurable; at least the Christian faith has denied neither side of the paradox,"[1] and it proposes a pattern that gives meaning to both the glory and the horror of existence. It has stated that meaning in many ways, among them a story which is an image: as a narrative, it has identity that can be traced through many variations; it refers to something greater than itself; and it reveals and conceals that greater thing. It is the story in Genesis of the creation of the world, of the fall of man, and of the consequent fall of the world.

For our purposes, it makes no difference whatever whether the story be taken as history, fantasy, or article of faith, because the story *as an image* says the same things in any case, just as Shakespeare's fictional *Romeo and Juliet* says almost exactly the same things about the romantic moment that Dante does about his actual confrontation with Beatrice.

The several Biblical accounts of the beginning are variants of one myth, and for Williams, a myth consists of a narrative that has acquired significance beyond its own immediacy—that is, a myth is a story functioning as an image.

In a sense, of course, history is itself a myth; to the imaginative, engaged in considering these things, all is equally myth. We may issue from it into other judgements—doctrinal, moral, historic. But so doing we enter into another kind of thought and judge by other tests—more important perhaps, but not the same. In the myth we need ask for nothing but interior consistency . . .[2]

Thus Williams wrote that World War II "is mythical in [the poets] already, and so they know it after the only true manner":[3] as an image of the universal conflict between defenders of antagonistic definitions of the good. Anything can become an image: Waterloo equally with Roncevaux, Winston Churchill with Aeneas, the concept of evolution with the Biblical myth of the direct creation of species. We are not inquiring here into the factual bases or references for the Hebrew-Christian myth of creation, but only into what it states about the structure of the universe which we now inhabit.

THE IMAGE OF CREATION

Stripped to its bones, the Genesis myth presents (1) an activity, "creation," (2) two different kinds of things, God and things which he made that were different from himself, (3) relationships among these things, and (4) the declaration that God considered the creation and the relationships to be "good," which so far can be taken only as indicating some sort of compatibility with himself. This framework, however, gives us a starting point.

(1) Things happen. There is energy, not merely potential but released into action. God does something, and that something involves further activities. The dry land brings forth grass; the great whales and the winged things disport themselves; the creeping things crawl. The energy of God produces a vast blur and buzz of movement within the creation.

(2) It produces also diversity. The power of God made things different from himself, and different from each other. It is hardly possible to overemphasize either the extent or the importance of these variations. Things differ in degree, in kind, in distribution, in style. Trees differ from stones or beasts, one species of tree from other species, individual trees within species, particular leaves on a single tree. Each

thing that exists is unique. No event is repeated. All things change
without ceasing. "And God saw everything that he had made, and behold, it was very good." Thus individuality, variety, distinctiveness,
alteration, are by definition good—that is, consistent with that from
which they are derived.

Two subsidiary aspects of the story develop more explicitly the significance of diversity *per se*. There is not the faintest suggestion that
matter[4] constitutes a lower form of existence than any other, or is less
compatible with God, less "good." The Biblical story allows "to matter
a significance and power which (of all the religions and philosophies)
only Christianity has affirmed."[5] It implicitly takes the material world
to be naturally good, not in spite of its materiality but expressly because
of that extreme difference from the various capacities or forms of
existence that are loosely grouped under the term "spirit," such as
mind, will, emotion, soul.

Also, God created certain living things in the disparity between male
and female. Having done so, he blessed them in their variation and
commanded them to multiply, to extend their original difference into
still other differences. The energy of life was to express itself by producing more and more things, and, because each new thing was different from all the rest, more and more diversity.

(3) These active, different things existed—according to the tale—
in relationship with each other. Then as now, grass grew in the soil;
the one depended upon the other in an orderly fashion. Fish inhabited
the sea, and generated others of their kind in accordance with a pattern.
Organic life consisted of a system of interdependencies: circulation
with respiration with digestion with circulation, and all with the struc-
tural components of skeleton and organ. Living things found their
nourishment outside themselves; in gathering food they altered the external world, withdrawing from it plants or other animals. In turn,
when the elements of that world were ingested, they changed the com-
position of the body that received them, if only slightly or temporarily.
And God saw that it was good.

Williams called this play of interaction among separate identities
"the Co-inherence";[6] he believed the source of its existence and continuation to be God, its basic principle of activity to be exchange, and

its fruits to be joy and love. Co-inherence is a Christian doctrine, but it belongs also to paganism and is much more than a doctrine: it is a natural fact, universally exhibited, although not universally recognized, valued, or enjoyed. We may or may not live *for* others, but whether we like it or not, we do live *from* others. It is an ultimate prerequisite for any life at all. Self-sufficiency, the absence of co-inherent exchange, is an outright impossibility for any sort of life known to man. All societies operate by means of exchange; thought develops from it; eating and breathing exhibit it; procreation requires it.

At the beginning of life in the natural order is an act of substitution and co-inherence. A man can have no child unless his seed is received and carried by a woman; a woman can have no child unless she receives and carries the seed of a man . . . The child itself for nine months literally co-inheres in its mother; there is no human creature that has not sprung from such a period of such an interior growth.[7]

A similar interplay of persons and functions sustains romantic love: the lover's vision depends upon his beloved; for the moment he lives from her, as also she from him, and both of them from other persons and things. Likewise, imagery presupposes the co-inherent union—the identity—of image and basis, and of thinking and the objects of thought. Co-inherence can be observed everywhere in all things, without special instruments or uncommon intellectual insight. It does not require that one postulate the Christian concept of God, or any concept of God at all, but only that he observe the ordinary conditions of ordinary life.

Judaism and Christianity, however, did say "God" and they said "good." They noticed further that exchange is frequently difficult, demanding, and painful, and that co-inherence results in destruction as well as in life. The carnivores prey upon other beasts or they die; herbivores destroy the—presumably innocent—lives of plants. An illimitable distress, if not agony, pervades this co-inherence which, by the Hebrew-Christian definition, is from God and is good. Their myth embodies this discordancy.

THE IMAGE OF ANTAGONISM

The myth of the double unity of man—"the Adam," male and

female[8]—in the garden of Eden declares that man was created good. The well-meaning may gaze upon the babe in the cradle and maintain that this is still the case, but the most casual consideration of the world around us indicates that if the infant has that perfection, he will not continue for very long in it, and that adults have long since fallen from that high state. On the other hand, if we are born flawed—why? Why are we not good in our origins? Because there is no God? or because God is not omnipotent and—or—not good? In this study, we are assuming the God of the Christian faith, omnipotent, omniscient, benevolent, but "something must have gone wrong somewhere. If (on the hypothesis) it cannot have gone wrong with God, it must have gone wrong with us."[9] How and why are the subject of the second episode in the myth, which is an attempt to explain by reason, and to frame "by something deeper than reason . . . the sense of a dreadful necessity."[10]

"The Adam had been created and were existing in a state of knowledge of good and nothing but good."[11] After all, there was then, by definition, nothing except good to know. The world was made up of God and that which he had created, which were compatible with each other, and the elements of the creation were mutually compatible, woven together in a web of interrelated activities. The Adam had been made in the image of God: they existed in their own right, separate from but related to him; they reflected him who was greater than they; and they were intrinsically like him. Their difference from him was such that they were not shadows or passive copies, but separate identities, and what powers they had were real, if limited. Their dependence upon God and interdependence with the rest of the world were the definitions of their existence and the preconditions of their joy.

But then, as now, the co-inherence contained the potentiality of an alternative to joyous exchange. "Some possibility of opposite action there must be if there is to be any relation between different wills."[12] God is said to have pointed this out to the Adam, showing them the tree of the knowledge of good and evil, and indicating that their difference from him allowed them a degree of freedom. They could choose to eat, or not to eat, of its fruit. Such freedom is "the only method by which he can praise his creatures; if they are not to be allowed to choose, neither can they enjoy his will nor he theirs."[13] God warned them that this fruit was not good for them; if they ate it, they would die as inexorably and impartially as if it were poisonous—which, of course, it was for them.

The possibility of alteration had been created as an element in the whole. That web of diagrammatized glory, of honourable beauty, of changing and interchanging adoration, depended for its perfection on two things—the will of God to sustain its being and its own will to be so sustained. He made—if we call it obedience we make the joy too dull (since we have, except at our momentary best and in our transient illuminations, lost the joy of obedience)—he made let us say the delight of a perfect response to his initiative a part of the working of the web.[14]

The options were strictly defined. The Adam might continue to know the good that they already knew, or they could know the good and something other than the good. At that point, the distinction lay only in the kinds of knowledge. And the Adam chose. They preferred their own wisdom to God's, and decided "to find out what the good would be like if a contradiction were introduced into it."[15]

They knew good; they wished to know good and evil. Since there was not—since there never has been and never will be—anything else than the good to know, they knew good as antagonism. All difference consists in the mode of knowledge. They had what they wanted. That they did not like it when they got it does not alter the fact that they certainly got it.[16]

The change in the Adam's manner of knowing produced, inevitably, a change in their actions. The unity of the Adam was broken: the man kept the name that means Man; the woman received from him the name that means Living. There was still relationship between them, but the relationship contained hostility as well as harmony. An ugly shame contaminated their princely difference. Their bodies continued to be what God had made them, and as good as God had made them, but the two persons now could not endure the distinctions between them. They made aprons, not for each other but for themselves. To that degree Adam withdrew from Eve and Eve from Adam. The simple seclusion developed, in their children, into open conflict. The farmer Cain killed his brother, the shepherd Abel. We do not have a tradition of the steps by which withdrawal deepened into the desolations of murder and warfare, but we do not need a tradition to trace them for us. We can see the process at work daily in individuals, in groups, in the community of nations. He who does not see things in right relationships, sees them in wrong relationships. Division in knowledge breeds antagonism in action, and evil is established in the universe as a positive force.

So the rhythm of day and night was and is good, but man hid in caves to escape the one and built fires against the other. By so doing he did not change the character of either day or night: they remained what they were, and their goodness was established in the foundations of the world. But man opposed the facts. He knew them as evil. He knew the good in and through his rejection of it. The differences between individuals, that had begun as opportunities for increasing the power and complexity of relationships, were twisted into the demand for uniformity or were appealed to in defense of attempts to control others. The craftsman's labor became drudgery. Intellectual and moral and emotional confusion replaced the lucidity of co-inherence. And the God who created, in the beginning, a world of whole and exquisite grace, permitted this antagonism to continue and to spread outward from man into the world that he inhabited. God

neither forbore to create because we were about to sin nor ceased to sustain when we had begun to sin. It is the choice of a God, not of a man; we should have been less harsh. We should not have created because we could not have endured; we could not have willed; we could not have loved. It is the choice of a God, not of a man.[17]

The analysis of Williams' profound and subtle interpretation of the Fall of Man had best start with what he is denying. He has postulated good, and declared that nothing except good existed before the Fall; he has not introduced a principle of evil to account for that event. For him, the image of the snake represents neither a personal Satan nor an impersonal force opposed to the Omnipotent Good. He rejects the metaphysical, as well as the ethical, dualism implicit in the notion of an evil power or principle or being that is outside of, and contradictory to, God.

Two questions arise at once from this refusal of dualism. Is Williams making the preposterous assertion that evil does not exist? No. On the contrary, he insists upon its reality, power, and pervasiveness. Is he then affirming that God is the source of evil? To this the inexorable answer is yes, and Williams faces directly the terrible implications of that affirmative.

There is no split second of the unutterable horror and misery of the world that he did not foresee (to use the uselessness of that language) when he created; no torment of children, no obstinacy of social wickedness, no starvation of the innocent, no prolonged and deliberate cruelty, which he did not know. It is impossible for the mind of man to contemplate an infinitestimal fraction of the persistent cruelty of mankind, and beyond mankind of the animals, through innumerable years, and yet remain sane. . . . The Omnipotence contemplated that pain and created; that is, he brought its possibility—and its actuality—into existence. Without him it could not have been; and calling it his permission instead of his will may be intellectually accurate, but does not seem to get over the fact that if the First Cause has power, intelligence, and will to cause a universe to exist, then he is the First Cause of it. The First Cause cannot escape being the First Cause. All the metaphors about fathers giving their children opportunities to be themselves fail, as all metaphors fail. Fathers are not the First Cause. God only is God. The pious have been—as they always are—too anxious to excuse him; the prophet was wiser: "I form the light and create darkness: I make peace and create evil: I the Lord do all these things."[18]

Man's knowledge and action had been fundamentally altered by the Fall, and the event could not be annulled. Like all events, it was irrevocable. Man's nature changed: he had been single and was now divided. He had been given dominion over nature, and his authority became the rule of inaccuracy and antagonism. The infection spread from him to animals and plants, and beyond them to the four ancient elements of nature.

> Loosed are the powers of earth and air,
>   fire and water in combat leap;
> space is now but a broken stair,
>   and the great sun runs on the edge of a steep
> dizzy with terror; for all around
> the elementals again abound
>   in clamour and freedom; water, fire,

earth and air unprison their powers,
   and no prayer reacheth the heavenly Sire
where he sitteth calm in his lucid towers.

Myriad atoms of man and beast
   strive apart as the kingdom strives;
within and without hath concord ceased
   for terror striketh the least of lives;
the summer gnat in his flight upsprings
for rage of the torment that takes his wings,
   the wolves for hunger but more for pain
howl and ravin about the moors,
   chaos is come upon earth again
and the pirates drive upon Logres' shores.[19]

The Fall, too, was an exclusive-inclusive event. The exclusive Adam chose evil, and that evil spread until it included all other things. But in the light of this, it needs to be recalled that according to the tradition, the original initiative in sin lay not with matter but with spirit. That which first fell was the will of man, and presumably the resulting degradation affected his volition and reason more seriously than his physical body, or nature in general. "Matter and 'nature' have not in themselves sinned; what has sinned is spirit, if spirit and matter are to be regarded as divided. That they so easily can be is due perhaps to that lack of intellectual clarity produced by the Fall."[20] The body is, "for all our difficulties with it, less fallen, merely in itself, than the soul in which the quality of the will is held to reside";[21] therefore the physical body may well contain more natural health than spirit, may express more readily the diagram of co-inherence, and may guide and encourage man both to know and to obey the primal law, physical and moral, of exchange.

AFTER EDEN

"In the old myth, the Adam, once they had insisted on seeing good as evil, were mercifully ejected from Paradise; how could they have borne with sanity that place of unrestrained good, all of which could be known as unrestrained evil?"[22] Yet the fundamental conditions of existence were not essentially altered by the Fall of Man. God had chosen to create a world, and he followed through on his decision: "nature was His original choice, and He has a supreme fidelity."[23] Specifically, the Fall did not destroy energy; it set forms of energy against each other. It did not diminish difference; it made diversity a sorrow and a burden. It did not abolish the principle or actuality of ordered relationship; it changed the order.

Man could not longer be innocent; he was corrupt, and his best efforts were, but for the new grace, doomed to death. But his best efforts were, and are, of no other kind than had been decreed. His blood might be tainted, but the source from which it sprang was still the same. His natural life was still, and is now, a disordered pattern of the only pattern, a confused type of the one original; it is full still of glory and of peace, as well as of bloodshed and despair.[24]

It is the co-inherence that makes evil possible and, since the Fall, inevitable. All evils borne and inflicted are grounded in the fact of interrelationship, and express the will of the Creator toward his creation: he will not abrogate its structure even when it presses toward its own destruction.

If this God is good, then goodness is exactly what Williams, in the person of his character Peter Stanhope, called it: "a dreadful goodness."[25] But: "Are our tremors to measure the Omnipotence?"[26] And of the phrase "terribly good":

"The substantive, of course, contains the adjective; not the other way round."
"The substantive?" Pauline asked blankly.
"Good. It contains terror, not terror good. . . ."[27]

Whatever the primal cause for sin, we do live, now, within antagonism. Division is inherent in our individual natures; our societies are saturated with conflicts that intensify our personal contradictions, so that the natural state of the natural human being is a kind of schizophrenia. "Lucidity and confusion are alike natural, and there is no corner into which antagonism to pure joy has not broken."[28] The child, born with both potentialities, enters a world that pulls him in both directions. His human origin determines that conflict shall characterize his entire being. For the moment, we need not question our generous conviction that the infant cannot be guilty because he is incapable of responsibility, although

it may be that we were "in" Adam very much more particularly than is often supposed; it may be indeed that we, in that pre-fallen state, *were* Adam, and that it was we who chose. *Fuimus ille unus,* said Augustine, *quando fuimus in illo uno;* we were the one when we were in the one. But popular doctrine in the Church has rather taken the view that we did not consciously choose that original sin, but are at most its successors and inheritors. The vicarious guilt of it is in us; the derived concupiscence is in us. There remains for us the eternal dying which is its result.[29]

All experience with children forces upon our attention that they protest as naturally as they co-operate, that irritable complaint against hunger and pain constitutes a wholly natural means of communicating their needs. This is a result of original sin, the antagonism which is natural to man, which is not learned by the child from his elders, but whose sturdy roots are embedded in his nature whether he is aware of them or not.

The myth defines a point in time for the genesis of original sin, but though the myth be rejected, the breach in nature within man and about him remains a fact, manifesting itself pointedly in the conflict between, on the one hand, the necessity for mutual interdependence among all things, and on the other, man's almost ineradicable impulse toward self-determination. The popular song of some years ago, "I Want What I Want When I Want It," sums up his desire. The "what" and "when" do not need to be defined: the "plight of self-circling adoration"[30] is equally apparent where any act expresses the choice by the natural self for its natural desires. This natural self can be directed to good ends; it

often applies itself unselfishly. It transfers its activities from itself as a centre to its belief as a centre. It uses its angers on behalf of its religion or its morals, and its greed, and its fear, and its pride. It operates on behalf of its notion of God as it originally operated on behalf of itself. It aims honestly at better behaviour, but it does not usually aim at change; and perhaps it was in relation to that passionate and false devotion that Messias* asked: "Think ye when the Son of Man cometh he shall find faith upon the earth?"[31]

So natural man contrives an uneasy balance between amelioration and endurance, in which he alters whatever inconveniences he can, and puts up with the remainder as graciously as may be. At its best, this results in a life of high nobility, but also of tragedy: man accepting himself and his world for what he finds them to be, spending his life prodigally to realize a dream that obscurely troubles him with its inadequacy.

Let us not minimize the achievements of natural man: he creates, he controls, he endures, to the shattering of credibility. "The difficult we do immediately; the impossible takes us a little longer." But neither let us overrate his accomplishments. Consider, in contrast, the requirement of the co-inherence that man freely obey its laws of exchange. The principle of co-inherence specifies that man shall subjugate himself to a process which exists independently of him, although he is a part of it, and promises him a fair return—but not one that looks entirely desirable. Such obedience led Christ to the cross, and, naturally, we do not want to be crucified. We do not want even to run the risk of being crucified, or to put ourselves in a position where we might conceivably be crucified in any sense whatever. Almost the only obedience which the natural man undertakes gladly is that which is impelled by love, when the lover spontaneously wishes what will give pleasure to his beloved. But then, to be in love is precisely to live co-inherently. In that state,

laughter and love convert for a moment the dark habitations within the soul to renewed gardens in Eden. The primal knowledge is restored, and something like pardon restores something like innocence. . . . It is a not unpleasant thought that the word Fall occurs in this experience also; as if the divine grace, after man had insisted on falling once into a divided and contradictory knowledge, had arranged itself to trick him into an unexpected fall into restored and single knowledge.[32]

That moment, as we have seen, is a kind of revelation, but it is not a renovation. The temporary beatitude bestowed upon the lover is sustained by passion rather than by will, and when the passion dies, the

* Williams preferred "Messias," an earlier form of the title, to "Messiah," which was invented by the translators of the Geneva Bible.

will returns to its naturally fallen condition. The lover cannot help but choose that the vision should persist; his very nature as man ensures that he shall impotently will for it to continue as it began. He wants what he wants, when he wants it.

The one thing that man cannot do is the one thing needful: he cannot heal the breach in his nature that forces him to fall out of love; he cannot free himself from sin. He can certainly will to be healed, but the very act of willing makes his divided self central. When he wills to obey, he is still choosing his own master, determining for himself what or whom he shall follow. And nothing in nature or human nature offers him a way out of this impasse. All his labors cannot save him from the division that constitutes his essential nature, and even his determined will not to will makes himself the decisive source of energy and the determiner of his own direction. Thus all his works are flawed, all his communications more or less seriously corrupt. He senses this, and attempts to correct matters by self-discipline, or legal enactments, or education, or further research. Natural man depends upon himself—naturally.

Here is the heart of man's problem: that antagonism cannot of itself produce anything except more antagonism, that disorder cannot generate order. The created world is permeated with evil, while confusion feeds upon itself to its own increase.

The Adam and their children had been involved in a state of contradiction within themselves. The law had done its best by imposing on that chaos of contradiction a kind of order, by at least calling definite things good and definite things evil. The prophets had urged this method: repent, "cease to do evil, learn to do well." But even allowing that, in all times and places, it was possible to know what was good and what was evil, was it as easy as all that? . . . How could the single knowledge be restored? Or if the myth itself were false, how could the single knowledge be gained—the knowledge of perfection in all experience which man naturally desires and naturally believes, and as naturally denies and contradicts?[33]

Within this context of helplessness, Dante falls in love and returns to the life of the Adam as he was first made, knowing all things as good because there is nothing except good to know. But the Adam fell from grace, and now Dante falls out of love because the inherent division in his nature cannot for long endure integrity. Beatrice has communicated a new knowledge, and what Dante has learned from her he may choose to become, but the decision defeats its own purpose by enthroning his divided will. Logically and practically, man is trapped.

4

THE CROSS

Messias is certainly to be trusted, but only after his own manner. "He is his own interpreter," as a once popular hymn justly remarks. He is; no one else could begin to think of his interpretations. "My thoughts are not your thoughts." One cannot object; that is the nature of God, but it makes things more difficult.

—HE CAME DOWN FROM HEAVEN, 100

THE APPROACH TO JUSTICE

In man's extremity of impotence, one option remains to him. As long as he can think, he can examine his situation and protest to the heavens against it. As Williams comments, with reference to those who say

in love or in laziness, "Our little minds were never meant . . . " Fortunately there is the book of Job to make it clear that our little minds were meant. A great curiosity ought to exist concerning divine things. Man was intended to argue with God. . . . The pretence that we must not ask God what he thinks he is doing (and is therefore doing) is swept away. The Lord demands that his people shall demand an explanation from him. Whether they understand it or like it when they get it is another matter, but demand it they must and shall. . . . Such a philosophical curiosity is carried on into the New Testament. It accompanies the Annunciation. The Blessed Virgin answered the angelic proclamation with a question: "How shall these things be?"[1]

In particular, man can raise with his Maker the fundamental problem of justice between man and God. Granting that man is responsible to a degree for the state in which he finds himself, God is responsible without degree. We cry out almost in spite of ourselves for justice against a God whose will, whose "love," has condemned us to such an existence.

The original act of creation can be believed to be good and charitable; it is credible that Almighty God should deign to create beings to share His Joy. It is credible that He should deign to increase their Joy by creating them with the power of free will so that their joy should be voluntary. It is certain that if they have the power of choosing joy in Him they must have the power of choosing the opposite of joy in Him. But it is not credible that a finite choice ought to result in an infinite distress; or rather let it be said that, though credible, it is not tolerable (to us) that the Creator should deliberately maintain and sustain His created universe in a state of infinite distress as a result of the choice. No doubt it is possible to Him.[2]

If this be love, then love is what Williams called it, an "intolerable charity."[3] If this be justice, then justice is a terrible thing, that makes for an appalling universe wherein goodness is to be dreaded, and the peace of God—this kind of God—becomes a chastisement from which man has no recourse. There is, however, a breath of comfort in that Christianity admits the fact. It

certifies to us that we are not fools in being conscious of the twisting of all goodness to ignominy. We may (if it may be put so) approach God with that at least cleared up. We are not being unjust to His creation in the distaste we feel for it, nor even in the regret we feel that He allows it to continue.[4]

Man's ache to reject life, his flights from reality, his cynicism and despair, are all justified; they are accurate responses to fact.

But the Faith goes farther. It contends that the Lord God Almighty has admitted before man his responsibility for suffering and sin, to the extent that he has allowed—that is, caused—man to bring him to trial, to condemn him, and to put him to death. He

put Himself then to His own law, in every sense. Man (perhaps ignorantly, but none the less truly for that) executed justice upon Him. This was the world He maintained in creation? *This* was the world He maintained in creation. This was the best law, the clearest justice, man could find, and He did well to accept it. If they had known it was He, they could have done no less and no better. They crucified Him; let it be said, they did well. But then let it be said also, that the Sublimity itself had done well: adorable He might be by awful definition of His Nature, but at least He had shown Himself honourable in His choice.[5]

In law and in equity, he paid his debt to man, enduring public shame, public torture, and public death that the whole world might see its Lord justifying man's accusation of him. God had given man freedom; he consented to suffer for the results of its misuse. He had established a possibility; he accepted responsibility for having done so. This is not to say that he was guilty: as Williams points out in a similar connection, to speak of God in such terms "is not only heretical but flagrantly silly . . . But let the imbecile phrase stand; it does at least express the dilemma in which our understanding is placed."[6] Obviously he was innocent of wrong; it is equally obvious that he was responsible, and he declared this by the act of submitting himself to the cross. That act

does enable us to use the word "justice" without shame—which otherwise we could not. God therefore becomes tolerable as well as credible. Our justice condemned the innocent, but the innocent it condemned was one who was fundamentally responsible for the existence of all injustice . . .[7]

Justice, however, is not enough, because it leaves man permeated by sin, ridden with antagonisms, and incapable of unmixed good. We need not only justice, but redemption.

THE WORK OF REDEMPTION

It is conceivable that after the Fall, God might have destroyed his creatures, or left them to destroy themselves, or that he might have forced his will for good upon them and turned them into puppets. But instead, he reaffirmed their integrity, and by so doing he permitted a situation to develop where redemption was possible only by the fulfillment of two opposing conditions. The breach in nature could not be healed by the abrogation of the energy, diversity, and ordered exchanges of co-inherence, without losing the primary conditions of existence itself. Any process of redemption would have to operate from within the created world if its integrity were to be preserved. Yet because the co-inherence was riddled with evil, and because the creation could not heal its own wound, redemption would have to come from outside that chaos, deprivation, and antagonism, if goodness were to be restored—or, abandoning the myth, attained. And the process needed to be entire: "Unless everything's justifiable, nothing is,"[8] "for on the achievement in the extreme all depends."[9]

As a matter of literal fact, "mankind by itself could not endure the results of its choice, the total deprivation of good, and yet recover joyous awareness of good."[10] Therefore a job needed to be done, a nasty, exhausting, agonizing business that no human being could handle, and that many people did not see the need for and would not co-operate in. Man had sown the wind, and the whole of the co-inherent creation reaped the whirlwind. Weakness had created a situation that only strength could resolve, and the strength that offered itself to that weakness was the Omnipotence.

He would not only endure; he would renew; that is, accepting their act he would set up new relations with them on the basis of that act. In their victimization, and therefore in his, he proposed to effect an escape from that victimization. They had refused the co-inherence of the original creation, and had become (literally) incoherent in their suffering. He proposed to make those sufferings themselves co-inherent in him, and therefore to reintroduce them into the principle which was he.[11]

His work was not so much to teach man what constitutes sin, or to enable man to refuse sin, as to heal the infirmity which was sin.

Williams' analysis of this change rests upon his diagram of the infinite interdependence among individual things which is the co-inherence, with its great characteristic exchanges of functions and powers. This pattern provides him with his standards for the definition of good and evil. Good, to him, means not a static condition but all that increases the number and complexity of co-inherent relationships; and evil includes all that limits or resists the co-inherence. Good thus consists of the energies and acts that promote exchange, and evil the energies and acts that obstruct exchange. And when good and evil are defined in terms of energy, the act of redemption becomes a matter of redirecting the energy of evil toward good, of turning it around, of converting it from sin to holiness. Redemption therefore is precisely a conversion of energy.

Examples of physical conversion of one kind of energy into another lie all about us, wherever heat is converted into mechanical energy or mechanical energy into heat, where reciprocal motion is transformed into circular motion, electrical or chemical energy into light or heat, nuclear fission into electrical power or bombs. But the conversion of energy, like the co-inherence itself, is not restricted to such material interchanges. It is as much a spiritual as a physical phenomenon. Evil can be converted into good and good into evil.

A striking illustration of the conversion of evil into good occurs at the climax of Williams' novel *The Greater Trumps*. By means of magic,[12] a storm is generated over England; it escapes from the adept's control and threatens to engulf the entire world in a never-ending blizzard. An energy of destruction has come into being, and though its source is supernatural, it is as effective in nature as any purely natural storm would be, and as obedient as other energies to the laws of the conversion of energy. On a strictly physical level, the storm is irresistible, but because of its supernatural origin, it can be redirected supernaturally. This the young heroine of the story does. Guided by her will to love, and scarcely knowing what she does, Nancy places herself where the full brunt of the storm falls directly upon her.

. . . everlasting destruction was near. Between that threat and its fulfilment stood the girl's slender figure, and the warm hands of humanity in hers met the invasion and turned it. They moved gently over the storm; they moved as if in dancing ritual they answered the dancing monstrosities that opposed them. It was not a struggle but a harmony, yet a harmony that might at any moment have become a chaos. The column of whirling shapes arose and struck, and were beaten abroad under the influence of those extended palms, and fell in other whirling columns; and so the whole of the magical storm was sent pouring back into the place of its origin. And out on the Downs, over villages and roads, over the counties and cities of England, over rivers and mountains, there fell but the natural flakes of a snowy Christmas.[13]

Evil was converted into good by Nancy's passionate love, as simply as the direction of a ball is changed by impact with a surface. Part of the ball's—or the storm's—thrust is absorbed by the surface against which it strikes—the floor, or Nancy. The remainder impels the object—ball or storm—upon its new course. Neither the floor nor the girl has an easy job, but that is another matter.

The harsh fact is that evil invariably produces some kind or degree

of death. The result is no more capricious than the consequence of
mishandling fire: if one treats fire in a manner contrary to its nature,
the flame will go out or else it will injure something, and so far as the
inevitability of the result is concerned, it makes no difference whether
lack of skill or the bad luck of a gust of wind precipitates the damage.
However, that evil and error do cause death, be it as miniscule as the
waste of a moment or as comprehensive as obliteration bombing, leaves
open the question: "Death—to whom?" The swiftest glance at the
world about us, or at history, gives the answer: "To anybody who happens to be in its way." A forest fire started by carelessness can very well
leave its originator not only unharmed, but ignorant that he has caused
it, and leaving aside a hypothetical Last Judgment, his sin may never
result in any death whatsoever to him personally. But the deathly effects
are not thereby annulled; they are borne by others, that is, by the
innocent—or those who are at least innocent of that particular error
or sin.

In some circumstances, the innocent deliberately take upon themselves the impact of an evil energy. Firemen do this, safeguarding the
forest or the city by placing themselves in jeopardy, substituting their
skills, equipment, and lives for the inadequacies of other citizens. It
is this kind of substitution and redemption which Jesus is supposed to
have effected by his passion and death. There, confronting a more
deadly evil than rampaging fire, he substituted his lonely competence
for our incompetence. The powers that tried, condemned, and killed
him were particular instances of evil, and imaged all the evil that
had been, then was, and would come. The hammer that drove the
nails was weighted with the whole sin of the whole world.

. . . in the last reaches of that living death to which we are exposed
He substituted himself for us. He submitted in our stead to the full
results of the Law which is He. We may believe He was generous if we
know that He was just. By that central substitution, which was the
thing added by the Cross to the Incarnation, He became everywhere
the centre of, and everywhere He energized and reaffirmed, all our
substitutions and exchanges. He took what remained, after the Fall, of
the torn web of humanity in all times and places, and not so much by
a miracle of healing as by a growth within it made it whole.[14]

Accepting the full impact of both original and actual sin, he converted them into good, and enabled anyone who desires a part in that act to change from natural man to redeemed man. If and when man accepts that new alternative, he becomes free of the impasse that was created by his fallen nature. He can, now, recover love. Or better, he can now accept the restoration of love.

It was said of Christ in mockery, "Others he saved; himself he cannot save." Of course. That is precisely the point. If the energy of evil is to be deflected or transformed, someone or something must suffer its impact. Always and inevitably, a savior *cannot* save himself, because to save himself would be to leave the work undone. The jibe is "an exact definition of the kingdom of heaven in operation, and of the great discovery of substitution which was then made by earth."[15]

We are to love each other *as* he loved us, laying down our lives *as* he did, that this love may be perfected. We are to love each other, that is, by acts of substitution. We are to be substituted and to bear substitution. All life is to be vicarious—at least, all life in the kingdom of heaven is to be vicarious.[16]

Since we cannot save ourselves, we must allow others to save us while we save them or someone else, but always it is Christ in them and in us, whether or not he be known and named in the acts of substituted and exchanged love. It will be well for his person to be recognized in those acts, and failure to do so may handicap the accomplishment of the work, but it does not prevent it. As he said, to call him Lord is of less moment than to live by his life.[17]

In one sense, obviously, there is nothing new about either substitution or redemption. We are always vicariously suffering for others' sins, whether we like it or not, and whether we choose to function redemptively in those situations or not. Likewise, we sometimes benefit by redemptions that are bestowed upon us apart from any apparent human or divine intervention: most of us can cite instances where a misfortune or evil was redeemed—where it produced unexpected pleasure or good—by what appeared to be, and very likely were, entirely natural means. Neither adherence to, nor knowledge of, Christianity needs to be presupposed in order to participate in such events, because substitution and redemption, like co-inherence, are natural facts. That which Christianity adds to the natural facts is the declaration that these exchanges are also, under certain conditions, more than natural: "co-inherence did not begin with Christianity; all that happened then was that co-inherence itself was redeemed and revealed by that very redemption as a supernatural principle as well as a natural."[18] Or, more bluntly, "Nature and grace are categories of one Identity."[19] God has substituted himself within nature and for it,

not by infusing grace only but by himself becoming what himself had made, in the condition to which it had, by his consent, brought itself. It is this particular act, done of free choice and from love, which makes the Faith unique. All the deities, and all the sacrificed deities, the sun-myths and the vegetable simulacra, all that look much like the God of Christianity, look in the last analysis much unlike the God of Christianity. There is over all of them a Fate, or else there is no union with man. But Christian dogma has denied all Fate behind the Omnipotence as Alfred denied it in his translation of Boethius a thousand years ago. "But I say, as do all Christian men, that it is the divine purpose that rules them, not Fate." It has asserted the indivisible union of the two natures in the single Person. It has asserted that this union accepted responsibility; at the hand of God himself God has required the life of man.[20]

He died; he rose from the dead. "Life has known absolutely all its own contradiction. He survives; He perfectly survives."[21] And he ascended into heaven.

THE REDEEMER

I do not think that a sense of justice between man and God can exist without the Incarnation and the Cross. You cannot have justice without proportion, and you cannot have proportion without a common term, and the Incarnation is the common term.

—"Dr. Joad and Sin"

The ambiguous being who—according to Christianity—was fully God and fully man did not simply claim that he knew or taught or demonstrated the Way, the Truth, and the Life. He said that he *was* these things, and that there was no way for man to attain them except by co-inhering in him. "No man cometh to the Father but by Me." If this be true, then it is imperative that we should be clear as to who and what he was. Our information about him rests upon copies of documents that were written some time after the events themselves occurred, and probably not by eyewitnesses to those events. But

if, *per impossible,* it could be divinely certain that the historical events upon which Christendom reposes had not yet happened, all that could be said would be that they had not *yet* happened. If time and place are wrong, they are at least all that can be wrong. If, by a wild fantasy, the foundations of Christendom are not yet dug, then we have only the architect's plan. But those foundations can never be dug on any other plan.[22]

The Christian doctrine of the Christ begins with the commonplace actuality of a man who was born of a human mother, who ate and drank and slept, who enjoyed parties, whose feet got dirty from walking the roads of Galilee and Judea, and who worked and died. Then it goes on to assert in the Nicene Creed that this person was also "God of God, Light of Light, Very God of very God; Begotten, not made; Being of one substance with the Father." The *Quicunque vult*—the creed commonly, but mistakenly, attributed to St. Athanasius—is even more explicit: it states that he was "God, of the substance of the Father . . . and man, of the substance of His mother." That is, Messias was derived from two sources: from God who is uncreated, and from the created world that is derived from God.

In discussing this double derivation, Williams follows the pattern suggested by Duns Scotus, which is orthodox but not commonly taught in our day, and which Williams summed up by saying that "the world exists for the Incarnation rather than the Incarnation for the world. But the Incarnation became the Redemption for the sake of the world."[23] A fuller statement of this position appears in *The Forgiveness of Sins:*

The beginning of all this specific creation was the Will of God to incarnate. God himself is pure spirit; that is, in so far as any defining human word can apply to him, he is pure spirit. He had created matter, and he had determined to unite himself with matter. The means of that union was the Incarnation; that is, it was determined that the Word was to be flesh and to be man.

It is clear that this, like all his other acts, might have been done to himself alone. It was certainly not necessary for him to create man in order that he might himself become man. The Incarnation did not involve the Creation. But it was within his Nature to will to create joy, and he willed to create joy in this manner also.

He willed therefore that his union with matter in flesh should be by a mode which precisely involved creatures to experience joy. He determined to be incarnate by being born; that is, he determined to have a mother. His mother was to have companions of her own kind; and the mother and her companions were to exist in an order of their own degree, in time and place, in a world. They were to be related to him and to each other by a state of joyous knowledge; they were to derive from him and from each other; and he was to deign to derive his flesh from them. All this sprang, superfluous, out of his original intention—superfluous to himself and his direct purpose, not superfluous to his indirect purpose of love.[24]

Thus Christ, having his source in both God and the creation, exhibits the fullness of reciprocal derivation. We are derived from him, but also he is derived from us. God had made man in his image; by the Incarnation man made God in *his* image, not in anthropomorphic conjectures but in unambiguous physical flesh; and thereby God "gave us the final privilege of owing everything to ourselves as well as to Him."[25]

The significance of derivation, in all its forms, should not need to be spelled out. Children are derived from their parents; all living things derive sustenance from outside themselves; minds grow by interaction with the surrounding world. Giving, we permit others to be derived from us; receiving, we accept derivation from them. Gratitude is the acknowledgment of derivation, courtesy an expression of it. Within the Godhead, so the great creeds tell us, the Son is derived from the Father by the process of begetting, and the Spirit proceeds from the Father and the Son. Derivation is one of the primary types of co-inherence, which the Christian faith

has declared . . . to be the root and the pattern of the supernatural as of the natural world. And the Faith is the only body to have done so. It has proclaimed that this is due to the deliberate choice and operation of the Divine Word. Had he willed, he could presumably have raised for his Incarnation a body in some other way than he chose. But he preferred to shape himself within the womb, to become hereditary, to owe to humanity the flesh he divinitized by the same principle—"not by conversion of the Godhead into flesh, but by taking of the Manhood into God." By an act of substitution he reconciled the natural world with the world of the kingdom of heaven, sensuality with substance. He restored substitution and co-inherence everywhere; up and down the ladder of that great substitution all our lesser substitutions run; within that sublime co-inherence all our lesser co-inherences inhere. And when the Christian Church desired to define the nature of the Alone, she found no other term; It mutually co-inheres by Its own nature.[26]

The phrase quoted in the preceding paragraph, "not by conversion of the Godhead into flesh, but by taking of the Manhood into God," comes also from the *Quicunque vult.* Williams sums up the import of this antithesis in his novel *War in Heaven,* where the Archdeacon meditates on it after a discussion of parish business with another priest:

That the subjects of their conversation should be taken into God was normal and proper; what else, the Archdeacon wondered, could one do with parish councils? But his goodwill could not refrain from feeling that to Mr. Batesby they were opportunities for converting the Godhead rather firmly and finally into flesh.[27]

It is the distinction between imposing a pattern upon man, and inviting him to participate therein. Order is not to be broken by divine fiat; the difference between God and that which is not God is to endure; "it is the actual manhood which is to be carried on, and not the height which is to be brought down."[28] The method of imagery supplies a useful illustration here: the God-bearing image does not confer revelation from above, but raises the beholder to the vision of God in a movement from nature to that which is above and beyond nature.

"How shall this be?" Williams gives to the Virgin Mary the lines:

He has thrust
into this matter his pattern of bones, as Eve's
towers of cheeks and arrogant torches of eyes
edify red earth into a pattern of manhood.[29]

But this pushes the question back by only a very short step. Elsewhere he quotes Durand, Abbot of Troarn, on the Incarnation as being "contrary indeed to the common course of human nature, but not contrary to the reality of the human body."[30] The essential "reality of the human body" consists of its co-inherence, its internal and external exchanges and interchanges, its derivations, its giving and receiving, its interdependence of structure and function. If God maintains and acts within the general co-inherence of all things, it is conceivable that he should operate upon Mary's body within that co-inherence to effect the Incarnation, even if that act remains "a thing in which the union of all opposites was more fantastic than in any riot of mortal thought."[31] He "came down from heaven . . . and was made man," says the creed of Nicaea; "not by conversion of the Godhead into flesh, but by taking of the manhood into God," the *Quicunque vult* antiphonally replies, completing the diagram of reciprocal movement. Dante sings that Mary, the physical bearer of the Son of God, is the daughter of her son; Williams writes that

it is these great doctrines of matter, of exchange, of perfect love, which are made apparent in the paradox of the line *"Vergine Madre, figlia del tuo Figlio."* This is the secret of the universe, the mortal maternity of Godhead; beyond is but the ray of Godhead which contains all. Dante gazes still; "look intently; look." But it was the face of the girl in Florence which first startled him into looking.[32]

The unity in Christ of the incompatibles, God and man, was described by Williams in the phrase, "the apparition and the presence are one,"[33] but the word "one" contains a disturbing note of ambiguity when associated with a compound subject and a plural verb. Elsewhere he makes the puzzling statement, "Substance was love, and love was substance."[34] A statement in the *Quicunque vult* brings together these quotations: it says that Messias was "one altogether, not by confusion of substance, but by unity of person," a declaration that as it stands is hardly remarkable for its clarity. But let us return to the double operation of the mind in using the techniques of imagery, and to the balance it maintains between the image and its basis, keeping the similarities and the differences separate and together. One may hold up to a light, for comparison, two drawings made on translucent paper. Neither design interferes with the other; they may be alike or very different, but their exact relationships can be seen simultaneously. And in so far as the two pictures repeat the same configuration, they are "one altogether, not by confusion of substance but by unity of"—in this case, pattern.

An illustration from romantic love carries the elucidation further.

The maculate and immaculate, mortal and eternal, Beatrices are categories of one identity, in which each functions in and through the other, yet each is dependent upon the other. The separate categories, like the two drawings, can be compared and contrasted, but they coinhere in the girl so as to constitute an indivisible entity. Her humanity does not interfere with her glory, nor her glory with her humanity, because she is "one altogether . . . by unity of person," and her two substances are neither divided nor confused. And so for Messias, whose very humanity and Very Deity are also categories of one identity. However, there is this essential difference between Beatrice and Christ: she is indeed divine, partaking in her own manner and measure of the nature of God; but he, according to Christian definition, is God.

Or, to state it in another way, the exclusive Jesus and the inclusive Messias are related to each other in the same way that Beatrice as image is related to her basis. Both Christ and Beatrice are functioning as God-bearing images, the difference between them being—so far— one of degree rather than of kind: he is a more adequate image than she is. The difference in kind lies at the point where Christianity declares that in the single instance of Jesus, the God-bearing image was himself God: this one time in history, the absolute and ultimate Deity imaged himself to man. The Gospels corroborate this supposition: they record Jesus as making statements that are either flat contradictions or else the definitions of a double nature. He is reported to have said, "I and my Father are one," and "He that hath seen me hath seen the Father," as if he were, on earth as in heaven, the ultimate reality, the absolutely inclusive thing. Also, he is quoted as speaking of himself with equal vehemence in exclusive terms, as when, being addressed as "Good Master," he rejected the attribution: "only One is good, even God." A similar exclusive-inclusive duality is apparent in the records of his life:

the Fourth Gospel . . . particularly stresses the fact that all the events in the life of our Lord, as well as happening in Judaea, happen in the soul; whereas the Synoptics made it crashingly clear that all events that happen in the soul happened in Judaea. Why this second fact should be thought a rather low business is always surprising. But so it was.[35]

Human reason finds it difficult to keep accurately aligned the difference in substance with the unity of person, the relation of the derived to the source, and the distinction between imposed dominance and growth from within, together with the relation of each of these principles to the others, to the records of Jesus' life, and to Christian doctrine. When one adds to this complexity that the Person and the events may also be treated as images, one tends tacitly to become docetist, relaxing his hold upon the reality of the image as it exists in itself while he examines that to which the image refers. And in fact, there are few if any places where thought itself is so dangerous or so exasperatingly difficult. It is all very confusing. But all of it can be reduced to terms of relationships among different identities. The problems arise principally because natural reason prefers to exclude one of the conditions: it elides difference, or tries to escape relationship. Yet if there be no difference, there can be no relationship, and where there is relationship there must be differences. Among all these things "there is, no doubt, a separation, but the separation is the union; and this is not so alien from our experience that we need reject [here] what we have to accept in mere living."[36] The separation provides the polarity which is the necessary condition for the flow of power that unites entities into organic unity. In the Divine-Human Thing, the diversities were held in exact balance; knowledge of him requires that the knowing mind repeat, in its own manner, that essential tension. In order to grasp the vital relationship-in-difference of the Christ, the mind must share that vitality and balance the same opposites. The two natures are one, although

we certainly have to separate them in thought, because of the needs of the mind, as we have sometimes to divide form and content in poetry. But as the poetry is in fact one and indivisible, so is the fact; so even is the doctrine. The thing as it happens on the earth and in the world, the thing as it happens on the earth and in the soul, are two stresses on one fact; say, on one Word.[37]

THE ALTERNATIVES FOR MAN

By conception, birth, nurture, and the continuation of life, we belong to the co-inherence. We exist within it, and it sustains us. This is the

minimal law of nature. We are invited to belong to it maximally, and
the acceptance of that possibility unites our wills and our lives with
Christ's. The catch in the business comes because the choice between
minimum and maximum is not eliminated nor emptied of meaning.
Williams tells the story of a London churchwarden

who had always supposed himself to be a true Christian until one day
he realized, in a flash of clarity, that Christ was dogmatically asserted
to have died for all men—especially some few whom he strongly dis-
liked and others whom he extremely despised. He therefore, with great
good sense, abandoned his profession of Christianity in favour of a free
hand with his emotions.[38]

"If there is a God, if there is free-will, then man is able to choose the
opposite of God. Power, Wisdom, Love, gave man free-will; therefore
Power, Wisdom, Love, created the gate of hell, and the possibility of
hell."[39] Nothing could be simpler. One either co-operates with the co-
inherence or he resists it. One cannot be prevented from participating
in the exchanges of derivation and substitution, and he cannot be forced
into it. Hell is one of the live options, perhaps not as a state of being
after death, but certainly as a condition in this life. Dorothy Sayers
writes:

If we refuse assent to reality: if we rebel against the nature of things
and choose to think that what we at the moment want is the centre of
the universe to which everything else ought to accommodate itself, the
first effect on us will be that the whole universe will seem to be filled
with an implacable and inexplicable hostility. . . . If we cherish and
fondle that grievance, and would rather wallow in it and vent our
irritation in spite and malice than humbly admit we are in the wrong
and try to amend our behaviour so as to get back to reality, that is,
while it lasts, the deliberate choice, and a foretaste of the experience,
of Hell.[40]

It was no mere poetic contrivance that led Dante to picture the damned
surging forward in their eagerness to reach their allotted places, or that
suggested to Williams that he show Lawrence Wentworth enjoying his
progressive corruption.[41] They have chosen incoherence, and they have
what they want, although as Williams points out, their degradation
cannot be considered tragic, "since there could hardly be tragedy,
whatever grief, in a man's obstinate determination to be damned."[42]

Such a choice by man between good and evil is necessary to fulfill justice. God was responsible for sin, but man was also responsible. God has acted to redeem sin; man must also act. Having chosen wrongly in the beginning, he is given another opportunity to choose, and not merely at one point in his life but—if Christianity be correct—at any, up until death or the destruction of his capacity for preferring one thing above another. Neither alternative guarantees him immunity from labor and anguish: Williams was not overstating the case when he wrote: "As for our Saviour, only in the high sense of mystical redemption can He so far be generally said to have made life more tolerable for anybody."[43] He gave a salvation that could be achieved only by suffering, and a life attained only by dying.

"The Spirit of glory is upon you," said Saint Peter, contemplating persecutions and martyrdoms. The very idea—the very distant idea— of more pain and distress than ordinary life supplies is enough to chill the blood in our already pallid happiness. It was the consciousness of the extreme surrender and the sadness which must accompany it that caused one Christian poet to compose a hymn with the refrain:

> *Jesus Christ is our Redeemer*
> *And we wish to God he weren't.*

His intelligence was lamentable but his emotion was comprehensible. We are unhappy enough anyhow, and if Christianity is to mean a little more unhappiness, more discipline, more trials—the prospect not unnaturally drives men to that plea for annihilation which (the Church declares) is the only thing the Omnipotence will never grant . . .[44]

Having said this, however, we need to say something else: that redemption, in the Christian sense, is not only the escape from an impasse that has been described in some detail in the preceding chapters, but is also the achievement of a state that has not yet been described at all. It has various names—sanctity, redemption, the in-Godding of man, the state of grace, and a thousand others—but all the phrases carry some reference to a God who not only loves but *is* love. Let us then turn to the meaning of the word "love," defined not in romantic or non-romantic terms, but in the consummation implied by the declaration "God is love."

5

LOVE IN THREE PERSONS

[Of a musical setting for the Quicunque vult:] *The men and boys of the choir exchanged metaphysical confidences; they dared each other, in a kind of rapture . . . to deny the Trinity or the Unity; they pointed out, almost mischievously, that though they were compelled to say one thing, yet they were forbidden to say something else exactly like it; they went into particulars about an entirely impossible relationship, and concluded with an explanation that something wasn't true which the wildest dream of any man but the compiler of the creed could hardly have begun to imagine.*

—THE GREATER TRUMPS, 109

Up to this point, the discussion of the theology of romantic love has been eased by the continual presence of finitude. Images, nature, and redemption—or Beatrice, the Adam, and the Christ—are all more or less directly known by natural reason, even if their immediacy constitutes only a part of their essential being. The study of the Godhead, however, is another matter, whether one is considering the Person in Himself, or his relationship to the created world. Words betray man when he applies them to the Lord God: for example, "The famous saying 'God is love,' it is generally assumed, means that God is like our immediate emotional indulgence, and not that our meaning of love ought to have something of the 'otherness' and terror of God."[1] But we have no other word, and he has used it of himself. And so for all the words.

It is our first intellectual descent from heaven; we are compelled to use terms which we know are inaccurate. Saint Paul gave us a new vocabulary, and the great doctors have continued the work. Theology, like all sciences, has its own proper language, but even the theologians are always sliding back into a one-sided use of that language. Their terms ought to be ambiguous; they ought to carry meanings at once in

75

time and outside time. It cannot be done; and if it cannot among those experts, it certainly cannot among lesser creatures. So one is compelled to talk of God foreseeing and God determining, of pure Act as divisible, of eternity as altering, of perfection as becoming.[2]

Among theologians, it is axiomatic that every definition of the Holy Trinity that has ever been formulated has at some time been officially condemned as heretical, because all statements about it are necessarily incomplete and are therefore false. Theologians do not conclude from this, however, that they should abstain from investigating the existence and attributes of the Deity, or the structure of the Godhead itself. Perhaps they should; more likely they are right in continuing their inquiries. "There is no humility in refraining from asking the questions; the humility consists in believing that there may be an answer."[3]

THE KNOWLEDGE OF GOD

From its inception, Christianity has accepted reason, and the two Ways of the Images, as legitimate means for acquiring and transmitting information about God. It has fully recognized that images—ikons, creeds, rites, institutions, history—have a tendency to obscure the Absolute Deity, but that also they provide the only ways by which man can perceive him at all: a thing must have "its sign, for otherwise it could not be known to either mortals or angels; you cannot know a thing if there is no way by which it can be known."[4] The Divine coinheres in the images (This also is Thou), but is not identical with the images (neither is this Thou), and we turn again to the *Quicunque vult:* "not by confusion of substance."

The Church's use of the Way of Affirmation began when the Spirit descended in flame at Pentecost and the congregation responded in tongues other than their own, but descriptive analysis of that way was delayed for thirteen centuries, until Dante wrote his *Comedy*. Williams suggests that

it may be that that Way could not be too quickly shown to the world in which the young Church lived. It was necessary first to establish the awful difference between God and the world before we could be permitted to see the awful likeness. It is, and will always remain, necessary to remember the difference in the likeness.[5]

God is *known* by the affirmation of images, but he is known to be *God* by their rejection, and any adequate concept of him must include both simultaneously. He is immanent—he is known through the images; and he is transcendent—he is not the image. He made man in his image, but he is wholly other. He can be recognized by human reason, but not comprehended. All things diagram his nature, but he is hidden beyond the diagram. Experience, in affirmation and negation, supplies the content of knowledge about him; reason provides the form for the organization of experience; the two work together to reveal him.

The discipline of reason by skepticism is, perhaps, more important in thought about God than in any other area.

"Reason," as Chesterton said, "is always a kind of brute force. . . . The real tyranny was the tyranny of aggressive reason over the cowed and demoralized human spirit." There is, certainly, a way by which Reason can avoid that brutality; it is not a way that St. Thomas took, but it exists. It consists of saying, at the very beginning, as that other great rationalist Euclid said: "Let us suppose. . . ." What we agree to suppose is another matter; it may be that logic can be trusted, or that things exist, or that I can think, or anything else. We cannot begin to prove anything without supposing something.[6]

This eminently sound qualification leaves reason unassailed in its own place, but it assigns boundaries to that place. However, to repeat constantly this "Let us suppose" would become unbearably monotonous for writer and reader alike; therefore I shall suppose that the point is grasped and held in mind throughout the discussion of God that follows.

The process of learning about God by imagery and reason does not begin with accumulating data nor with asking questions, but with assenting fully to the facts of our present situation, and particularly to the fact of our ignorance.

Man was created as a finite being. It seems not to have been the Creator's intention, even at the first, that man should know the entire pattern of reality, but only that he should know accurately the portion of it that was needful for his life and joy and obedience. Given the Fall, however, man is doubly limited, by sin as well as by finitude. Thus "we cannot be sure that we have all the relevant facts; indeed (our intellects being finite) we know we have not, and that therefore all deductions may be wrong."[7] And because of sin, the self is warped to a degree that precludes complete accuracy in perceiving and reasoning. As Lord Arglay in *Many Dimensions* recognizes, "I know that any god in whom I believe will be consonant with my mind. So if I believe it must be in a god consonant with me. This would seem to limit God very considerably."[8] Is sanctity then a precondition for knowing the true God? No more than the knowledge of God is a precondition for sanctity, and no less. They are, perhaps, one thing, the one culmination that is offered to man. "There is only one sorrow, not to be a saint."[9] We start with ignorance and sin, and if there be any way out of these states, it lies in the direction that Williams indicated when he said, "Unless devotion is given to a thing which must prove false in the end, the thing that is true in the end cannot enter."[10]

In the *Divine Comedy*, Dante's imagery was both psychologically and theologically sound when he pictured himself accepting the dubious wisdom and virtue of Virgil to guide him to Beatrice. How can a citizen of hell lead a man to heaven? Virgil images—among other things—a natural goodness that falls short of Christian goodness, but that was more sound and exalted than anything Dante possessed at the moment of their meeting or for a long time thereafter. In placing himself under Virgil's direction, Dante gave himself up to the best that he knew, or rather, to the best that he was then capable of experiencing. He still remembered Beatrice, but the distance between them was too great for her to speak with him there in the dark wood. "The glory is apt to dazzle the beholder unless he already has a mind disposed to examine the pattern of the glory,"[11] and Dante's mind was not ready until he had passed through hell and purgatory.

To repeat: "Unless devotion is given to a thing which must prove false in the end, the thing that is true in the end cannot enter. But the distinction between necessary belief and unnecessary credulity is as necessary as belief; it is the heightening and purifying of belief."[12] If Dante had not followed Virgil, he could not have regained Beatrice nor reached the glory of which she was only an image. But also, Dante had to lose Virgil before he could meet Beatrice, and he had to turn away his eyes from her before he could see God. The requirement is, in the end, no more strange than a baby's abandonment of the elaborate co-ordinations of crawling when he learns to walk: he originally learned to crawl in order to make crawling unnecessary. It is true that some children do not crawl at any time, but proceed from other forms of exercise directly to walking. Similarly, some people seem to know God more easily, more swiftly, more directly, than others. But they have received no more of the grace of God than those who struggle for that awareness: the end is the same and the difference is intended for delight: "our handicaps are all different, and the race is equal. The Pharisees can even catch up the woman with the mites."[13] Being fallen, we wish everything were easy; being still imbued with the image of God, we set ourselves to the work that has been given to us individually, with the final reminder and warning of the impossibility that we confront: "If indeed the existence of God were certainly probable to human reason—but it cannot be; at best, we cannot admit more than a reasonable likelihood."[14]

THE GLORY OF GOD

The classic formulation of the doctrine of the Holy Trinity was given to the Faith by the Council of Nicaea.

The question there asked was capable of translation into all categories, including the category of exchange. Was there, in the most Secret, in the only Adored—was there that which can be described only by such infelicitous mortal words as an equal relation, an equal goodwill, an equal love? was this in its very essence? was the Son co-eternal with the Father? If there had been no creation, would Love have practised love? and would Love have had an adequate object to love? Nicaea answered yes. It confirmed, beyond all creation, in the incomprehensible Alone, the cry of Felicitas: "Another is in Me." The Godhead itself was in Co-inherence.[15]

St. Hilary condensed the Trinitarian dogma into an epigram: "We confess neither a solitary nor a diverse God."[16] The entire unity of the Godhead is not a static integration of uniformities or the repetition of monotony. "Co-inherence depends upon individuality, as much as individuality on co-inherence."[17]

Dorothy Sayers has expounded the Christian doctrine of individuality as follows:

The higher the created being is, and the nearer to God, the more utterly it is itself and the more it differs from its fellow-creatures. The lowest and least of created things—the prime matter—is formless and homogeneous: and inorganic matter has very little individuality. Plants have much more; animals are real individuals; and a human being is more than that: he is a person. When we come to the angels . . . they are thought of as possessing such super-personalities that the Schoolmen refused to think of them as being merely so many members of a species; they said that every angel was a separate species all to himself.[18]

Even in human relationships, one person cannot join with others, cohering or co-inhering, until he has something to relate with, that is, until he has sufficiently divided himself from all other persons and things that he is an individual; and the more individuality he achieves, the richer his relationships will be. The doctrine of the Three Persons expresses the ultimacy of this fact. The Godhead consists of the Alone, Creator and Father; the Son who is the Word, the Name and perfect expression of God, whose presence contradicts but does not negate the nature of the Alone; and the Holy Spirit, who "moves us to be, by every means to which we are called, the Images of Christ,"[19] and who is "the Life of the human Image toward its divine Original."[20] The three do not cohere, " 'stick to' each other," but they co-inhere, " 'abide in' each other,"[21] as the unborn child abides in its mother, the lover in his beloved, spirit in body, the Word in flesh. This is "a union very much beyond our powers to conceive; more than a union, a unity,"[22] and a unity so heightened in its perfection that Christianity makes good its claim to monotheism. "We worship one God in Trinity, and Trinity in Unity," says the *Quicunque vult,* and it goes on to specify that the Godhead is all one: one eternal, one uncreated, one almighty, one Lord, and—for our abiding comfort in our perplexities—one incomprehensible.

In the Godhead, the exchanges among the different persons *are* the life and the singleness of the life, and God created, according to his essential nature, not a multiverse but a universe that depends for its

own proper life upon interchange among separate identities. Relationship, like separation, is an ultimate metaphysical reality and the substantial basis for being. And in Williams' phrase, this substance is
Love, who is not a quality but a person who loves and can be loved
without "confounding the Persons nor dividing the Substance."[23]

This unity of the Godhead is like the unity of the City of God, in
that each person "is unique and is the subject of due adoration so, and
yet, all being unique, 'none is afore or after other, none is greater or
less than another.' "[24] Because each is unique, they reign conjointly,
and their existences are equal. There is, however, a correlate to this:
their functions are different. The Father creates by means of the Word
who is his Son; the Incarnate God redeems; the Holy Spirit acts within
man as well as outside and beyond him: it is at once the Inner and the
Outer Light. In Williams' theology, the difference in function implies
a hierarchy of function which in no way conflicts with the co-ordinate
principle of the equality among existences. He wrote that "existence is
equal, function hierarchical,"[25] and he explained the phrase by references to both nature and God. The activities of the brain not only
seem to be, but are, higher than the processes of digestion: the latter
nurtures minimal life; the former extends toward maximal sensitivity
and integration. The apostles and prophets are, as St. Paul said, higher
than "healings, helps, governments, diversities of tongues," so that the
Church rightly raises the priest above the laity. The servant is not
above his master, nor the wife above her husband. The most thorough-
going democracy cannot avoid lifting some above others into positions
of special responsibility and therefore of acclaimed superiority, and
beyond this, men's inherent capacities differ both in kind and in
degree.

However, the brain functions through the courtesy of digestion and
of circulation and of the hard armor of the skull that protects it from
damage. Therefore the "lower" processes share the dignity of the
"higher." Existence is equal.

> There is no prestige in any blessed priesthood,
> only the priesthood; no prestige in any
> true thing, but God and the thing itself.[26]

The intricate working of the co-inherence depends as much upon what

St. Paul termed the "uncomely parts" as upon those to which we give "more abundant honour." All, being parts of the one physical, social, or spiritual body, partake of the glory of the one, and each—in eternity if not before—glories only in that it belongs to the whole, and that it accomplishes there whatever exact function has been assigned to it.

In his poem "The Founding of the Company," Williams seals this doctrine with delight. One of Arthur's knights, speaking to the poet Taliessin, calls him "lieutenant . . . of God's new grace in the streets of Camelot," and Taliessin protests: to accept the ascription would be to arrogate to himself an undue and inappropriate authority. Within the Company (the Co-inherence, the City of God), such degrees cannot properly be claimed or given. His friend replies:

> "Sir, God is the origin and the end God;
> cause is comfort and high comfort is cause.
> Catch as catch can—but the higher caught in the lower,
> the lower in the higher; any buyer of souls
> is bought himself by his purchase; take the lieutenancy
> for the sake of the shyness the excellent absurdity holds."[27]

The term "excellent absurdity" carries, in this context, at least three implications that are significant for Williams' doctrine of equality and hierarchy. First, where equality is based upon uniqueness, as in the Godhead and Taliessin's company, pride of place is laughable. Second, "importance" is a relative matter: at one time or in one situation, the highest function for a given person may be eating, or for a given society may be the production and distribution of food. In other times or situations, poetry or prayer may be more needful than anything else for the individual or the society. Functions are hierarchical, but the position of any specific activity within the hierarchy continually changes: "at every moment the hierarchy alters, and the functions re-ladder themselves upward."[28] No function, activity, vocation, holds a fixed relation to other functions, activities, and vocations: throughout the co-inherence runs this theme of the perpetual alteration of authority and subordination between equals as they exchange places upon the ladder of the hierarchy. The natural phenomenon images, and is derived from, the supernatural Godhead, wherein

the Son is co-equal with the Father (as Origen held, and as was afterwards defined), yet the Son is obedient to the Father. A thing so sweetly known in many relations of human love is, beyond imagination, present in the midmost secrets of heaven. For the Son in his eternal Now desires subordination, and it is his. He wills to be so; he co-inheres obediently and filially in the Father, as the Father authoritatively and paternally co-inheres in him. And the whole Three Persons are co-eternal together—and co-equal.[29]

The principles of exchanged and hierarchical functions are on earth as they are in heaven, and because they are in heaven. Eternally, all created things are equal in uniqueness, and eternally they exchange places in joy.

Third, Taliessin's lieutenancy is absurd because, in the last depth of analysis, nothing which is outside God is in any real sense necessary. The Eternal remains unmoved in his perfection no matter what man does or leaves undone. We are amazed by it, as we are amazed that the sun should rise when our personal worlds have been shattered. And at times we resent that inflexibility. We are not necessary to God? No. Our redemption increases his effective love, but our damnation does not diminish it by a hair. Then surely we are at least necessary to others? No. Nothing which is outside God is necessary to any other being.

We are, so often and so often, anxious to be necessary to—A or B; we have been taught, so often and so often, the duties of giving, that we overlook the joy of being superfluous even to A or B, let alone to God, of having nothing whatever that we can give. Yet—ask Irene in her happiest state if she wishes to be only and wholly *necessary* to Crites, and not at all superfluous, and will she not hesitate on her answer? From what other source spring all Crites' own poems attributing love to her will and definite choice? Can the beloved do without us? Yes; her passion, if accorded, is greater so.

This is but an analogical argument, but it will serve. How burdensome the opposite view, that creation is necessary to God! heretical, though taken by distinguished minds. . . . The web of created glory, exterior to Himself, is unnecessary to Himself. So the Divine Word need not have had a Mother, but exquisitely decreed that he would. So we need not love, but mightily decide that we will.[30]

Man is superfluous. He was not created because God needed him, or needed a world. The Lord created in the "free generosity of love,"[31] and the sole duty, as the sole necessity for man, lies in enjoying God and all that he is and does, in the way and for the reason that God enjoys them. This is the excellent absurdity, that man is superfluous, but that God so loved these superfluous creatures that he died for them—that in the eternal present he dies daily for their joy. Because of the Fall, man can reach that joy only by traveling through and beyond the pain of existence, and he is able to accomplish this journey only because of the Redemption. But it is the joy that matters—God's joy, not man's, but man's because it is God's.

The organic structure of unity in trinity, of hierarchy in equality, of necessity in superfluity, is what Williams means by the phrase "the Glory of God," but "the glory is not something bestowed on the organism; it and the organism are one."[32] Occasionally it seems to be visible to the physical eyes, as to Moses on Sinai, to three disciples on the Mount of the Transfiguration, and to Dante when he beheld Beatrice and entered upon the Affirmative Way. It is the Shekinah, the indubitable manifestation of God, the eternal radiance of the web of exchange and of the operation of love through every unique thread of that web. In C. S. Lewis' phrase, it is "Order, envisaged not as restraint nor even as a convenience but as a beauty and splendour."[33] Williams writes of "the pattern of the glory";[34] he continually refers to its mathematically meticulous accuracy. "The word glory, to English ears, usually means no more than a kind of mazy bright blur. But the maze should be, though it generally is not, exact, and the brightness should be that of a geometrical pattern."[35]

It is this glory which is detailed in the poem "Taliessin in the School of the Poets," where "the young poets studied *precision*" in "*patterns* of *multilineal* red / sprinkled and spreading everywhere, / and *spaced* to one design." They contemplate "the crowned form of *anatomized* man, / bones, nerves, sinews, / the *diagram* of the style of the Logos," and Taliessin speaks of "the *weighed* gold of butterflies' wings," "the *straight*, absolute spine," "the *measuring* hazel wand." His "voice sharpened / on Virgil's *exact* word . . . he *defined* the organisms of hell."[36] Williams calls God's messengers *logothetes*[37]—accountants—and says that "the prophets are sent out from the visible mathematics of the glory to proclaim the moral mathematics of the glory. Morality is either the mathematics of power or it is nothing."[38] He defines theology as "the measurement of eternity in operation, of the bright cloud and the rushing wind."[39] To live within this exact order of interchange is to be in love—surrounded and supported by, and grounded in, love.

THE RETURN TO LOVE

If there had been no creation, Love would have practiced love and would have had an adequate object to love.[40] Love is whole, and wholly himself, the substance from which all lesser substances and loves are derived, at once the end of desire and knowledge, and the means to that end.

The best maxim towards that knowledge was yet not the *Know thyself* of the Greek so much as the *Know Love* of the Christian, though both in the end were one. It was not possible for man to know himself and the world, except first after some mode of knowledge, some art of discovery. The most perfect, since the most intimate and intelligent, art was pure love. The approach by love was the approach to fact; to love anything but fact was not love. Love was even more mathematical than poetry; it was the pure mathematics of the spirit. It was applied also and active; it was the means as it was the end. The end lived everlastingly in the means; the means eternally in the end.[41]

In *Many Dimensions,* the Stone was the Tetragrammaton, the Name of God, and Williams wrote of it that "the way to the Stone is in the Stone."[42] In the Gospel of John, it is written that the Word of God said "I am the Way." In practice, what it comes to is this: "If the pattern's arranged in me, what can I do but let myself be the pattern? I can see to it that I don't hate, but after that Love must do his own business."[43] Love in this sense is not only dogma but the active principle of nature and supernature; it is moral obligation and description of natural facts and a Person who is loved and who efficiently loves.

None of these assertions can be proved or disproved. They are definitions of terms, and declarations of the same type as Peter Stanhope's statement that life is "either good or evil . . . and you can't decide that by counting incidents on your fingers. The decision is of another kind."[44] We must suppose one thing or the other: this definition of

"God is love" is true, or it is false, and either we follow or we abandon it. Let us, at least for the moment, suppose that it is true; then "the glory of God is in facts. The almost incredible nature of things is that there is no fact which is not in His glory."[45] Boethius' dialogue with the Lady Philosophy traces the theme to its inevitable conclusion:

There was no way of eluding the result, nor did the imprisoned Roman elude it; he followed his meditations to their only end—"Then all fortune is good." "Every lot is good . . . whether be it harsh or be it pleasing." So Philosophy; and Boethius: "At this I was afraid, and said: 'What thou sayest is true; yet I know not who would dare to say so to foolish men, for no fool could believe it.' "[46]

Williams agrees with Boethius on both counts: "all luck is good,"[47] even when it is indeed a terrible good, and he who finds it so is no longer a fool in ultimate matters, though Greek and Jew deride him. This is the intellectual return to Eden, to the paradisal knowledge of all things as good because, in very truth, they are good.

Let it be added, however, that Christianity does not expect us to adjust our emotions into conformity with this dictum, but only our judgments: to approve is not at all the same thing as to be pleased, and the latter ought never to be forced. "The world is painful in any case: but it is quite unbearable if everyone gives us the idea that we are meant to be liking it"[48]—thus C. S. Lewis describes Williams' attitude. Indeed, in so far as we remain fallen, we cannot like the good, because to be in sin—original or actual—means to dislike the good.

"The I AM (and indeed, all life) is experienced in an evil manner, but the I AM has sworn that he and it shall be known as good, and only good, to whoever chooses."[49] "To whoever chooses": that is, not by revelation but by the lifting up of the manhood into God, or more simply, by man's becoming, "without a miracle . . . the perfection he has seen."[50] The Adam before the Fall was right in knowing all things as good, and after the Fall he was wrong in knowing some things as evil. This one learns—if at all—in defiance of the obvious and almost in defiance of sanity.

Men had determined to know good as evil; there could be but one perfect remedy for that—to know the evil of the past itself as good, and to be free from the necessity of the knowledge of evil in the future;

to find right knowledge and perfect freedom together; to know all things as occasions of love.[51]

This refers in part to the infinite possibilities for redemption of evil into good, and in part to the nature of forgiveness. But beyond these, it reaches to the place of the unredeemed and the unforgiving. Actually, as well as potentially, they are contained within the order which is God's glory; they testify to the glory that will not let them go.

On a fairly elementary level, Paradisal knowledge can be described in such terms as the tendency of confusion to stimulate the search for order, or the way a misunderstanding between lovers can lead to a more accurate understanding and thus increase their felicity. More profoundly, it includes the supposition that errors of choice rest upon the magnificent fact of freedom, and that cruelty implies the existence and acceptance of relationship, even while it is a wrong relationship or wrong action within the relationship. But so far, this is merely the frequently sentimental recognition that "there is some good in everything." It is not yet the knowing after another manner, the "passionate intention to know all things after the mode of heaven, and it is impossible to know evil as good if you insist on knowing it as evil."[52]

Some confusion is inevitable here for all of us who come short of that intricate and sublime accuracy. We who are outside beatitude can hardly comprehend how heaven perceives the relation of evil and good, or how one thing can be at the same time real evil and real good. As C. S. Lewis reminds us, it would be grossly inaccurate to ignore or approve "the infinite menaces of life, the unremitted possibility of torture, maiming, madness, bereavement, and (over all) that economic insecurity which, as he [Williams] said in *War in Heaven,* poisons our sorrows as well as modifying our joys."[53] These are natural facts and genuinely evil—within nature. To know them as evil is to be accurate but also to be limited by nature. To know them as good, it is necessary to enter a world of being and discourse that transcends, but also includes, nature. In that larger context, evil has a double nature, and it is up to us to have double sight.

The story of the greatest evil recorded in history echoes with both ways of knowing evil, the one in Jesus' statement about Judas, "It were good for that man if he had not been born," and the other in the incredible moment when the two men kiss in greeting and Jesus calls Judas "Friend."

> Think that our Lord
> saw his enemies as his best and fairest friends
> coming to do what he could not do for himself,
> even he; that is, to die at the will of another,
> and could not help loving them for that kindness.[54]

Later, the reconciliation of natural with Paradisal knowledge is exhibited in the resurrected body of Christ, because

when he returned, he returned with his scars. The Resurrection is something other than the spiritual survival. It is the continuation of the physical in the highest degree; the continuation of the past into the present. But the past was now exposed. His glory secluded the scars no more; therefore it did not seclude the sin that led to them.[55]

Neither did that glory deny that sin was sin, nor that pain was pain, nor that death was death. The new Adam and the new Eden are complex: the wounds are healed but the scars remain; the evil is not forgotten, but remembered, so that it may be taken into God and there transformed into good, and recalled with joy. Even here and now, it is possible to know that God "has only Himself to give, and He, even He, can give it only in those conditions which are Himself."[56] "This also is Thou," whatever the "this" happens to be, and the "Thou" is unchangeable love.

Now at last we can return to the problem faced by the lover when he discovers that his love has died, and that he cannot restore it. His situation remains unaltered in that his will is still corrupt and therefore cannot take him back to that which was lost. His situation is changed in that a new alternative is offered him: a technique of redemption by substituted love which is a means of grace, and a manner of loving that offers the hope of glory. What he can do, even in the blackness of sin, is to will love—not that he should again love his beloved or anyone, nor that she should love him or anyone, but that love *is*. His point of freedom lies in the choice between recognizing and allying himself with all loves, whenever and wherever they occur, and

recognizing and allying himself only with his personal loves. A fragment of conversation between Joseph and Mary in *Seed of Adam* sets
forth the distinction. The Annunciation has just taken place.

Joseph.   Mary, you are changed; you are in love.

Mary.   Yes, Joseph.

Joseph [*starting up*].   Ah, ah! but who . . . ?

Mary.   No one, Joseph.
          Only in love.

Joseph.   It must be then with someone.

Mary.   Dearest, you did not hear: we said *in love*.
          Why must, how can, one be in love with someone?

Joseph.   Because . . . but that is what *in love* means;
          one is, and can only be, in love with someone.

Mary.   Dearest, to be in love is to be in love,
          no more, no less. Love is only itself,
          everywhere, at all times, and to all objects.
          My soul has magnified that lord . . .[57]

Mary does not love from herself; she is a vehicle of Love, a means by
which it relates all things to each other—and at that, an unnecessary
means, since Love can very well do its own loving. "The God-bearer
/ is the prime and sublime image of entire superfluity."[58] Yet the superfluous may adorn necessity and contribute to delight: "If an image
lacks, since God backs all, / be the image, a needless image of peace /
to those in peace."[59] In like manner, Dante's Beatrice is the vehicle of
Love, but her death deprives him only of *his* love for *his* beloved. Bitter
though that may be, he can look about him and see that others love,
and in whatever grief at his separation from love, he can acknowledge
its continuing life. In time, he may even be glad thereof.

To will love, and to will that it appear where and as it chooses, is to
will necessity and to be free of necessity. The God who is Love made

the delight of a perfect response to his initiative a part of the working
of the web. We could not otherwise become at once perfect servitude
and perfect freedom. They are one and interchangeable, at least in
consciousness: even now, in some states of love, it is possible at once
to delight in being bound and to delight in being free. As Blake said:

"Contraries are not negations." Much less there. In this world they tend to become opposites; that too perhaps is the result of what then happened [at the Fall].[60]

It is not necessary that we join ourselves to necessary love. Again and again, man is free to resent and resist necessity, to hate love, to refuse joy, and nothing in heaven or earth can prevent him from following that course. But he is also free to love, and he who loves will find that all luck is good to the ends of the world—future and past—in God.

6
NATURE AND SUPERNATURE

The "supernatural" must . . . in some sense include the "natural."
"A new earth" was promised as well as "a new heaven." Whatever the
promise means, that earth is presumably in some relation to this earth.
Matter, certainly, is by definition the opposite of spirit. It is ap-
parently as far the opposite of God (leaving will and morals out of the
question) as God chose to create. But it did not therefore become less
significant of Him than that less technical opposite which is called
spirit.

—"NATURAL GOODNESS," 76

The definition of love as an omnipotent Person, and the description of
universal natural law as love's will, raises a number of problems that
center upon the restrictions imposed upon love by time, space, and
matter. One of the oldest of these questions has to do with the "virtuous
pagan" who has never heard proclaimed the gospel of exchanged love,
or who in all honesty and goodwill cannot accept it. Closely related to
this is love's apparent inability to alter the dreadful past, or to reach
beyond physical death. Does nature in fact circumscribe love? or if not,
how can love overcome these physical limitations without destroying or
contravening the physical world?

Williams' answers to these questions are complex, subtle, and so distinctive as to require from most of us a fairly radical effort of the
imagination. He is a supernaturalist in that he predicates modes of
existence other than those which are perceived by our physical senses
and adequately known—or knowable—by natural reason. Four such
worlds, or kinds of being, or "provinces," or "themes," appear in his
writings: God, eternity, nature, and a world which in his Arthurian
poetry he named Broceliande. Broceliande includes, among other
things, witchcraft and faerie; C. S. Lewis described it as being "what

the Greeks called the *Apeiron*—the unlimited, the formless origin of forms."[1]

Strictly speaking, only God is above or beyond nature, so that he alone is truly supernatural, and eternity, Broceliande, and nature, are alike natural. Common practice, however, identifies nature with the world of matter, space, and time that are ordinarily perceived and taken for granted, and in this discussion there is no good reason for running counter to that usage. Therefore supernature, here, will refer in general to the created worlds of eternity and Broceliande, as opposed to nature, and in specific to Williams' definition of supernature as that word was understood in the classical and early Christian periods:

The use of the word supernatural has been rebuked, and indeed it is a little unfortunate. It did not imply then, nor should it ever have implied since, any derogation from the natural order. But it did imply that that order was part of and reposed on a substance which was invisible and which operated by laws greater than, if not in opposition to, those which were apparent in the visible world.[2]

Again to speak strictly, only God has ultimate and unqualified reality; all created realities are derived from and dependent upon him. Within the creation, there seem to be many kinds of realities which, so far as we can tell, are equally real but different. Nature, even apart from supernature, exhibits this: an idea has as much reality as a stone, although the thought lacks physical weight and dimension, and the stone lacks other, less easily definable characteristics that are shared by all mental products. Friendship is as real as a skein of geese, but no more real, and London is as real as the City of God, but differently real. However, we shall not be concerned here with degrees of reality: we shall have work enough establishing the primary distinctions between nature and supernature, the position of Broceliande between nature and eternity, and the ways in which exchange takes place among the worlds.

SUPERNATURE: ETERNITY AND BROCELIANDE

As a preliminary, a notable difference between nature and supernature consists in the fact that for man in nature, entrance into supernature is optional. The process of natural living does not constrain anyone seriously to predicate, or to study, or to be aware of, any part of supernature. Christian orthodoxy does insist upon the theoretical and practical acceptance of God as transcending nature, as well as immanent within it, and traditionally it has permitted the exploration of other modes of being, such as the mystical—though often without any great enthusiasm—but it has not required them. And Williams states his central theses in terms of supernature, but one can grasp and even adhere to them without committing himself to belief in super-natural realms or processes.

Some people, however, are "caught by a rumour"[3] of worlds or a world other than nature and God. A drive from within, a lure from without, impel them toward mysticism, sorcery, faerie, or some other of the regions of supernature. It presses upon them and will not be gain-said. The works of W. B. Yeats and of Walter de la Mare echo with it. Wordsworth said in his *Prelude,* "my brain / Worked with a dim and undetermined sense / Of unknown modes of being." C. S. Lewis wrote that supernature is

what most romantics are enamoured of; into it good mystics and bad mystics go: it is what you find when you step out of our ordinary mode of consciousness. You find it equally in whatever direction you step out. All journeys away from the solid earth are equally, at the outset, jour-neys into the abyss. Saint, sorcerer, lunatic, and romantic lover all alike are drawn to Broceliande . . . Dante and D. H. Lawrence, Boehme and Hitler, Lady Julian and the Surrealists, had all been there. It is the home of immense dangers and immense possibilities.[4]

Williams' most detailed description of the elemental perception of supernature appears in his book on the history of witchcraft, but is equally valid for all the realms of supernature.

The predisposition towards the idea of magic might be said to begin with a moment which seems to be of fairly common experience—the moment when it seems that anything might turn into anything else. We have grown used—and properly used—to regarding this sensation as invalid because, on the whole, things do not turn into other things except by processes which we realize, or else at least so frequently that we appreciate the probability. But the occasional sensation remains. A room, a street, a field, becomes unsure. The edge of a possibility of utter alteration intrudes. A door, untouched, might close; a picture might walk; a tree might speak; an animal might not be an animal; a man might not be a man. One may be with a friend, and a terror will take one even while his admirable voice is speaking; one will be with a lover and the hand will become a different and terrifying thing, moving in one's own like a malicious intruder, too real for anything but fear. All this may be due to racial memories or to any other cause; the point is that it exists. It exists and can be communicated; it can even be shared. There is, in our human centre, a heart-gripping fear of irrational change, of perilous and malevolent change.

Secondly, there is the human body, and the movements of the human body. Even now, when, as a general rule, the human body is not supposed to mean anything, there are moments when it seems, in spite of ourselves, packed with significance. This sensation is almost exactly the opposite of the last. There, one was aware that any phenomenon might alter into another and truer self. Here, one is aware that a phenomenon, being wholly itself, is laden with universal meaning. A hand lighting a cigarette is the explanation of everything; a foot stepping from a train is the rock of all existence. If the first group of sensations are due to racial fear, I do not know to what the second group are due—unless indeed to the Mercy of God, who has not left us without a cloud of witnesses. But intellectually they are both as valid or invalid as each other; any distinction must be a matter of choice. And they justify each other, at least to this extent, that (though the first suggests irrationality and the second rationality) they both at first overthrow a simple trust that phenomena are what phenomena seem.[5]

Such experiences are like the Beatrician in that they can be followed or abandoned, but he who follows them will find that all the forces and alternatives that exist in nature are present in supernature to a heightened degree. Therefore it is dangerous. Passions there are more extreme, risks more severe, disasters more overwhelming, laws more strictly binding. Goodness is more intensely good in supernature than in nature, and evil more sharply evil than anything we experience in ordinary life, so that it is more imperative that moral judgments be accurate.

Further, the annals of mysticism and romanticism, and the traditions of witchcraft and faerie, agree that after a certain point in the exploration of supernature, one cannot turn back to the ordinary world.

In sorcery as in sanctity there is no return. The master in any art who abandons the methods of his mastery and falls back on prentice habits runs a fearful risk. No lover, of any kind, not even the lover of himself, can safely turn from maturity to adolescence. His adolescence is in his maturity. The past may be recalled and redeemed in the present, but the present cannot be forsaken for the past.[6]

Dante wrote of that moment: "I have set my feet in that part of life beyond which it is not possible to go with any intention of return."[7] "That part of life," "a certain point"—the literature does not specify how one identifies that truly continental divide, or precisely at what stage one confronts it, or whether the crossing be the matter of a single choice or the cumulative result of many trivial choices. But it does specify that those

> who enter
> come rarely again with brain unravished
> by the power of the place—some by grace dumb
> and living, like a blest child, in a mild and holy
> sympathy of joy; but the rest loquacious with a graph
> or a gospel, gustily audacious over three heavens.[8]

Among the "blest children" are those who have seen the Glory, the Shekinah of which Dr. Joseph Sittler has said, "Once you have seen it, you can have no argument with it, but only argument under it."[9] The "gustily audacious" include those who establish and follow the esoteric religions that offer panaceas to their initiates, and the control of extraordinary powers to their adepts. This is not the place to argue whether the cultists and magicians actually accomplish what they claim; the point is simply that all supernaturalists seem to concur on some of the characteristics of supernature, and that this evidence comes from remarkably diverse sources.

NATURE AND ETERNITY

Whereas nature functions in time, eternity is timeless, and with the word "timeless" we confront immediately the popular misconception that equates timelessness with infinite duration. We speak of the eternal rest of the dead, meaning that their repose is unending, or of eternal joy, or of an eternity of torment, with the implication of an interminable state. Williams, however, interprets timelessness as precisely the absence of time, a condition of absolute and infinite contemporaneity.

In nature, man commonly recognizes past, present, and future, and accepts his inability to act except within the running present. The past cannot be recovered or altered, and the future is accessible only in that it is affected by the present.

"*Now* is the accepted time; *now* is the day of salvation." In this sense there is nothing but *now;* there is no duration. We have nothing to do with duration, and yet (being mortal) we have to do with nothing but duration.[10]

Eternity, however, contains only the present—but it contains in a blinding simultaneity all present moments that have been, are, and will be. Every instant in time, with all that takes place therein, exists in eternity. Every person, every blade of grass, every period of passion or sleep or sin, every meeting or parting, has eternal life. Nothing which ever is ever ceases to be, and everything that is now in process of happening has already been completed. "Each of us has already died; there only remains for us to discover the manner of our dying."[11] Our natural life shows us, as it were, successive fragments of a painting which exists in its entirety beyond our purview, but which in eternity we see complete. So when we pray that God's will be done on earth,

the events for which we sincerely implore that fulfilment upon earth are already perfectly concluded by it in heaven. Their conclusions have to be known by us on earth, but they already exist as events in heaven. . . . In that simultaneity the passion of the prayer is already granted; all that is left for us to do is to discover in the process of time the conclusion that we have implored in time.[12]

Eternity and nature have in common the double present, temporal and eternal, where the two worlds intersect. At that point, one who yet lives in time can enter the eternal present by means of the temporal present, and the exchanges of substitution, redemption, and love can cross the barrier of time without abrogating the separate laws that govern the separate worlds.

What Williams means by the intersection of time with eternity will be more forcibly expressed, and more completely summarized, by one of his own illustrations than by any number of propositional statements. In his novel *Descent into Hell,* a young girl, Pauline Anstruther, is introduced by the poet Peter Stanhope to the theory and practice of substituted love. Later, her attention is drawn to the history of her ancestor John Struther, who had been burned for his religious convictions four centuries earlier, and who was reported by those who had witnessed his martyrdom to have entered the fire "in a tumult of joy." Pauline is tormented by the old tale, and by her awareness that she cannot give the martyr such assistance as she had received from Stanhope. Her grandmother challenges her on this point: " 'But how could he take it before I'd given it?' Pauline cried, and Margaret said: 'Why do you talk of *before*? If you give, you give to It, and what does It care about *before*?' "[13]

Pauline accepts the principle, and finds herself in John Struther's cell on the morning of his death. There and then she frees him from his fear, as she had been freed by her friend. Her offer of release is made in the temporal present, is received into the eternal present, and re-enters time in the sixteenth century, four hundred years before she had tendered the gift.

The doctrine that Williams here presents in fictional terms, he elaborates in his theological works, especially in *He Came Down from Heaven*, where he writes:

The vicarious life of the kingdom is not necessarily confined to sequence even among the human members of the kingdom. The past and the future are subject to interchange, as the present with both, the dead with the living, the living with the dead.[14]

This holds no implication that what had happened in the past was made not to have happened; it explains why the past occurred as it did, by referring to another event that took place later in time, but concurrently in eternity. The events of the past remain irrevocable and irreducible. But one of the facts (in the story) was that John Struther had cried out triumphantly, as the flames engulfed him, "I have seen the salvation of my God."[15] And it was Pauline's intervention that produced his triumph. It is worth emphasizing that apparently Williams intends this not as a speculation but (accepting the limitations of language) as literally true, an accurate description of a metaphysical reality. "If indeed all mankind is held together by its web of existence, then ages cannot separate one from another. Exchange, substitution, co-inherence are a natural fact as well as a supernatural truth."[16]

No derogation or limitation of man's freedom is involved here. Does the fact that you know today the decisions which you made yesterday predetermine their character? Of course not. *Then* they were made; *now* they are known to have been made. In eternity, decisions are not known in advance because in eternity there is no "in advance." It has its own mode of being that cannot be bound into the terms of time, or into words written and read consecutively. *Descent into Hell* continues to provide the clarification: since the martyr had, in fact, been released from his fear, was not Pauline predetermined to save him from it? To Williams, freedom of choice is primary: the girl is utterly free to accept or to reject any participation whatsoever in the event. However, if she refuses, another will take up the work, or has already done so, freely giving what she freely withholds. Or the event would have occurred otherwise, and history reported some other end for the martyr.

The difficulties in this may be eased by pointing out that "in the place of the Omnipotence there is neither before nor after; there is only act."[17] Obviously one can know and participate in events that are in the process of happening where and when one is: it is no more complicated than conversing with one's family, or lending a book to a neighbor, or sharing work with a friend. So long as one is contemporaneous with the others, of course he can exchange with them. All that Williams does is to stretch our notions of contemporaneity, and to demonstrate man's capacity for operating within that larger present. At the table of exchange, all times are now, and no one who seeks to receive or give aid is denied. Therefore anyone in the present can contribute to the salvation of any other person from fear, sin, pain, ignorance, or any other disorder. On this basis, the early Church practiced baptism for the dead, and Williams suggests seriously that one who has been nurtured by Virgil or Plato or Isaiah can now help to introduce them to the ranges of joy of which they were deprived by the circumstances of their temporal existence. In his poem "On the Death of Virgil," Williams shows Virgil's Christian students gathering at his death to give the pagan poet the opportunity for Christian love that he had lacked in life, and lifting him by their love into its full glory.

Unborn pieties lived.
Out of the infinity of time to that moment's infinity

they lived, they rushed, they dived below him, they rose
to close with his fall; all, while man is, that could
live, and would, by his hexameters, found
there the ground of their power, and their power's use.
Others he saved; himself he could not save.
In that hour they came; more and faster, they sped
to their dead master; they sought him to save
from the spectral grave and the endless falling,
who had heard, for their own instruction, the sound of his calling.

Virgil was fathered of his friends.
He lived in their ends.
He was set on the marble of exchange.[18]

To many, this will sound fantastic, and indeed, from the point of view
of the assumptions commonly made about the nature of the world and
of time, it is in the worst sense fantasy. Those who so react to it had
better leave it alone, except in so far as they should, in courtesy, note
that others testify, "This we have seen; this we have done." Williams
may be talking rubbish, as St. Thomas Aquinas may have been when
he "declared that the denial of sorcery was heretical,"[19] but he talks it
soberly and circumstantially, and other witnesses confirm him in the
same measured terms.

As time is the natural correlate, and image, of eternal contemporaneity, so the image and correlate of space in nature is, in eternity,
speed. Nature contains examples of this: how far apart are New York
and London? The answer can be given in miles or in time: by sailing
vessel they are weeks apart, by plane hours, by radio the distance can
be computed only by delicate instruments, so swiftly do those waves
travel. In eternity, distance between entities depends upon intention,
and only the hesitant impulse or the lack of training in movement increases the length of any journey to any time or place. In *All Hallows'
Eve,* when the two dead girls run through the streets of the eternal city
toward their living friend,

Lester lost ground; she did not know clearly why she went, but Evelyn
did; therefore the one ran faster and the other slower, for still in the
outer circles of that world a cruel purpose could outspeed a vague pity.
But the cruelty could not reach its end.[20]

So Pauline hurries to meet her ancestor; so the Archdeacon of Fardles runs off with the Holy Grail in a very fast car; so the Unicorn, imaging the swiftness of God's grace, blesses the Breaking of Bread in the Wesleyan chapel.[21] This immediacy is the measure of God's distance from man: "The thing we call 'grace' is here and there and gone and back, like the lightning of the living creatures, and a greater: 'so shall also the coming of the Son of Man be.' "[22] Motion is of eternity's essence, swift and slow, broken and continuous, directly in speed and indirectly in rest, through all times and places corresponding with space in nature.

Williams has separated and united time and eternity in terms of the double present and of the correspondence of space with speed; similarly, he divides and joins body and flesh with the concept of matter. "Mind is never to put off matter,"[23] he writes, and "the spirit waits for the letter and the letter for the spirit; both together are love."[24] This stands in direct contradiction to the view which pictures eternity as inhabited by disembodied spirits, but it belongs to orthodox Christian doctrine, and is buttressed by the content of the romantic moment. "The flesh and the soul are one: that is the nature of the experience of beatitude."[25]

The knowledge of this singleness of man's being was broken by the Fall. At that time or in that timeless state,

the breach between body and soul, the breach in the indivisible, was fully established. The great physical ratification of that breach was Death. Whether something like Death—some change, some conversion—existed before the Fall we cannot know. But the Bible is full of suggestions that Death, as we do know it, is a result of the Fall. It is an outrage; it is a necessary outrage. It is a schism between those two great categories of physical and spiritual which formed the declaration in unity of one identity.[26]

The proposition that flesh, and person or mind or soul or spirit, are categories of one identity can also be expressed by saying that the spirit is the inward correlate of the outward body, or that they are different manifestations of the unique and indivisible person. In any case, the individual is one thing: his flesh is inseparable from his spirit in the

same way that a poem is inseparable from the words of which it is
made and by which it is communicated. Without the words, the poem
has no existence, and without matter, spirit does not exist.

Two lines of Williams' poetry convey the difference within the union
of these diverse modes of the single existence: "Flesh knows what spirit
knows, / but spirit knows it knows."[27] The identities obey the same
laws, are held within the single order, and in their various ways fulfill
the principle of difference. Their interdependence functions to constitute the final oneness of being. "Partnership has become a more intense
unity."[28] Again we find "in its twyfold Nature the golden Ambiguity"[29]
that the *Quicunque vult* declares: "neither confounding the Persons
[the modes of being] nor dividing the substance."

The individual identity that is man exists in nature as physical flesh,
and in supernature as eternal body, the former being the whole man
functioning in time and space, the latter the same whole man functioning contemporaneously in unrestricted movement. Both physical flesh
and eternal body are material—but we shall do well to remember, at
this point, the theory of modern physics that matter is energy organized
in a particular way. Williams touches on this in *The Greater Trumps,*
where he describes Nancy going into a church.

. . . her intelligence reminded her, even as she entered, that the apparent quiescence, the solidity, the attributed peace of the arched
doorway was one aspect of what, in another aspect, was a violent and
riotous conflict of . . . whatever the latest scientific word was. Strain
and stress were everywhere; the very arch held itself together by extreme force; the latest name for matter was Force, wasn't it? Electrical
nuclei or something of that sort.[30]

This suggests, if it does not imply, that that which is individual about
any entity is its configuration, its unique pattern of organization, and
not the elements ("electrical nuclei" or whatever) of which it is composed. It seems clear that the natural flesh of man is a system of organically related energies; his eternal body may be also a system of
organically related energies, organized according to the same pattern as
his natural flesh, so that physical flesh and eternal body are two manifestations of the single man.

Our information about such eternal bodies rests chiefly upon the reports about the one that was clearly displayed in history: that of the resurrected Messias. Two of its characteristics are important here. One has already been mentioned: his resurrected body so reproduced his physical flesh that it was scarred. If the wounds in Christ's flesh marked the timeless matter, it is possible that anyone's smile and gesture will be the same in eternity as in time, along with the carriage of the head and the characteristic pattern of mental activities. Christianity

has proclaimed, against experience, against intelligence, that for the achievement of man's unity the body of his knowledge is to be raised; no other fairer stuff, no alien matter, but this—to be impregnated with holiness and transmuted by lovely passion perhaps, but still this. Scars and prints may disseminate splendour, but the body is to be the same, the very body of the very soul that are both names of the single man.[31]

Second, Christ's resurrected body was not immediately recognized as his by his friends. The identity between flesh and body contains a difference. Natural flesh is not, and eternal body is, consummated; therefore the eternal body includes and exhibits at once all its ages and experiences in their genesis as well as in their fulfillment. This sort of completion does not commonly appear before man; no wonder that it seems alien, or that we hurry to interpret the strangeness in terms of an incorporeal semblance of a body. But

the result of that kind of evasion of "sensuality" is the destruction of "substance." The only "uplift" permissible is that of the Ascension, and it was a real body (the very root of all sensuality) which there withdrew through all the dimensions. "Handle me and see—."[32]

BROCELIANDE

In Williams' diagram of the worlds, Broceliande lies between nature and eternity, and some of the roads connecting them—not by any means all—traverse it. Pauline, in her act of substituted love, entered eternity directly from nature; so also the Christian mystics usually take the direct route, and not the perilous by-pass through Broceliande.

Williams describes Broceliande as a "sea-forest"; C. S. Lewis quotes him as saying that "the chief fact about a wood is that in it you have no horizon," and defines horizon as "a hard, straight line which at once unites and separates heaven and earth."[33] Much of the evidence for such a realm comes from the public domain of the fairy tale, which, Lewis says, appeals to "the sense of something older, wilder and more earthy than humanity,"[34] and from the esoteric lore of witchcraft, which appeals to a similar sense of something older and wilder but less earthy. Broceliande resembles nature in that it contains time, space, and matter, although its standards for measuring time and space are not those of nature, and what matter there is does not always occupy the same space as here. It has its own conditions of being, and man has no access to it except in so far as he meets those conditions deliberately or by accident. Serious belief in Broceliande is not popular in our time: dogmatic science condemns it as vigorously as dogmatic religion once did Galileo and Darwin, so that it is respectable now to express the sense of this numinous world only in poetry or science fiction or fantasy: they can be dismissed with a tolerantly superior smile.

Two hundred years ago, Joseph Addison stated a more genuinely tolerant view. " 'I believe in general,' he wrote, 'that there is such a thing as witchcraft; but at the same time can give no credit to any particular instance of it.' "[35] The statement could be applied with equal cogency to faerie. Most of the records of the purported events in these realms can be set aside as projection, wish-fulfillment, escape mechanism, deliberate falsification, or artistic invention, but even a radical rejection of the content of these stories leaves a residual difficulty: the experience of this kind of "otherness," which is as distinct and as authoritative as the experiences of any other sort of reality. If we categorically refuse this experience, then we must equally discount the others.

It is, however, logically and psychologically possible that these fanciful tales represent modes of describing something that actually exists and has been actually perceived, and that they are as appropriate for their own purposes as "particle" and "wave" are for describing other sorts of existence. Physicists insist that sub-atomic units are neither waves nor particles, yet they continue to use the words and the concepts indicated by the words; so one may refuse belief in fairies, dragons, the tree Igdrasil, or the witches' sabbath, without locking the mind against the chance that these terms refer to a reality of some sort. "All rubbish, of course," a police officer says in *War in Heaven,* of a report of witchcraft in London, "but he must have had *something* in his mind."[36] During a great part of Western history, the phenomena of witchcraft have been the object of serious, and in many periods of intelligent, belief. But we in more recent times have not studied the subject in order to separate wheat from chaff, nor tested the basic principles. For the most part we have simply refused to *think* in this area. Therefore we should demonstrate a decent intellectual humility with respect to it, neither affirming nor rejecting the hypothesis until we have examined the evidence and—perhaps—accumulated further data.

The extent to which Broceliande ought to be studied is a moot point. So far as faerie is concerned, the tales suggest that man cannot find that realm by seeking it, which makes deliberate investigation unlikely if not impossible. With respect to witchcraft, Williams says that

of the present position it is almost impossible to say anything with certainty unless by belonging or having belonged to the secret schools of sorcery; it is a condition that no record of the history of witchcraft is important enough to make desirable. Even if one accepted it, the condition would invalidate its own conclusions. No accuracy could be expected from anyone who had seriously accepted the practice of sorcery—except perhaps in the practice of sorcery. The exactitude of diabolism is confined to itself alone.[37]

But there may be other regions in that forest: it may have been there that Blake and Yeats saw their visions, and Williams associates still other forests and trees with Broceliande: Arden and Birnam, Westermain, Igdrasil, Eden.[38]

In any case, the same fundamental ethical laws of exchange control all the worlds, so that some supernatural operations are unquestionably forbidden to the Christian, if not to all men. For example, after the coming of Christ,

there could be no more foretelling, and that for two reasons at least. The first was that the future should not be foretold, since it depended on the Will of God and the free will of men. God might know what would happen, but even if He did He knew it as much because it was already present to Him as because He merely foresaw it. But no-one else should; the future had to be treated as unknown if man was to be treated as free. But secondly the future, apart from man's moral choice, could not *matter*. "All luck was good"; whatever happened was fortunate. Knowledge was not so much immoral as irrelevant to the reality of Love loving and being loved at every moment. That was what did matter.[39]

Other uses of witchcraft are extensions of evils that also occur in nature, and fall under condemnation for the same reasons, as in Gilles de Rais' murders, and Mme. de Montespan's magical rites compelling (she believed) Louis XIV's love. The spiritualists' attempt to force communication with the dead, to control eternity for their own ends of knowledge or comfort, belongs here, because the participants approach supernature in the pretense, if not the reality, of being its masters. They may speak about "serving the spirits," but their actions betray that they call upon them to come, and this—whether with table rappings or on one's knees—constitutes a demand by nature upon supernature. But the Christian may properly make demands only upon God himself, and the mature Christian probably will not do this. He comes to all the worlds, natural and supernatural alike, in obedience and love.

THE PATTERN

Before we turn to the study of the ways by which the romantic experience becomes the life of love, we shall do well to summarize the theology of romantic love as set forth by Charles Williams.

He begins with the world that he sees and touches and hears about him, and that reverberates with suggestions of greater realities lying beyond it. The romantic moment confirms and strengthens these impressions. It convinces him that the entire universe, in all its variety and contradictions, is completely coherent, a system of interdependent entities which he calls the Co-inherence.

Interdependence is at once the basis and the culmination of his diagram of the Glory. Each thing derives its being from all other things, and in its turn supports the lives of others. Therefore the primal law of exchange both describes the situation that in fact exists, and defines the universal moral standard: good fosters exchange; evil inhibits it. But since nothing can exist at all without some form or degree of exchange, "mere being," Williams points out, "is in itself admirable, and must be coloured with definite evil before it can be lost."[40]

Our physical bodies are the clearest exemplars of the nature of co-inherence and of the processes of exchange.

All things are finally worked out in the body; all mysteries are there manifested, even if still as mysteries. It is the only crucible of the great experiment; its innocent, even if debased, purity endures the most difficult transmutations of the soul.[41]

Physical flesh creates and changes, takes and gives, accepts and rejects. Undiscriminating acceptance endangers physical, as well as intellectual and spiritual life; the rejection of that which would harm or which cannot be integrated into the whole is equally imperative for all levels of being. The gross body, the microscopic cell, the eternal man, maintain themselves by that process of affirmation and rejection, exhibiting the Ways of the Affirmation and the Rejection of Images by which the mind is nurtured and by which societies live.

Such is the natural fact. At the root of the physical nature of man (so long as free choice exists) lie exchange of liking, substitution, inherence. The nature of man which is so expressed in the physical world is expressed after the same manner, only more fully, in the mental and spiritual.

The formal threefold division is a nuisance, but it may momentarily stand. What unites the three worlds is precisely this business of "living from others."[42]

To practice living from others "is not the reward of sanctity; it is a way of sanctity, but also it is the only way of bearable life."[43] It is at once the key to existence and to joy, to freedom and to love.

This structure images the God who created it. Within the Trinity-in-Unity itself is the reciprocal derivation which is the substantial ground of being, and which is named love. This love, however, is not merely a quality or a power: it is a person who has qualities and powers. He loves and can be loved—and he can be denied or hated. That is, love can be known accurately as love, or inaccurately as the opposite of love. It was St. Catherine of Genoa who said, "The fire of Hell is simply the light of God as it is experienced by those who reject it."[44] Like the fire in Dante's *Comedy*, love tortures the damned who "refuse living and learning, postponement and irony, whose dwelling is necessarily in their undying and perishing selves."[45] It purges those on their way to heaven. It is a flame of rapture leaping within and upon those who adore it. The fire, single in its nature, operates to very different effects. God is not mocked: he will be known, one way or another, and man is not free to avoid that confrontation but only free to choose between hating and loving it. The one love radiates upon all things, but some hate it so that its presence is an agony to them, while to those who love it, it is unspeakable bliss.

"Hell is always inaccurate."[46] The result of inaccuracy is to prevent exchange; the refusal of exchange produces inaccuracy. The damned refuse both, by deliberate choice. But when interchange, the ground of being, has been rejected, nothing is left except nothingness, the infinite continuation of the living death, the unlimited consciousness of chaos, impotence, disgust, and pain. This is horror enough, but for Williams hell has still another quality that is worse: it is infinitely, interminably boring. It does not offer night to relieve day, nor warmth to vary coolness, nor one sound or idea to supplant another. There is nothing except idiocy, the reign of nothingness that Wentworth entered at the conclusion of *Descent into Hell:*

this depth where anything might be anything, and was anything, for he did not know what it was . . . So there entered into him still a small, steady, meaningless flow of sound, which stung and tormented him with the same lost knowledge of meaning; . . . there expanded an anarchy of unintelligible shapes . . . the blankness of a living oblivion . . . he was drawn, steadily, everlastingly, inward and down through the bottomless circles of the void.[47]

He had withdrawn from relationships until he grew incapable of sustaining any relationship, but he remained in the hands of the God who respected his resolution and who empowered him to endure his heart's desire. It is one of the alternatives, one of the two Ends, and those who truly seek hell shall surely find it.

Those who seek God shall find love. They shall be upheld by the reality to which they have given themselves and from which they receive increasing life. In heaven all is change and interchange, one joy immediately apprehended in many varieties of joy. Over against the monotony of hell, Williams sets the insight of Sybil, in *The Greater Trumps:*

Drinks and baths and changes were exquisite delights in themselves; part of an existence in which one beauty was always providing a reason and a place for an entirely opposite beauty. As society for solitude, and walking for sitting down, and one dress for another, and emotions for intellect, and snowstorms for hot drinks, and in general movement for repose, repose for movement, and even one movement for another, so highly complex was the admirable order of the created universe.[48]

As on earth, so in heaven the blaze of newness and the sweet assurance of sameness radiate in all things. Difference is exalted, so that every glance reveals a fresh delight, and every touch holds at once the perfected security of habitual contact and the incredulous awe of a first meeting. Here each submits joyously to necessity because necessity is the consummation of love.

Man was created in order to share the perpetually changing glory in which he knows as he is known, in the splendor of love. He was created for heaven, and he takes his place therein as he gives himself to the work of exchange in the form that has been decreed for him. Every man, like Dante,

was created in order to do his business, to fulfil his function. Almighty God did not first create Dante and then find something for him to do. This is the primal law of all the images, of whatever kind; they were created for their working and in order to work. Hell is the cessation of work and the leaving of the images to be, without any function, merely themselves.[49]

Yet if any man fails in his work, love does not fail: it has taken from man's back the intolerable weight of responsibility for himself and for the world. The task that one person leaves unfinished is accomplished by others—or by Another, and "once you have grasped the principle," C. S. Lewis remarks, "it is not chastening but liberating to know that one has been almost wholly superfluous."[50] God sent his Son to demonstrate that he, and not man, is finally responsible, and finally will give man more than his heart desires, only on the condition that man does not will to refuse it. This applies to all men, whether or not they consciously refer their exchanges to the power of the Incarnate Lord, because it is he who upholds all the exchanges. He gives the principle; he is the reality of co-inherence, and its image, and its original operation in nature and supernature alike: "this universe also carries its salvation in its heart."[51] Without the recognition of his part, we live but we live in penury. Recognizing him, we inhabit a world suffused with richness and scintillating with infinite possibilities for exchanged joy. The exposition of the principle was born into time, but the fact is out of time. It is temporal and eternal, natural and supernatural, bone of his bone and flesh of our flesh. This love said to Dante, "I am the centre of a circle to which all parts of the circumference are in a similar relation; but you are not so."[52] And Williams adds: "If under the influence of the centre where Love is, we have wished to be at the centre with Love, then we have to get to the centre."[53] So we come to the ways leading away from that center, and the ways leading toward it, and this, in turn, will further clarify the theology.

PART III

The Co-Inherent Life

Anthony
I thought I spoke the truth.

The Flame
I know you did.
But then the Faith is much truer than you thought.
—*The House of the Octopus,* 95

7

THE PERVERSION OF LOVE

The alternative to being with Love at the centre of the circle is to disorder the circumference for our own purposes.
—THE FIGURE OF BEATRICE, 48

When Dante saw Love in Beatrice, he acknowledged that Love as Lord, but also he realized that he was not wholly *in* Love nor Love wholly in him. Failing of that perfection, he was in sin—and he knew it. The word "sin" did not perturb him as it has some more recent students of love: he was persuaded that goodness existed apart from his private judgments about it, and that sin meant departure from that goodness in any direction and for any reason. He found himself in sin; he wished to be in love. His method of proceeding from one to the other called for the accurate appraisal of the distance between his present position and the end which he hoped to reach.

Like Dante, Charles Williams knew that the lover must learn to recognize sin, and like Dante he followed the Christian faith in affirming that sin is grounded in the good, and constitutes the perversion of the good. "Deep, deeper than we believe, lie the roots of sin; it is in the good that they exist; it is in the good that they thrive and send up sap and produce the black fruit of hell."[1] Without existence and exchange, without prevenient love, there is nothing for sin to corrupt, no reality to give it being. Therefore all discussion of sin must continually refer to the glory from which it is derived.

The doctrine of original sin, like all dogmas, is an "epigram of experience"[2] summarizing long observation that self-interest and rebellion are as native to man as co-operation and delight. "Why this man should hate may be strange; that he should, cannot be."[3] This is original sin. In addition, man perceives in himself and in others "actual

113

sin," the deliberate perversity which, if persisted in, destroys his capacity
for distinguishing between good and evil, beauty and ugliness, love and
malice. Whether actual sin necessarily follows from original sin is not
clear; that it commonly does is attested by abundant evidence. "Man
having got himself into a state when he was capable of willingly shedding blood, the shedding of blood could no longer be neglected."[4] Who
has not contravened love at some time in his life, by rebelling or by
subjecting himself to a lesser lord? Who has not wished to reject some
fact, or submitted to an evil when he should have fought to transform
it into good? Who instantly and invariably distinguishes evil from
good, or better from best?

The Adam had desired to share the knowledge of the God; they had
wished to experience good as something else than good, to discover a
hostility in the good. So they did. Their descendants, in the situation in
which they were involved, had (and have) the same choice. They can
prolong the Fall by their will. They can introduce their own prudence
and wisdom into the nature of the good. It is something deeper than
impiety or immorality, though it involves them. It is the preference of
their own wisdom; it is sin.[5]

All sin militates against co-inherent love and entangles the whole
man who is sinning, but each of man's activities is particularly sus-
ceptible to certain sins, and most of them can be grouped as they
primarily invade man's reasoning, emotional responses, or decisions.
In the following discussion, only the most obvious sins against Christian
romanticism can be dealt with at all, and the emphasis will be upon
those which are especially germane to the Way of the Affirmation of
Images. Following the stages on that Way, we shall examine succes-
sively: (1) the sins that most immediately arise from the emotional
shock of the Beatrician experience—self-indulgence in love; (2) those
that afflict the lover in interpreting that experience—the loss of "the
good of intellect"; (3) those into which he may fall when he chooses
what action to take on the basis of the experience and his interpretation
of it—self-assertion in love; and (4) an analysis of two of Williams'
evil characters, Nigel Considine and Simon the Clerk, to show certain
of the corruptions of the whole romantic way.

Self-indulgence, failure of intellect, and self-assertion have all been mistaken for romanticism at some time or other, by critics of or by adherents to that way, but to Williams they are forms of what he calls "pseudo-romanticism." In denying them a place in true romanticism, he not only attacks what he believes to be evil, but also he clarifies the meaning that he gives to the terms "romantic" and "Christian."

THE FLYING MOMENT

Williams writes that "Hell has made three principal attacks on the Way of Romantic Love. The dangerous assumptions produced are: (1) the assumption that it will naturally be everlasting; (2) the assumption that it is personal; (3) the assumption that it is sufficient."[6] These are the sins which create the pattern of pseudo-romanticism that is sometimes called "Hollywood love." But let us not underrate that phenomenon: "Hollywood has a touch of Dante's heaven,"[7] and the kind of love that it glorifies can, if followed intelligently and faithfully, lead to the paradise of eternal love.

"(1) The assumption that the Beatrician state is everlasting is false."[8] The departure of love is one of the oldest themes of common sense, and one of the firmest assertions of the psychological sciences.

"It won't last." Or, at least, it does not. An opaqueness, even if a beautiful and dear opaqueness, takes the place of that translucency. The sensitive awareness of perfection disappears, and the spring joy of Beatrice and Love arriving at once. Why then? There are, no doubt, many reasons. Time seems to change it, and custom—"heavy as frost and deep almost as life." One grows (despite oneself) tired of beholding beauty; the mere monotony of the revelation wearies, and beauty ceases, in one's own sight, to be beauty, and the revelation to be revelation. It may be added, for fairness, that Beatrice—in a closer and more prolonged life than Dante was permitted—is not always celestial. Sin on both sides—original or actual—is a fact; we are too quickly "disobedient to the heavenly vision."[9]

No passion endures, not even the passion of love: "It is temporary, it is a 'flying moment.' "[10] Herein the emotions resemble all the other natural energies that man has studied. The sun's output of heat varies; the wind rises and falls; the metabolic rate of the body incessantly changes. It appears to be possible to produce, under laboratory conditions, an absolutely uniform flow of energy, but only by the use of such meticulous care that its achievement can hardly be called natural. Because of this persistent fluctuation, he who depends upon the emotions aroused by the Beatrician moment to keep him on his course will change his direction with each change of mood; he cannot be steadfast in traveling the long road to the City of God or to any other distant point. This is not to say that the emotions of love are undesirable or evil: on the contrary, properly used they reveal the way and the end more clearly, perhaps, than any other of the signposts given to man. But the sign points beyond itself. The wayfarer who expects the sign to substitute for the end, or to carry him along the road, will find himself without shelter when night comes.

Romantic theology insists both upon the instability of passionate love, and upon the necessity for such instability. It points out that the intensity of the vision gives it such authority over the lover that temporarily it limits his freedom. While it lasts, he is subject to it and cannot but acknowledge its claim upon him. But revelation of God though it be, Godhead is not to be imposed upon the flesh; rather, the manhood is to be lifted into God. Beatrice as visible love must die in order that her lover may

become, by his own will, the *caritas* which was, by God's will, awakened in him at the smile of Beatrice . . . "There hath passed away," wrote Wordsworth of another revelation, "a Glory from the earth." Religion itself knows such withdrawals; "the dark night" is asserted to be an inevitable stage of the Way. Dante knew the death of Beatrice, and many other young lovers have known the disappearance of the peculiar Beatrician quality. This is the meaning of the death in the whole pattern. It is not, however, an unfortunate accident which is a conclusion. It is a state of being, a quenching of sensitive knowledge, which is a necessary—or all but necessary—part of the Way of Romantic Love.[11]

The disappearance of the glory forces man's intellect and will into action; were the glory always to remain, emotion would stupefy these other capacities and arrest the intellectual and moral labor that are necessary before reason and volition also can be restored to Eden.

The clouding of the translucency may be at the will of the translucency, and the withdrawal of the glory at the will of the glory. Here too, if we may continue the similitude of the young Beatrice with the True Light, it is perhaps the glory which says: "If I go not away, the Comforter will not come unto you, but if I depart, I will send him unto you." . . . The young lament the vision; the old warn the young—sometimes with tenderness, sometimes with abominable gusto—that the vision will go. Few remit to the vision itself the control of its own manifestation.[12]

Love chooses to reveal and to hide himself, as Messias chose to enter and then to leave history, and as God chose that he should appear and then disappear from his Son's consciousness. Close to death, "the Image of Godhead demanded of Godhead 'Why hast Thou forsaken me?' "[13] It is Dante's cry when Beatrice dies, and that of every lover when the glory fades from his—or her—beloved. The answer is the same for all: "one must will charity and humility; it is not enough that they shall be communicated by joy."[14] Only thus can the Holy Spirit establish maturity in love.

"(2) The second assumption is that the state of love is a personal possession."[15] This sin takes two principal forms: jealousy, "a desire to retain the glory for oneself, which means that one is not adoring the glory but only one's own relation to the glory";[16] and envy: "The envious man identifies the kingdom with himself, and by a frantic effort to retain the outward manifestation of the kingdom destroys it in himself, and with it his capacity to see it outside himself."[17]

Lawrence Wentworth, in *Descent into Hell,* succumbed to jealousy when a rival was awarded an honor which he coveted and when the girl whom he loved turned her attention to another man—a reaction so natural as to elicit generally only the most tender criticism. In so far as Wentworth was naturally disappointed, his response involved no more than original sin, the almost reflexive motion to grasp or to keep that which one desires. Had he refused to nourish that impulse, submitting to the fact of his sin but not consenting to it, the sin might have been redeemed. Instead, he chose to linger over the sweet taste of resentment and injured pride, and so he committed actual sin, the sin of Cain who incarnates "the self-desirous spirit which troubles the divine glory in all lovers."[18] Cain had tended his flocks and laid his sacrifice on his altar. Wentworth had worked hard at his profession and had opened his heart to a girl. Both felt that they deserved reward; more exactly, both felt that they personally deserved the kind of re-

ward they wanted, in defiance of the straightforward fact of experience that

usually the way must be made ready for heaven, and then it will come
by some other; the sacrifice must be made ready, and the fire will strike
on another altar. So much Cain saw, and could not guess that the very
purpose of his offering was to make his brother's acceptable.[19]

The jealous do not merely regret that one sows and another reaps;
they loathe it and fight against it. Wentworth moved from love to gloating over his possession of the objects of his love; when it became apparent that in fact neither belonged to him personally, he clutched at
pretense of ownership until nothing remained to him except illusion.
He ended in idiocy.

While the jealous claim possession of the glory as their right, the
envious claim an exceptional or an exclusive right. They desire more
of the glory than others; at the extreme, they will not grant the presence of the glory in any except themselves, lest their unique identity
with it be jeopardized. Such is the case with the missionary priest
Anthony, in *The House of the Octopus*. With a pagan invader threatening his small group of converts, he prays:

> Give me therefore grace . . .
> to be to them a tender father and wise;
> grant that on the foundation they find in me
> they may build a true church, low but well-roofed.
> Grant this, blessed Spirit, and bless
> me to my task, whatever their present want.[20]

Beneath this petition lies an intention of which he is unconscious until
the Flame of the Holy Spirit draws out of him the truth: that he
wishes to be a partner, perhaps an equal partner, with God.

> I would be again
> all that which I was to these once,
> their father, their centre, almost their creator. . . .
> I wish you to spring from me and live from me. . . .
> I do not wish you to live from God alone;
> I wish always to be your means of God.[21]

The discovery of his sin horrifies him and he turns from it: "Most men when at last they see their desire, / fall to repentance—all have that chance."[22] At the last, Anthony is in love and love is in him.

Love cannot be possessed, and the greed for personal possession of love leads not to love but to infinitely insatiable greed. Man was created to function by loving and being loved, but the jealous or envious soul has become "incontinent to its function; it treats its function as created for it."[23]

"(3) The third assumption is even easier than the others: that it is sufficient to have known that state of love."[24] Then love is not enough? Not the kind of love that ends when the Beatrician moment ends, whatever its depth of mutuality or its duration. To limit love to the moment of vision is to fall into "the sin of indulging oneself in love instead of devoting oneself to the duty of love, the perverse and selfish twisting of the 'falling-in-love' to nothing but one's own satisfaction."[25] Dante illustrates this sin with the story of Paolo and Francesca, the fair lovers in the first circle of hell who in life had surrendered themselves to passion, and in death are blown eternally on the monotonous wind of their fulfilled desire for each other. Williams comments that

lussuria is the word Virgil uses of this circle, and it is *lussuria,* luxury, indulgence, self-yielding, which is the sin, and the opening out of hell. The persistent parleying with the occasion of sin, the sweet prolonged laziness of love, is the first surrender of the soul to hell—small but certain. . . . and could the soft delaying indulgence of the soul so delay perpetually, the imagination and the will might be almost content to lose heaven for *that.*[26]

But dalliance with self-gratification need not be sexual. Wentworth's ritual preparation for sleep exhibits precisely the same sin.

He made it a rule to think of pleasant things as he stretched himself in bed: his acquaintances sometimes, or the reviews—most of the reviews—of his last book, or his financial security, or his intentions about his immediate future work, or the permanent alterations he hoped he had caused in universal thought concerning Caesar's employment of Balearic slingers during the campaigns in Gaul. Also, deliciously, his fancies would widen and change, and Caesar would be drawing out cheques to pay his London Library subscriptions, or the

Balearic slingers would be listening to him as he told them how they used to use their slings . . .[27]

The modern name for *lussuria* is lechery, the craving for sensations which, if indulged in, demands increasingly extreme sensations until the lecher trips headlong into "the Pit of destruction and self-destructive madness to which the way of sensation leads."[28] It is not that the emotions of love inevitably lead to that pit: any lover will have moments when passion submerges his other faculties and when he should allow it to do so and enjoy it for what it is. The distinction lies in the difference "between a temptation and a capacity; desire may be summoned either for the lover's own satisfaction or for a proper fulfilment of the moment";[29] it can be an excuse for lechery or an expression of love's integrity. Those who are adult in love are gladdened by more than emotion and more than its interminable repetition.

In *The House of the Octopus,* an official of hell speaks to a subordinate:

> Every pious man—and, of course, woman—
> has one—just one—surface where religion and he
> are so delicately mixed in his soul as to be
> indistinguishable; he is never quite sure—
> and does not (believe me!) ever want to be sure—
> whether his religion or he is being soothed
> into a lascivious spiritual delight.
> All of them, Prefect, are at bottom religious lechers,
> fornicating with their fancies.[30]

This is a very acute observation, and although Williams gives the analysis to an exponent of evil, I have no doubt but that he intended it as the accurate description of a tendency that afflicts all men. Release from such lechery comes not by denying that the self and religion are so conjoined, nor by attempting to separate them, but by the serious application of intelligence to love—intelligence which does not destroy passion but which balances it. "As every heresy is a truth pushed disproportionately, so with every sin; at least, with every physical sin."[31] But with the introduction of intelligence as a factor in romantic love, we move from the romantic shock itself to its interpretation, and to the sins that destroy what Dante called "the good of intellect."

THE FAILURE OF INTELLECT

Confusion and perversion of reason are sins against love, and so also is the absence of intellect. The last of these is admirably illustrated by the story of Gawaine and the Unasked Question from the myth of the Holy Grail. The story is simple enough: Gawaine has been sent from Arthur's court to the Castle of the Hallows, where the wounded King Pelles guards the chalice of the Last Supper. There he is shown the Pageant of the Grail: the two maidens bearing the cup and the spear, the third maiden and the figure of the child, and above and beyond them all "a King crowned, nailed upon a rood, and the spear was still fast in his side."[32] Grief and pity and ecstasy master Gawaine, so that he forgets to fulfill his mission, which is to ask the question "What serves the Grail?", the answer to which would have healed the king and bestowed upon the land a transcendent good.

That it was a vision from God which numbed his mind explains why he failed to think at that critical moment, but does not condone the sin nor ameliorate its effects. The country is left in its desolation, Pelles in his agony, and the Grail in its seclusion. "The refusal to ask the question is precisely that refusal to inquire which accompanies so many a temptation and encourages so many a sin."[33] Not to think is itself sin, wherever the capacity for intellectual activity exists.

Obviously, no more can be asked of the mind than it is able to give: a child usually cannot comprehend subtleties that are clear to the saints; for that matter, neither can some adults. Recent studies in the psychology of learning indicate that some people lack the ability to work with symbols, and that others cannot comprehend more than the rudiments of linguistic skills. Their minds simply do not work in those ways, so that in particular areas they may be nearly unteachable, even though they may be surpassingly competent in other mental processes. Intellectual talents vary in kind, as athletic and manual skills do, and there is no sense in boggling at the fact. But not to use those which one has, is sin.

That ignorance as such can be culpable was implied by Messias "in that first word of the Cross which entreated pardon for them [his executioners] precisely on the ground of their ignorance: 'forgive them,

for they know not what they do.' "[34] They who condemned and killed
him had capacity and opportunity to discover what they were doing,
but they had closed their minds against that knowledge. So doing, they
committed actual sin, building upon that original sin by which, always,
our minds are clouded. None of us can know all the ramifications of
all our actions, or indeed of any of them, so that we also do not know
what we are doing, and need forgiveness. But we can at least try to
escape the actual sins of refusing to consider evidence, of failing to investigate deeply and without prejudice where it is our responsibility to
do so, or of following Mr. Batesby, of *War in Heaven,* in concluding
that it does not matter what one thinks so long as he does the right
things.

"Morals are more important than dogma," Mr. Batesby says. "Conduct is much the biggest thing in life, I feel. 'He can't be wrong whose
life is for the best.' "[35] In *The House of the Octopus,* the officer of hell
says to the priest, "We shall agree / that dogma is less important than
fair living / and a free giving of exchange."[36] The issue is a serious one,
and has harried the Faith since its earliest days: To what extent is
intelligent understanding necessary for Christian belief and life? During long periods in the Church's history, she has felt that "it mattered
a good deal what he [the Christian] thought and consequently did not
wish to leave him to think for himself."[37] It was her considered judgment that the examination of theological ideas ought to be left to those
who were qualified by capacity and training to handle them, very much
as today we take for granted that the practice of medicine and law
should be restricted to persons who have demonstrated their competence in those fields. This is a position with great, and unmistakable,
merit.

But we individually, whatever our intellectual equipment, must
make choices, and the ultimate source of choice is thought, as the source
of morality is what one's "intellect has led him to decide to believe is
the nature of the universe."[38] It is one thing to confess finitude, another
to take refuge in it or protract it. In the first, man disclaims omnis-
cience; in the second, he repudiates intellect. The command "do" is
an imperative, but so also is the command "know." Messias himself
"compelled always from his uncertain followers not only decision but

definition."[39] In that respect, our position today is no different from that of his disciples.

Probably the most common form of intellectual confusion in romanticism consists of misinterpreting the relationship between the Beatrician image and its basis. Specifically, the lover is apt to conclude that the glory "is the personal adornment of the beloved,"[40] so that he makes of his Beatrice an idol. Or he supposes that the glory can be revealed to him only through that one person.

But the doctrines of Romantic Theology will have no such easy satisfaction. Maintaining that the beloved is there seen in her proper and heavenly perfection, they maintain also that such a perfection is implicit in every human being, and (had we eyes to see) would be explicit there. . . . that perfection is the arch-natural state of human beings as such, seen after that arch-natural manner. It is everyone's or it is no-one's; on that there can be no compromise.[41]

Or even more disastrously, the lover can be caught in the dilemma which all but destroyed Palomides,[42] the Saracen knight of the Arthurian saga.

At the court of King Mark of Cornwall, Palomides fell romantically in love with Iseult the Queen.

> In the summer-house of the Cornish king
> I kneeled to Mark at a banqueting,
> I saw the hand of the queen Iseult;
> down her arm a ruddy bolt
> fired the tinder of my brain
> to measure the shape of man again;
>
> .   .   .   .
>
> Blessed (I sang) the Cornish queen;
> for till to-day no eyes have seen
> how curves of golden life define
> the straightness of a perfect line,
> till the queen's blessed arm became
> a rigid bar of golden flame
> where well might Archimedes prove
> the doctrine of Euclidean love . . .[43]

For a long moment Palomides held the vision intact and glorified it, but suddenly he stopped: "division stretched between / the queen's

identity and the queen. / Relation vanished, though beauty stayed
. . ."[44] Iseult remained to him the most beautiful and most desirable
of women, but she was no longer in relationship with anything greater
than herself. She had manifested, been identical with, Euclidean love;
then on the instant she lost that identity. Where there had been relationship was now nothing, the intolerable nothingness where the
Questing Beast scratches forever.

It is relevant to note that Williams gave this incident to a Moslem.
As C. S. Lewis explains in his exegesis of the poem,

Islam denies the Incarnation. It will not allow that God has descended into flesh or that Manhood has been exalted into Deity. . . .
It stands for all religions that are afraid of matter and afraid of mystery, for all misplaced reverences and misplaced purities that repudiate
the body and shrink back from the glowing materialism of the Grail.[45]

Palomides had experienced Iseult as a God-bearing image, and the
revelation had been so explicit and so authoritative that he was forced
to accept it. On the other hand, he could not accept it because, as a
Moslem, he believed that God has neither incarnations nor images; only
God is God. The dilemma being neither soluble nor endurable, Palomides set off into the nothingness to kill the Questing Beast. He failed,
of course: the beast is as eternal as the nothingness that results from
the breaking of relationships. But though one cannot destroy it, one
can leave the barren rocks where it prowls, for there are lands that it
cannot enter because the web of relationships leaves no place for it.

To the sins of the absence and the confusion of intellect must be
added a third grave sin of the mind: the perversion of reason, the deliberate twisting of ideas into conformity with one's preferences. This
is heresy.

Once an idea has been enunciated, it lies open to three sorts of
treatment: partial or complete agreement; partial or complete disagreement; and perversion, whether deliberate or accidental, gross or trivial.
Of these, only deliberate perversion constitutes heresy, which is not a
matter of refusing an idea but of distorting it. To borrow an example
from Miss Sayers,[46] the norms of accurate thought allow one to enjoy
or not to enjoy *Hamlet*, but it does not allow anyone to misquote,
misinterpret, or rewrite the play, no matter what his motives or excuses

are. If, having accurately comprehended a given idea—let us say, Christian romanticism—one believes that it is erroneous, he may be a pagan or a classicist or almost anything else—he may very well be right—but he is not heretical with respect to that doctrine. In contrast, sentimentality, sensualism, and "spiritualizing" are heresies of romantic love not because they are fallacious, but because they claim to be true romanticism when (at least according to Williams) the term is properly defined so as to exclude them. Likewise, docetism and Arianism are not Christian heresies because of their fundamental error, but because they define themselves as Christian, contrary to the decision of the Church. Therefore the Church rightly has proceeded more violently against the heresies than against other faiths, such as Buddhism. And Buddhists are not heretics: they accept their difference from Christianity. They disagree, but it is honest disagreement; they do not corrupt. Most of them do not claim—as some who call themselves Christian have done—that they and Christianity are really saying the same things in different ways, and they are to be honored for that honesty and accuracy.

One may fall into heresy without knowing it; his idea is then heretical, but he is not yet essentially a heretic. One becomes a heretic by "clinging to a particular thought or idea because it is one's own, although it is against the known decision of the Church—the disintegrity of the intellect, the justification to oneself of error and evil."[47] It is justifiable to insist that one's own ideas are right, regardless of their compatibility with a given doctrine. But to maintain that one's ideas reflect that doctrine, when they clearly contradict it, cannot be excused or explained away. Hence the significance of Dante's description of hell as the place of those who have "lost the good of intellect," and of his emphasis upon the obduracy of the heretics. They have deliberately and obstinately perverted the meaning of words and ideas, until they are no longer capable of determining what an idea means, or of relating ideas to each other. "Meaning is lost, accuracy is lost, and accuracy is fruitfulness—it is the first law of the spiritual life."[48] Hence also the stress that Williams places on the heretic's awareness of his sin.

A heretic, strictly, was a man who knew what he was doing; he accepted the Church, but at the same time he preferred his own judgement to that of the Church. This would seem to be impossible, except that it is apt to happen in all of us after our manner. . . . he justified error and evil to himself, and propagated the justification. The temptation to it is a Medusa's head, for it petrifies. It is an incredible state— yes? yet "much more than you would believe, the tombs lie laden." This is apt to be the doom of the false Romantic. The Beatrician doctrine has its own dangers there also; it is very necessary that it should be subdued to that clear communion of intelligences which is the City.[49]

So defined, heretics combine the sin of intellectual perversion with the sin of self-assertion: they "have petrified their minds into themselves and their desires."[50] Self-assertion, however, includes more than heresy; it forms the nucleus for another group of sins which develop at the point where the lover chooses what he shall do about the vision of Beatrice and his understanding of that vision.

THE REFUSAL OF EXCHANGE

On Williams' hypothesis, men "are ruled by that single principle of exchange deepening into co-inherence which governs the whole created universe."[51] According to this pattern, the heart of original sin consists of the inability to participate fully in the process of exchange, and the heart of actual sin consists in the refusal to do so—essentially, in the refusal to give and—or—the refusal to receive.

Most of us have been, since childhood, thoroughly imbued with the apostolic teaching that "it is more blessed to give than to receive,"[52] and we tend to forget that all giving depends upon prior acts of receiving. Before we can have anything at all to give, before we can desire to give, we must accept life from our parents, food from the earth, oxygen from the air, instruction from our mentors and companions. Further, no gift can effectively be given unless someone can be found who will accept it. Because this necessity for receiving is so often unrecognized, Williams' insistence upon the refusal to receive as a sin against love requires special emphasis.

This is the sin which Williams sees as characterizing the Satan whom Milton portrayed in *Paradise Lost*. "He objects to having anything given him; he objects to the nature of love."[53] Specifically, "the mark of Satan and the rebel angels is that they will not consent to be derived from anyone else,"[54] not even from God. They "imagine themselves 'self-begot' . . . and they imagine God to be of the same nature, only more powerful."[55] The intellectual denial of their derivation from, and therefore dependence upon, God is reinforced with emotional aversion to any dependence, that is, with pride. To accept the fact of their derivation from the creator of the universe would require them to humble themselves before him, and this they will not do. Still less will they admit dependence upon any being inferior to God.

But he who will not accept dependence cannot learn nor love, and in the end he cannot live. The door to love opens when the lover receives illumination and joy from another, and when he recognizes his dependence upon that other as the source of his joy. The first shock of the romantic moment is an act of acceptance, whole-hearted and single-minded. However, it is entirely possible to insulate oneself against that shock, and against the humility which it generates, as Rosamond, in *Shadows of Ecstasy,* did. On the very verge of love, she refuses to countenance its existence: "She would neither fight it nor flee from it nor yield to it nor compromise with it. She could hardly even deny that it was there, for there was no place for it in her mind."[56] Succumbing to it would have meant shattering "her vision of her unsubservient self,"[57] that self-esteem which over long years she had fostered at all costs.

She had been self-possessed, but all herself was in the possessing and nothing in the possessed; self-controlled, but she had had only a void to control. . . . She was alive and she hated life; not with a free feeling of judgement but with servile fear.[58]

Consequently she hated the king whom she refused to love, and hated everything that reminded her of him, following the path to hell that Williams described with reference to Milton's Satan, who

goes on to hate the free love itself because it follows its own nature and not his. He has rebelled, in the name of freedom, against the central nature of freedom. He is to be free but God is not to be free, because if God is free heaven will be heaven. And it is precisely heaven being heaven to which Satan so violently objects. Recognizing (one might say) the force of his objection, heaven obligingly, so far as he is concerned, turns itself into hell. . . . He can never be reconciled to Love,

because he hates Love. He cannot hope; he will not fear. There can
then be no change but to plunge from agony to agony, in despair which
is complete hell and yet opens on deeper hells: "*all* good to me is lost."
All that can be done is to go on madly warring with heaven's matchless
king; perhaps somebody can be hurt somewhere.[59]

Satan cannot be forgiven this sin, because the nature of the sin makes
it impossible for him to desire forgiveness, or to accept it if it is offered.
It is

the choice which so many men have made, the preference for the existence of their own will as the final and absolute thing as against the
knowledge (whatever that may be) of some "great commanded
Good." The only choice which a man can make in such a crisis is
between submitting to that good or refusing to submit to it, and if he
refuses to submit he does so precisely because so, and so only, he can
hold "divided empire with heaven's king." Every bold bad baronet in
the old stories did the same thing. He cannot get rid of the good, he
cannot destroy it. He can only know, and refuse, and hate it, and be
equivalent to it.[60]

Man naturally craves self-importance, self-gratification, self-sufficiency; he naturally dislikes pain, frustration, and intrusion. Love,
however, does constitute an intrusion upon the self, and thereby demonstrates how vulnerable the self is, how flimsy its security, how false its
sense of assurance. In the face of such intrusions, the self confronts
alternatives which are simple and mutually exclusive: one protects
himself from such intrusion, or he accepts it. The former is represented
not only by Satan, but also by Simon the Clerk in *All Hallows' Eve,*
who

had refused all possibilities in death. He would not go to it, as that
other child of a Jewish girl had done. That other had refused safe-
guard and miracle; he had refused the achievement of security. He
had gone into death—and the Clerk supposed it his failure—as the
rest of mankind go—ignorant and in pain. The Clerk had set himself
to decline pain and ignorance. So that now he had not any capacities
but those he could himself gain.[61]

Having chosen to see nothing except what his limited wit showed him,
ultimately Simon saw eternally only his own reduplicated faces reflect-
ing back to him the blast of loathing with which he stared at them.

This protest against intrusion is repeated in sexual perversion. Williams describes King Arthur lying with his sister Morgause: "she had his own face."[62] C. S. Lewis, commenting on the poem, says: "That is the horror of incest: it offends against the law of exchange, the strain gives itself not to another strain but only back to itself."[63] Similarly, by interweaving two closely similar creatures, the homosexual relationship approaches the forbidden enjoyment of oneself—forbidden not merely by statute or because of undesirable social consequences, but because it minimizes the distinction between lover and beloved, isolating each from the invasions of difference that nourish love-in-co-inherence.

Beyond the homosexual evasion of love there is a deeper iniquity.

The Lord's glory fell on the cities of the plain, of Sodom and another. We know all about Sodom nowadays, but perhaps we know the other even better. Men can be in love with men, and women with women, and still be in love and make sounds and speeches, but don't you know how quiet the streets of Gomorrah are? haven't you seen the pools that everlastingly reflect the faces of those who walk with their own phantasms . . . The lovers of Gomorrah are quite contented, Periel; they don't have to put up with our difficulties. They aren't bothered by alteration, at least till the rain of the fire of the Glory at the end, for they lose the capacity for change, except for the fear of hell. They're monogamous enough! and they've no children—no cherubim breaking into being or babies as tiresome as ours; there's no birth there, and only the second death. There's no distinction between lover and beloved; they beget themselves on their adoration of themselves, and they live and feed and starve on themselves, and by themselves too, for creation, as my predecessor said, is the mercy of God, and they won't have the facts of creation.[64]

Williams retells an old legend that before Eve's creation, Adam saw his reflection in a pool of Euphrates and worshiped himself. Therefore Lilith came to "deceive him with himself . . . draw him to adoration of himself."[65] Seeing this, God decreed:

> ". . . nor god nor jinn nor man but We
> shall be to man the self whom he adores,
> when the appointed time brings forth the hour.
> Now therefore since himself alone he knows,
> let difference in himself foretell that hour
> of difference which is We; adore and know

what stroke within him prophesies of Us."

   .   .   .   .

                    . . . for such cause
the Eternal shaped a woman and no man
out of the sleeping Adam, that his flesh,
more than the drowsy and deceiving mind,
might know amidst illusions of content
heart-rending union; and thereafter comes
heart-healing separation.[66]

The disjunction which is necessary for love is built into human bodies, making the sexual and spiritual relationships a mutual invasion, and thereby breaking down both selves so that both can be transformed by the love that they both receive.

Because exchange consists of giving and receiving together, the refusal to give is as serious a sin as the refusal to receive, but not to give is so generally recognized as sin that there is no need to discuss it here. There are, however, two other ways of refusing to exchange that do need mention: the will only to give, and the will only to receive, either of which can be coupled with the refusal of giving or of receiving. Thus, one may wish neither to accept nor to give, enclosing himself in a carapace against any interchange at all; or he may refuse to accept but desire to give, to be "by himself, the centre of all the derivations."[67] It was this sin which, in the fifteenth century, was specified as the sin of Satan: " 'he desired to be,' says the *Malleus Maleficarum*, 'to those related to him by a certain dependence, the only source of good.' "[68] Incessantly giving, one feels important and others acknowledge his importance. Or if the attitude be cloaked with religion, he feels blessed and impels those around him to declare him blessed. "But generosity, though an easy indulgence, is not an easy virtue."[69] It can be a type of self-assertion that destroys even the appearance of exchange between life and life. Not all giving is of this character, and even giving where there is no possibility of direct return from the recipient can be a genuine act of exchange, as will be seen later in the analysis of substituted love. But that giving can be used to serve only the self, cannot be denied.

The pagan Assantu, in *The House of the Octopus*, represents the urgency to receive without giving. According to his religious beliefs, he must devour others or else be devoured, and naturally enough he prefers the former.

> I wish not to be eaten, but to eat others;
> I wish to grow great and thrive on others;
> and if others will not, I wish them to be compelled.
> I will be a belly to them and they food to my belly.[70]

He is willing to accept his dependence upon others, but that dependence is to be of one kind only. His insatiable craving recalls the imbruted Lancelot raging in the form of a wolf—"the fierce figure of universal consumption,"[71] and the she-wolf of Dante's *Inferno*, "lean with infinite craving."[72] "I want . . . I need . . . this is mine . . . give me," cries the self, and it rends others that it may gorge itself into death. Take but do not release; accept sacrifices but do not immolate yourself; bear the burdens of others but do not give your burdens to them. Mind and spirit can no more sustain life under such a regimen than the physical flesh can, and the condition which it produces is not a punishment but an inevitable consequence. He who does not receive *and* give dies, not because sentence has been passed upon him, but because life is constituted by giving and receiving. Exchange is life. Willed and joyous exchange is love. Therefore, "the spirit, angelic or human, which refuses love, discovers Love destroying him";[73] but he would rather burn in hell than consent to the double action of exchange in giving and receiving.

TWO CORRUPTIONS OF NATURE

Williams' first and last novels contain portraits of two extremely serious perversions of romanticism. Nigel Considine, in *Shadows of Ecstasy,* images the turning of the romantic vision to the service of natural man; Simon the Clerk, in *All Hallows' Eve,* embodies the attempt to dominate nature by supernatural methods and forces. "Hell, like heaven, has many mansions":[74] these are two of the sins against romanticism which, in one way or another, have peculiar relevance to our time.

Shadows of Ecstasy centers upon the figure of Nigel Considine, the leader of African forces that have invaded England, proclaiming as their purpose "the restoration to mankind of powers which have been forgotten or neglected,"[75] and appealing for support

to those among the peoples of Europe who know that their lives have origin and nourishment in the great moments of the exalted imagination . . . to all who owe their devotion to music, to poetry, to painting and sculpture, to the servants of every more than rational energy; greater than those and more numerous, to all who at this present moment exist in the exchanged or unexchanged adoration of love . . .[76]

Considine himself is a figure of great power and beauty. Everything about him combines to attract the most discerning and high-minded elements in the Western world. He proceeds by the methods of the experimental sciences in his search for the conquest of death. He affirms the necessity for passion as a supplement to intellect. He achieves wholeness, power, ecstasy, and he invites his followers to "a more intense life than the talk of your learned men—a more intense passion for discovery, a greater power of exploration, new raptures, unknown paths of glorious knowledge."[77] And he is selfless in his dedication: he does not care whether it is he or some other who succeeds, because he has no doubt but that his doctrines will, sooner or later, prevail. As another character sees him: "It was Man that stood there, man conscious of himself and of his powers, man powerful and victorious, bold and serene, a culmination and a prophecy."[78] Considine moves fearlessly and joyously through the book as through the streets of London, centering his life in the illusion of man autonomous and omnipotent, master of life and death, building the Kingdom of Man, as opposed to the Kingdom of God. In Considine's own words,

I bring you achievement, I bring you the fulfilment of desires, the lordship of love and death. . . . He that has mastered love has mastered the world, and he that masters death is lord of that other [world] . . . I have always, so far as I could, done according to the gospel which moves in me and my friends, the doctrine of transmutation of energy, of the conscious turning of joy and anguish alike into strength and will, and of that passionate strength and will into the exploration of all the capacities of man. . . . I tell [men] that they are themselves gods, if they will, and the ecstasy of that knowledge is their victory.[79]

Isabel, wife of one of his followers, defines the alternative to him:

· "But those that die may be lordlier than you: they are obedient to defeat. Can you live truly till you have been quite defeated? You talk of living by your hurts, but perhaps you avoid the utter hurt that's destruction."

He smiled down at her. "Why, have it as you will," he said. "But it isn't such submission and destruction that man desires."[80]

The key phrase is the last, where Considine admits that he seeks that which man desires. Because natural man—that is, man who has not been redeemed—always and always revolts against the imperative "Ye must be born again." He does not want to die even in order to be reborn, nor to despair even though that may be the road to life in God. Basically he is satisfied with himself, and the greater the development of his natural capacities, the more emphatic his insistence that he does not need to be reborn, that he needs and wants nothing for his fulfillment except what his own abilities ultimately can supply. Human morality, human science, human art, human effort, are or will be sufficient to him. Considine represents an exalted form of this belief: it is notable and credible in the book that he readily accepts intrusion, delights in exchange, welcomes passion but is not overwhelmed by it, and insists upon the rigorous discipline of intelligence. He is confident but not proud, and untainted by spiritual lechery or avarice.

Considine desires knowledge and power in order to serve mankind. The redeemed, however, seek to become nothing in order that God may work through them without hindrance. Williams quotes from Kierkegaard's *Christian Discourses:* "It is now the only wish of the worshipper to become weaker and weaker, for with that the more worship; the only need worship feels is that God may become stronger and stronger."[81] Character-building and personality-development may make the natural man into a considerably nicer and more effective person, but they do not make him Christian. Rather, they tend to confirm him in his self-determination. "If any man would come after me, let him deny himself"—although since one can hardly deny a non-existent self, self-development is probably an inevitable stage on the way to the glory of God: "you will have to find your heart, and your real heart, before you can leave it."[82] Personality, character, selfhood, are created in order that they may be re-created, but the old man has to die before the new man can arise. The self, like any other image, has to be both affirmed and rejected before it can lead beyond itself, and before that which is disclosed by its rejection can return upon man to give him a new kind of life. Of the self that does not die, Williams writes:

> . . . thinking you are someone, you become someone
> to be caught by sin—and only someone so.
> A nothing in God cannot despair. I heard
> a voice cry when I saw the naughting of myself
> that the Faith was truer than I thought. O truer!
> A man is only himself to see himself
> in his own naughting . . .[83]

Behind this lies Christianity's eternal insistence that man cannot save himself, whether by character-building, self-discipline, self-sacrifice, asceticism, or any other method. He cannot even love by his own efforts to love.

According to the Apostle, self-sacrifice by itself was as remote from the way of salvation as self-indulgence. As a technique, as a discipline, as a method, it might be useful: no more. But so may—if not self-indulgence at least things gratifying to the self. . . . Neither self-sacrifice, as such, nor self-gratification, as such; both may be sacraments of love at any moment, but neither is covenanted. The denial of the self affects both. "It is no more I that live, but Christ that liveth in me" is the definition of the pure life which is substituted for both.[84]

All man's efforts to save himself are, in the end, attempts to convert the Godhead into flesh, to do God's work for him, in contrast with letting God do his own work of lifting man into himself. This is true even when man clothes his impulse toward redeeming himself in the majesty of a worthy cause—universal education, freedom, peace, justice, eradication of poverty—pursuing them for their own sakes or for the sake of humanity. Only when they are love's spontaneous expression of itself do they become sanctified in the Person of Love.

C. S. Lewis makes the contrast explicit when he speaks of

what Williams called "heavy morality"—the ethics of sheer duty and obedience as against the shy yet (in the long run) shameless acceptance of heaven's courtesies flowing from the "homely and courteous lord" . . . the defeat of fine and tender and even frolic delicacies of goodness by iron legalism, the "fallacy of rational virtue."[85]

"Heavy morality" ought not to be despised, for—as was quoted earlier —"unless something is done, nothing happens. Unless devotion is given to a thing which must prove false in the end, the thing that is true in the end cannot enter."[86] Williams wrote of his character Damaris Tighe, "The years of selfish toil had had at any rate this good—they had been years of toil; she had not easily abandoned any search because of difficulty, and that habit of intention, by its own power of good, offered her salvation then."[87] Perhaps we cannot do more than Damaris until we are at the center of the circle with love, although in the end love will not be

content with so moderate a maxim. It is indeed almost an encouragement to the "imperfect fruition" of joy, and any romantic explorer into spiritual things who is content with it thwarts the purpose of his journey before it is begun. The necessary thing for him is not the comfort of knowing that there is a much greater sin, but the discomfort of believing that there is a much greater good.[88]

Considine believed that there was no greater good than that which man could achieve by his own intelligence, will, and passion. Williams does not indicate whether he has damned himself eternally, but it is perfectly clear that he who persists in attempting to make man ruler of the universe does end in hell, if only because anything that tries to become more or other than itself automatically divides its intention from its essential nature, and thereby becomes first less than itself and finally nothing.

Where Considine tries to dominate nature by natural means, Simon the Clerk tries to dominate both nature and supernature by supernatural means. To this end, he uses witchcraft, but the reader does not need to believe in the efficacy of such methods for the novel to be relevant to his condition. In fact, he will lose much of its impact if he restricts the application to that extremely limited area, and fails to recognize that Simon's magical operations image perils that beset all who acknowledge Broceliande and eternity, whether in terms of magic, mysticism, or the power of prayer to be more than self-expression.

Simon, desiring to supplant God, has obtained almost complete control over the body and spirit of his daughter Betty, and he plans to separate these two aspects of her nature while maintaining life in them both, and his mastery over them both. The tool that he uses for this purpose is the Tetragrammaton, the most sacred Hebrew name for God, pronounced backward.

The principle underlying this technique comes from one of the oldest and most widely spread beliefs in history: that the word for a thing shares the life of that thing, so that one who knows the word has power over that which it denotes. For this reason, in some cultures a person's true name is known only to himself and a very few others, lest he become subject to those who might injure him by using it. Words also are used for spells and conjurations; for example, Dante is referring to a well-known practice when he describes Virgil's use of "words of power" in silencing Charon and Minos.[89] These various usages presuppose an identity between the word or name and its referent. The word or name functions as an image, so that by means of the word, one not only comprehends something of the true nature of its referent, but also, the invocation of the word effects communication with the greater reality which it images. Christianity has not repudiated this theme; it has developed it. St. John began his Gospel with "In the beginning was the Word" which was God and was with God, existing separately from him who uttered it, and perfectly imaging him. "Hallowed be thy Name": indeed, that name *is* holy, whether we give it reverence or not.

Against this background, Simon's procedure can be seen as triply corrupting. First, in speaking the Tetragrammaton backward, he invokes the opposite to God.

Great pronouncements had established creation in its order; the reversal of those pronouncements could reverse the order. . . . He would come presently to the greatest—to the reversal of the final Jewish word of power, to the reversed Tetragrammaton itself. The energy of that most secret house of God, according to the degree in which it was spoken, meant an all but absolute control; he thought, an absolute.[90]

Second, language as such is a medium of exchange, but Simon used it not for the holy purposes of give-and-take, but as a means for outraging nature. He manipulated the currency of communication for his private ends. Taliessin, in the King's Council, spoke at once of words and of coins when he said, "I am afraid of the little loosed dragons."[91] Where language is used without disciplined accuracy, used carelessly or ignorantly, with deliberate malice or in order to mislead, it perverts individual and social exchange: "when words / escape from verse they hurry to rape souls."[92] Flattery, overblown advertising, demagoguery—Simon's intention to dominate Betty with a word is not, perhaps, very remote from sins that are committed around, and by, ourselves.

Third, Simon reverses the balance of exchange among the worlds. The four realms—nature, Broceliande, eternity, and deity—exist in a hierarchy of power: supernature can control nature; eternity can control both Broceliande and nature; and God is over all. But God has reserved to himself action from above to below; it is not for man to loose upon nature supernatural energies against which nature has no protection. It is one thing for man to call upon supernature to increase the variety and effectiveness of exchanged love, and another to use supernature for the coercion of nature, by reversing the Tetragrammaton or—to take one out of many other instances—by turning intercessory prayer into a kind of bullying of the one for whom the prayer is offered.

The old self on the new way has always enjoyed himself most at prayer. He can pray fervently for other people's delivery from other people's sins; he can indicate to Messias where X is wrong; he can try and bring supernatural power to bear on X to stop him or divert him or encourage. It is precisely because he is playing with a real power that this is so dangerous. It is dangerous, for example, to pray that Nero may be delivered from killing Agrippina; it looks a fairly safe petition but . . . What do we know of Nero, of Agrippina, of Messias? But it can never be dangerous, without particularizing, without fluency, intensely to recollect Nero and Agrippina "in the Lord," nor can it be dangerous to present all pains and distresses to the kingdom with the utmost desire that Messias may be, and the recollection that at that moment he is, the complete reconciliation . . .[93]

We, as well as Simon, play with real supernatural powers, and real powers are sometimes used upon us. But coercion by prayer is yet coercion, even though it seldom reaches the extreme that Simon imposed upon his disciples, who became "men who were beetles, beetles who were men."[94] One of Williams' early sonnets, " 'Thy Will be done,' " replies to a friend who had written "I prayed for you," with an acute sense of the coercive power of prayer, and with self-mockery:

What hast thou done? what hast thou sought? Alas,
 And what shall the high God who knows thy aim
And is determined to bring all to pass
 Which by his saints required is in his name,
What shall he work upon me in delight
 So to fulfil thy purpose and his own?
O no more sacrifice me, night by night,
 But leave that prayer unto my lips alone!
For there, by many infidelities,
 My slippery soul from formal plea escapes,
But thou being once set firmly on thy knees
 Bring'st God's will on me in how many shapes!
Hallo no more those hounds upon my track:
They know thy voice; halt, turn, and call them back.[95]

Simon is defeated not by counteracting his black magic with white, nor by the supernatural rites of the Church, nor by the energy of prayer, but by the eternal principles of the universe, which is so organized that there are limits beyond which no evil can go—limits set by the essential nature of evil as derivative from good. While Simon repeats the reversed Name, another sound breaks into the syllables. "He could just utter his own word as he willed, but he could not banish from it the other song."[96] Neither the languages of the world nor the magical words of power can, in any final sense, silence the language of heaven.

"The supreme achievement of hell is to make interchange impossible."[97] In our day, the thesis that the wages of sin is death is in disrepute; we have forgotten—if we ever knew—the Christian claim that as there are two births possible for man, there are two deaths. One results from original sin, and falls upon all; it is the gate of eternity. The second results from actual sin, and is suffered only by those who deliberately refuse life or the conditions for life. Whether the first death shall be for a man the entry into the second death is for him to decide.

8

THE WAY OF EXCHANGE

If under the influence of the centre where Love is, we have wished to be at the centre with Love, then we have to get to the centre.
—THE FIGURE OF BEATRICE, 36

All that has hitherto been presented of the theology of romantic love is, in one way, only a preparation for these two final chapters on the interchanges of love among individuals and within communities. Williams' analysis of the structure of the universe has indicated that it is possible to love; his discussion of sin has defined the alternatives to love. With this foundation completed, we can at last examine "the sanctity which is known and understood in romantic love and to which that love was meant to lead."[1] Because that which the romantic moment offers to the lover is precisely sanctity—that life where one is essentially and habitually in love, and love in him.

Since this study of loving stresses sanctity, which tends to be strenuous, it will be well to quote at the outset Williams' comment on the balance that must somehow be made between sanctity and sanity:

In morals, as in everything, there are two opposite tendencies. The first is to say: "Everything matters infinitely." The second is to say: "No doubt that is true. But mere sanity demands that we should not treat everything as mattering all that. Distinction is necessary; more-and-less is necessary; indifference is necessary." The contention is always sharp. The Rigorous view is vital to sanctity; the Relaxed view is vital to sanity. Their union is not impossible, but it is difficult; for whichever is in power begins, after the first five minutes, to maintain itself from bad and unworthy motives. Harshness, pride, resentment encourage the one; indulgence, falsity, detestable good-fellowship the other.[2]
. . . Relaxation is no less holy and proper than rigour, though perhaps it can hardly be preached so. But the lovely refreshments of this

world in some may not be without their part in the lordly rigours of
the others; the exchanges of Christendom are very deep; if we thrive
by the force of the saints, they too may feed on our felicities. The life
of the Redeemer is at the root of all . . .³

"This also is Thou; neither is this Thou."

No rigid pattern can be laid down to guide the aspirant to love, or
to define the balance—among, let us say, intelligence, faith, and
works—that will express any lover's personal style in sanctity. "Deportment may be of many kinds; the deportment of an angel and the
deportment of a panther and the deportment of a young man are all
proper to themselves,"⁴ and individual variation among saints is no less
extreme. They are identical in perhaps only one characteristic: the
swiftness and intimacy with which they co-inhere in all other life. Even
so, each participates in the exchanges of co-inherence according to the
manner that is peculiar to himself.

Love must carry itself beautifully; it must have style. It may seem
absurd, in such high matters, to use so common a literary term, and yet
there is hardly any word so useful. . . . *Le style, c'est l'homme même*
—style is the man himself, said the French maxim. . . . His style is his
particular manner of courtesy; his lack of style is his lack of courtesy.
It may be sedate or glorious, distant or intimate, firm or even flam-
boyant. Only, if it exists at all, and to the level at which it exists, it will
not be insincere or partial.⁵

" 'Love,' wrote Tyndale, translating Saint Paul, 'suffereth long and is
courteous.' "⁶ The courtesy of love springs out of humility, which in
turn is based upon the recognition that each created thing is ordained
by God to be itself and not some other thing, and that naturally and
supernaturally,

the harvest is of others, as the beginning was in others, and the process
was by others. This man's patience shall adorn that man, and that
man's celerity this; and magnificence and thrift exchanged; and chas-
tity and generosity; and tenderness and truth, and so on through the
kingdom. We shall be graced by one and by all, only never by ourselves; the only thing that can be ours is the fiery blush of the laughter
of humility when the shame of the Adam has become the shyness of the
saints.⁷

In this chapter, the basic methods of exchanged love will be ex-

amined: the use of the body as an index of love, the development of
the feeling intellect and of faith, and the primary acts of love—the
bearing of burdens, sacrifice, and forgiveness. The discussion ends with
a section on what it means to love necessity and to become free in love.

THE HOLY AND GLORIOUS FLESH

When God took flesh and dwelt among us, he confirmed the ancient
declaration that man was made in the image of God, and he demonstrated to all men that the physical body—his and ours—is indeed the
body of our salvation: not spirit dissociated from matter, not some
alien substance, but the full humanity of man. God's Son "is incarnate . . . not a mirage in a desert of piety."[8] The blood that he
shed on the cross was human blood, and the mysterious and perfect
union of God and man that was exhibited in his body is exhibited
equally mysteriously, though imperfectly, in our own. "It is in our
bodies that the secrets exist,"[9] our bodies that proclaim with a more
than Mosaic emphasis the Christian doctrines. "We experience, physically, in its proper mode, the Kingdom of God: the imperial structure
of the body carries its own high doctrines—of vision, of digestion of
mysteries, of balance, of movement, of operation."[10]

The flesh not only supports all love, even the most "spiritual," but also,
every part and every function of the body can be understood as an
image of co-inherent interrelationship and—in the phrase that Williams
took from Wordsworth—an index to love. As the words of an index
repeat words in a text, so the qualities of the body, and of its members
and operations, repeat the qualities of essential love. For example, the
eyes

are an index of vision; they see and refer us to greater seeing. Nor has
the stomach a less noble office. It digests food; that is, in its own particular method, it deals with the nourishment offered by the universe.
It is a physical formula of that health which destroys certain elements—
the bacteria which harmfully approach us. By it we learn to consume;
by it therefore to be, in turn, consumed.[11]

Carrying the image further, the digestive system parallels, in its own
manner, the function of the will. In accepting and rejecting, it images

the inevitable acceptances and rejections in any decision, and the re-joicings and repentances of Christian growth. As Taliessin says to Gareth, at work among the sewers and privies of Camelot, "without this alley-way how can man prefer? / and without preference can the Grail's grace be stored?"[12] Unless man selects, he cannot cleanse him-self from sin nor receive the grace that nourishes him; so long as his flesh endures that sacred function of selection goes on within him: his body binds him to co-inherent exchange.

Taking another example, Williams writes: "I can never see why the buttocks are funnier than any other part of the body; they support us when we sit, they are balance and (in that sense) justice."[13] He ampli-fies this in "Taliessin in the Rose-Garden": ". . . the imperially bot-tomed glory; / and the frame of justice and balance set in the body, / the balance and poise needful to all joys / and all peace."[14] "Scandal to the Jews, folly to the Greeks!" he goes on—and scandal or folly it is apt to be to us, whose notions of the flesh as holy to the Lord ordinarily stop short of our entire humanity. Yet man cannot sit or stand or walk without these rounded muscles, and that they have an erotic connota-tion in no way hinders the image, but rather enriches it.

Williams gives place to the hands as images and tools of intellect. He describes Rome as the city of the twins and the twinned hands, where the Pope performs "the heart-breaking manual acts"[15] of the Mass. At the opposite side of the world, where the headless, and therefore mind-less, emperor walks in P'o-L'u, his "indecent hands" are hidden: "lost are the Roman hands; / lost are the substantial instruments of being."[16] In *The Greater Trumps,* when the cat claws Nancy's hand, she thinks:

"It's got no hands," and this seemed to her so horrible that she nearly lost control. It had no hands, it had no spiritual instruments of inten-tion, only paws that patted or scratched, soft padded cushions or tear-ing iron nails—all four, all four, and no hands.[17]

The romantic lover sees in the body of his beloved that " 'the means of grace and the hope of glory' are in our bodies also, and the name of them is love."[18] Beatrice's flesh is "the physical Image of Christ, the physical vehicle of the Holy Ghost,"[19] not merely because it is hers, and not merely because it images things greater than itself, but because in its own right it is holy. It shares the co-inherent nature of very love—which is what it means to be holy. "Flesh knows what spirit knows, / but spirit knows it knows":[20] our bodies are not conscious of their imaging function, and here again they serve as an index: perfection is to be known in others rather than in ourselves. Dante discovers the glory in himself only as Beatrice's eyes reflect it back to him.

Williams does not claim that the sanctity of the body is unmixed with sin, original and actual. The Adam's preference for their own will contaminated their bodies, and ours suffer the consequences, in disease and in those states where "our virtues are not at ease together."[21] At times—not always—the flesh interferes with our mental or spiritual impulses toward holiness; at times it corrupts our intentions; and at times it bears us to hell. These dangers increase if we forget or ignore the principle of the body as index to Incarnate Love, or if we assume that the occasions of antagonism between flesh and intellect or spirit exhibit the normative relationship between them. Romantic theology confirms what Richard Furnival, in *All Hallows' Eve*, realized of Lester, his wife: "the body that had walked and lain by his, was itself celestial and divine. Body? it was no more merely body than soul was merely soul; it was only visible Lester."[22] Similarly, Lester saw Richard "in his whole miraculous pattern, all the particles of him, of the strange creature who was in every particle both flesh and spirit, was something that was both, was (the only word that meant the thing he was) a man."[23]

Williams' concept of the whole body as an index to love supplements and corrects the preoccupation with sex that has often clouded the discussions of the body in love. It is not that the theology of romantic love minimizes the sexual element—as will be seen later—but that it also proclaims the beauty and importance of the other bodily organs and processes. And this description of the body carries implications that reach far beyond itself: it implies a doctrine of reason that Williams, again borrowing a phrase from Wordsworth, called "the feeling intellect."

THE INTELLECTUAL GLORY

It follows from the thesis, "Flesh knows what spirit knows,"[24] that body and mind, passion and intellect, are cognate functions, categories of one identity; therefore they are not fundamentally opposed. Thus "Donne spoke of the lady whose body thought: but his own mind felt. His own intellectual emotion discovered her corporeal intelligence."[25] The clearest illustration of this complex unity comes from the romantic moment, where Dante sees in Beatrice the perfection that his reason demonstrates to him, and thereby, if only for that moment, he possesses

an intellect so swiftly capable of ordering its emotions that it may itself be said to "feel." It knows, and feels as it knows. This activity of the intellectual love includes in itself all other lesser tendernesses. "All that friendship, all that love, can do" are to be there to complete the man.[26]

Yet to think and to feel are different categories of the one identity: they are no more the same thing than to reason and to imagine. Nor do these operations always reinforce each other. Their union in the feeling intellect is normative, the state for which man was made; it is not normal in the sense of being commonplace.

Williams makes no suggestion that it is easy to achieve or to maintain the feeling intellect. He begins his essay "The Cross" by asserting: "It is almost impossible to state what one in fact believes, because it is almost impossible to hold a belief and to define it at the same time."[27] Similarly, "the maxim for any love affair is 'Play and pray; but on the whole do not pray when you are playing and do not play when you are praying.' We cannot yet manage such simultaneities."[28] Attempting them, we are likely to find ourselves confusing the two categories of identity, allowing sentiment to direct our reason, or adulterating an emotional response by a fiat of the will. Passion and intellectual analysis must each purify its specific function before the two can unite perfectly. To obscure their extreme difference would be, as it were, for a man who is not quite a man to marry a woman who is not quite a woman. C. S. Lewis supplies the explicit corrective:

Can we, in virtue of the maxim *This also is Thou,* regard the apparent differences as superficial or even subjective? Is Felicity simply one? . . . Whatever may be the truth, that certainly is not. Felicity not only alters, it "alters from its centre." The *differentia* is central: a lifetime of distinguishing would not be enough to mark and adore the utter difference, even the incommensurableness, of our diverse experiences.[29]

But adoration requires a whole person. Neither passion alone nor intellect alone enables the whole person to participate fully in the complexity and delight of the co-inherence. On earth as in heaven, union depends upon separation, and separation makes union possible.

However, the feeling intellect needs for its fulfillment more than internal harmony among reason, emotion, perception, and vision. It must have enrichment from the experiences of others, and rectification by other minds.

Much was possible to a man in solitude; perhaps the final transmutations and achievements in the zones on the yonder side of the central Knowledge were possible only to the spirit in solitude. But some things were possible only to a man in companionship, and of these the most important was balance. No mind was so good that it did not need another mind to counter and equal it, and to save it from conceit and blindness and bigotry and folly. Only in such a balance could humility be found, humility which was a lucid speed to welcome lucidity whenever and wherever it presented itself.[30]

One who believes in the co-inherence is forced by logical necessity to include in his deliberations as much of the experience of others as he can learn of, weaving it with his own into a coherent unity. Knowledge, as well as being, depends upon exchange.

Man has always to proceed by hypotheses. But to accept a hypothesis as a hypothesis is precisely to admit that some other possibility may exist. Are we to comment on our own hypothesis in the light of other possibilities? and do not other people exist, holding other hypotheses? and must we not regard their convictions as some kind of "compensation" for our own? must we not be, in that sense at least, a "double man"?[31]

In the intellectual exchanges, man submits his personal experiences and ideas to others for illumination and qualification, and he scrutinizes and evaluates their reports. That is, he subjects himself to their authority and exercises his own. "The recognition of authority is the desire for union, but also it is the knowledge that the individual by himself is bound to be wrong. . . . However right a man's ideas, they were bound to go wrong if he nourished them by himself."[32] The balance of individual insight with authority does not infallibly protect man from error, or guarantee the truth of his analyses, or subject individual judgment to majority rule. Neither does it liberate man from the need to determine for himself how much weight he shall assign to a given experience, his own or someone else's. It does provide a check upon both the overweening and the insufficient intellect; it increases the probability of his avoiding the major aberrations of reason and passion alike; and it unites him with others in a web of reciprocal derivation.

Failure to participate in these intellectual interchanges led John Wilmot, Earl of Rochester, into a basic error. "God, his passion cried, did not reveal His secrets to men; for God, his pride added, had not revealed them to the Earl of Rochester."[33] He had taken the first step in skepticism—he doubted others—but not the necessary second step of equally doubting himself, that would have enabled him to assign appropriate authority to those others. To that degree he was credulous, and "hath God anywhere promised that he will save credulous men from being deceived . . . ?"[34] Others have followed that road further than Rochester: denying others' knowledge and experience, they have committed themselves to arbitrary unbelief, which is equally yoked with arbitrary belief. Skepticism opposes them both. The skeptic, knowing all human knowledge to be doubly limited by finitude and by sin, holds his beliefs lightly even when he holds them seriously.

There is a great deal of skepticism in believers; and a good deal of belief in non-believers; the only question is where we decide to give our better energy. . . . "Lord, I believe; help thou mine unbelief" may, and should, be prayed two ways.[35]

The stages of belief, as traditionally understood, have been summarized by Williams as follows: "I believe Christ, I believe in Christ, within Christ I believe. The progress is from formal belief to real belief, and then to unitive belief."[36] The first is essentially intellectual assent; the second and third are degrees of faith which, he writes, "is another kind of thing,"[37] embracing not only intellect and will, but also imagination.

Imagination is "the faculty which deals with images and their relation. Faith indeed is much the same capacity whenever it is recognized as having authoritative control over our actual lives."[38] Or in other terms, "Faith was not a poor substitute for vision; it was rather the

capacity for integrating the whole being with truth. It was a total dis-
position and a total act."[39] It is an act of faith when a lover walks
proudly: his whole being is integrated with the fact of being in love.

Sometimes the romantic falls into faith as he falls into love, without
a conscious decision. But if either faith or love is to become stable in
him, he must ratify it by a deliberate choice. He has confronted a dozen
or a hundred views of the nature of the world, of which the Beatrician
is only one. No doubt all are inadequate, but presumably some are
more nearly adequate to the unknowable reality than others, and certainly none of them can be absolutely proved. Therefore "no-one can
possibly do more than decide what to believe."[40]

. . . we have on inadequate evidence to make up our minds on the
principles of things; it is the old gamble. "Then the wise course is not
to gamble." "Yes, but you must; you are not free to choose." The
agnostic, the anti-romantic, gambles as much as the believer and the
romantic—nor is he any more certain of the great classic end. He is
indeed less certain, for he has ceased to explore the distances; he has
given up measuring the times; he has, that is to say, abandoned proportion. But on proportion the classic whole depends. That whole has
a place for the romantic beginning; it puts the romantic into its place
certainly, and firmly keeps it there. But the anti-classic has no place for
any image at all—either of the beginning or of the end, only for a
makeshift.[41]

We are not the creators of our worlds. Whether God does or does not
incarnate himself depends upon him, not upon our belief or disbelief in
it. But we choose how we shall understand our world; we decide
whether incarnation shall be for us fiction or reality, and whether
Beatrice shall be for us only herself or both herself and the God-bearing
image. At stake are our premises, and the thoroughness and honesty
with which we follow the chosen premises to their conclusions in the
active life of faith. Hard thinking is necessary, and disciplined imagination, and rigorous translation of thought and imagery into action,
before the feeling intellect can mature into the life of faith. Acceptance
of the Christian premises

may come violently and catastrophically; it may come gently and continuously. It may be welcomed; it may be resisted. But when the
intellect becomes aware of it or assents to it, then the intellect is condi-

tioned by it. To say it conditions is not to say that it deforms or limits, except indeed as all premises must limit. The intellect working in a world in which the Incarnation has happened is not obviously in the same position as the intellect working in a world in which the Incarnation has not happened. But it has to learn to operate on the new premises.[42]

Do we believe in the Incarnation of Love in Christ? Then our job is to know and to welcome him, and in him, all the lesser incarnations of love that we can find, whatever form they take. Do we believe in the co-inherence? Then our job is to discover how to love co-inherently, and to practice the exchanges of co-inherent love in order to know more fully, and to act with increasing swiftness and skill.

THE PRACTICE OF SUBSTITUTED LOVE

The bearing of burdens: "The pattern of the glory is a pattern of acts."[43] Williams names many acts as characterizing that pattern, among them derivation, exchange, interchange, substitution, vicariousness, and the bearing of burdens; it is the last of these which he takes as the archetype. In *He Came Down from Heaven,* he states the principle; in *Descent into Hell,* he illustrates a variety of ways in which burdens can be borne, the results of this activity, and the results of refusing to bear others' burdens or to be borne by others.

Pauline, the central character in that novel, lives under the shadow of a recurrent and terrifying event: at irregular intervals, she sees herself on the street—not a similitude of herself or a ghost, but her very self, the doppelgänger—and she knows that when she finally meets it she will go mad or die. Her acquaintance, the poet Peter Stanhope, suggests to her that the basic difficulty in the situation lies not in her encounter with the doppelgänger but in her fear of it. "The fact remains—but see how different a fact, if it can't be dreaded!"[44] he says, and later, "If meeting is a pleasure, as we so often tell people, you may as well enjoy the pleasure."[45] Since no one can destroy fear merely by commanding himself not to be afraid, Stanhope proposes to release Pauline from her fear by taking it upon himself. He asks her,

". . . Haven't you heard it said that we ought to bear one another's burdens?"

"But that means—" she began, and stopped.

"I know," Stanhope said. "It means listening sympathetically, and thinking unselfishly, and being anxious about, and so on. Well, I don't say a word against all that; no doubt it helps. But I think when Christ or St. Paul, or whoever said *bear,* or whatever he Aramaically said instead of *bear,* he meant something much more like carrying a parcel instead of someone else. To bear a burden is precisely to carry it instead of. If you're still carrying yours, I'm not carrying it for you—however sympathetic I may be. And anyhow there's no need to introduce Christ, unless you wish. It's a fact of experience. If you give a weight to me, you can't be carrying it yourself; all I'm asking you to do is to notice that blazing truth. . . ."[46]

An analogy may help here. The emotional energy of terror exists in Pauline; as a specific pattern of energy, it has existence and direction of its own that, on the principle of the conservation of energy, cannot be destroyed. But like various other energies, it can be transmitted to another part of the energy system: it can be moved about in a field as if it were a thing. Because Pauline is fearful, her fear has to happen, so to speak, but she can alter the locus of that fear. She gives it to Stanhope.

"When you are alone," he said, "remember that I am afraid instead of you, and that I have taken over every kind of worry. Think merely that; say to yourself—'he is being worried,' and go on. Remember it is mine. If you do not see it [the doppelgänger], well; if you do, you will not be afraid. . . ."[47]

Emphatically this is not repression, which is a matter of retaining the energy below conscious levels. Pauline's fear continues to exist; she recognizes that it continues to be fear and her own fear, only Stanhope has taken it over. On that basis she proceeds about her business without fear.

The technique of taking up another's burden is sufficiently important in Williams' theology that it must be considered in his own words.

The one who takes has to set himself—mind and emotion and sensation—to the burden, to know it, imagine it, receive it—and sometimes not to be taken aback by the swiftness of the divine grace and the lightness of the burden. It is almost easier to believe that Messias was probably right about the mysteries of the Godhead than that he was merely accurate about the facts of everyday life. One expects the burden always to be heavy, and it is sometimes negligible; which is precisely what he said.[48]

This is how Stanhope acts upon that principle:

He recollected Pauline; he visualized her going along a road, any road; he visualized another Pauline coming to meet her. And as he did so his mind contemplated not the first but the second Pauline; he took trouble to apprehend the vision, he summoned through all his sensations an approaching fear. Deliberately he opened himself to that fear, laying aside for awhile every thought of why he was doing it, forgetting every principle and law, absorbing only the strangeness and the terror of that separate spiritual identity. . . . it was necessary first intensely to receive all her spirit's conflict. He sat on, imagining to himself the long walk with its sinister possibility, the ogreish world lying around, the air with its treachery to all sane appearance. His own eyes began to seek and strain and shrink, his own feet, quiet though actually they were, began to weaken with the necessity of advance upon the road down which the girl was passing. The body of his flesh received her alien terror, his mind carried the burden of her world. . . . The experience itself, sharply as his body took it, was less sharp for him [than for her]; not that he willed it so, but because his senses received their communication from within not from without, and there is in all holy imagination from goodwill a quality of greatness which purifies and stabilizes experience. His goodwill went to its utmost, and utmost goodwill can go very far. It went to all but actual vision, and it excluded his intellectual judgment of that vision. Had he been asked, at that moment, for his judgment, he would have answered that he believed sincerely that Pauline believed sincerely that she saw, but whether the sight was actual or not he could not tell. He would have admitted that it might be but a fantastic obsession of her brain. That made no difference to his action. If a man seems to himself to endure the horrors of shipwreck, though he walks on dry land and breathes clear air, the business of his friend is more likely to be to accept those horrors as he feels them, carrying the burden, than to explain that the burden cannot, as a matter of fact, exist.[49]

Stanhope's poetic vision assisted his act of substitution, but lack of that kind or degree of imagination does not hinder the act itself. The bearing of burdens depends upon intention, not upon imaginative genius. The act of taking up a burden can be, and frequently is, as simple and direct as—in *All Hallows' Eve*—Lester's putting herself at Betty's disposal when Simon began his magical attack. She did not know what

Betty wanted or needed, so she waited, offering herself to be used in any way that might be required.[50] And the spell, directed against Betty, redounded upon her friend, and through her was taken into God.

How does one let a burden go? The first requirement is intellectual acceptance of the possibility. A person who denies that such an exchange *can* happen, who refuses it even as a working hypothesis, is not likely to experience its reality, and is in no position to test it. Second, one releases a burden of fear, pain, guilt, or anxiety, by the same methods used in turning any other kind of a job over to someone else. One tells his co-worker what needs to be done and then—it is devoutly to be wished—goes away and leaves the other to do it. Essentially there is no difference between asking a friend to carry one's fear, and hiring someone to scrub a floor, or ordering a subordinate to draft a report, or letting a neighbor run an errand. All these are forms of substitution: A substitutes his labor for B's. If there is love on the part of either, this is substituted love.

In the specific form of substitution where one casts his burden upon the Lord, obviously it is merely stupid to stand around kibitzing. His capability can be assumed; his willingness has been promised. "Come unto me . . . and I will give you rest." Making such a contract with the Omnipotence has the advantage that it requires of man principally the act of giving up the burden. Presumably God already knows what the difficulty is, so that it need not be defined for his benefit, although no doubt it would be salutary to do so for our own intellectual clarification. But it seems as if it is not enough to call upon him.

"Mystical substitution" we have heard from the text-books, or from other books that are less than the text-books. It is supposed to be for "nuns, confessors, saints, not us": so much the worse for us. We are supposed to be content to "cast our burdens on the Lord." The Lord indicated that the best way to do so was to hand these over to someone else to cast, or even to cast them on him in someone else. . . . The commerce of love is best established by commercial contracts with man.[51]

From the point of view of the one who gives up his burden, the procedure in giving it to a friend is identical with giving it to God. It may be humiliating so to ask for help: "a pride and self-respect which will be content to repose upon Messias is often unapt to repose on 'the brethren.' "[52] It is natural to protest, with Pauline, "Would I push my burden on to anybody else?" And Stanhope:

"Not if you insist on making a universe for yourself," he answered. "If you want to disobey and refuse the laws that are common to us all, if you want to live in pride and division and anger, you can. But if you will be part of the best of us, and live and laugh and be ashamed with us, then you must be content to be helped. You must give your burden up to someone else, and you must carry someone else's burden. I haven't made the universe and it isn't my fault. But I'm sure that this is a law of the universe, and not to give up your parcel is as much to rebel as not to carry another's. . . . "[53]

When reluctance to transfer a burden stems from generous hesitation to impose upon another, it reveals one's misunderstanding of the process. The new bearer of the burden can carry another's because he does not carry his own—they are borne for him by another. As Pauline comes to see,

everyone carrying everyone else's [burden], like the Scilly Islanders taking in each other's washing. Well, and at that, if it were tiresome and horrible to wash your own clothes and easy and happy to wash someone else's, the Scilly Islanders might be intelligent enough.[54]

There may be also a feeling that one ought to stand on his own feet in order to increase his strength and self-reliance. It is true that he would accomplish this end, but self-sufficiency destroys the life of the co-inherence, and himself with it. In taking that option, man isolates himself from exchange and so descends into hell.

There are, of course, duties that ought not to be given away. A task may be difficult to perform but not burdensome, because one enjoys doing it. Conversely, another task may require little effort, but constitute a burden because one rebels against it. Or one faces a work that he is eager to accomplish but which lies beyond his capacity by reason of some inadequacy—a lack of skill or knowledge or materials or physical strength, or because of an impossibility inherent in the work itself. So St. Paul confronted the Law, and every man confronts the perfections that are demanded of him daily. What, exactly, is the burden? Illness, or the frustration and impatience and annoyance that prevent one from settling down to the work of healing? Grief, or resentment against the circumstances that caused the grief, against the universe that allowed the tragedy to occur? A warped childhood, or the confusions and the tendencies toward sin which that background encouraged, and which afflict one in the present? The burden may be any of these—the illness, the grief, or the past; or it may be the emotional response to the work. But it is important to know what the nature of the burden actually is, before one gives up a labor that would have brought him into joy, or wastes his forces upon an unnecessary undertaking.

Substitution, if true at all, is independent of time and place. These are categories of nature, not restrictions upon the acts of exchange. So in circumstances where the substitution cannot take place at the time when the burden needs to be borne—as in Pauline's wish to carry her ancestor's fear—the act can be performed in eternity, the infinite contemporaneity of all things. The acceptance of one's participation within the eternal glory involves one in all its operations, so that any burden borne by any person at any moment and in any place may be laid upon anyone who lives by interchange. What matters is not sequence or distance, but the living web of acts that makes up the Glory of God. The exchanges and the derivations belong to nature because they exist in the eternity that supports nature, and they extend beyond nature. One's times and occasions may sequester him from others of like mind, but he still can call upon the power of all who live by the exchanges of love.

One called: *What of him that hath not?* but who could be that had not? so universal, in itself and through its means, was the sublime honour of substituted love; what wretch so poor that all time and place would not yield a vicar for his distress, beyond time and place the pure vicariate of salvation?[55]

One can give up a burden without knowing who receives it, or one may find that beyond or even contrary to his will, he has been placed within a situation as a bearer of a burden. Substitution works through him, and he cannot withdraw from it, nor govern its direction, nor determine its manner of operating, unless he withdraws from the coinherence itself.

We know very little about what happens in bearing each other's burdens; we know still less what could happen. Yet this much is clear and needs to be said: first, C. S. Lewis has written, in connection with the doctrine of bearing burdens and from intimate knowledge of both Williams himself and his work, "This Williams most seriously maintained, and I have reason to believe that he spoke from experimental knowledge."[56] Second: Williams consistently declared that in the end, all bearing of burdens depends upon him who bears our griefs and carries our sorrows. Even though his part may not be known and acknowledged, the act finally is his in whom all things are possible, and it is ours only as we unite ourselves with it.

The "good works which thou hast prepared for us to walk in" are those that belong to "that holy fellowship"; they are therefore those peculiarly of exchange and substitution. They are prepared and they are there; we have only to walk in them.[57]

The walking requires effort, however, at the very least the effort of attention, and often much more. "It is therefore necessary (a) not to take burdens too recklessly; (b) to consider exactly how far any burden, accepted to the full, is likely to conflict with other duties. There is always a necessity for intelligence."[58] The Faith lists prudence among the primary virtues. Common sense precludes attempting more than our available strength can manage, strength here meaning not only spiritual and intellectual energies but physical as well, because the substitutions draw upon the finite resources of the body. Exhaustion is a discourtesy to ourselves and to others; forgetfulness is a failure of accuracy as well as of love. But our finiteness does not limit God's act: if we cannot undertake or fulfill a task, some other will, or has, and ultimately the lost good will be restored.

There is, it seems, a law in things that if a man is compelled to choose between two good actions, mutually exclusive, the one which he chooses to neglect will in course of time avenge itself on him. Rightly considered, this is a comfortable if chastening thought, for it implies that the nature of good is such that it can never, not even for some other mode of itself, be neglected. If ever it is, for whatever admirable reasons, set on one side it will certainly return.[59]

Two special kinds of burdens need further comment: bearing others' sins, and bearing their physical pain or disease. Williams ruled out the former when he wrote *Descent into Hell,* but later he reversed that judgment, for reasons which he gives in his introduction to Evelyn Underhill's collected letters.

On one of the few occasions on which the present writer met Evelyn Underhill, she permitted herself to speak of one of his own novels [*Descent into Hell*]. . . . In it he had written of two characters: "He endured her sensitiveness, but not her sin; the substitution there, if indeed there is a substitution, is hidden in the central mystery of Christendom." It was a well-meant sentence, but she charmingly corrected it. She said something to this effect: "Oh, but the saints do— they say they do. St. Catherine said: 'I will bear your sins.' " She spoke from a very great knowledge of the records of sanctity, but I should be rather more than willing to believe that she spoke from a lofty practice of sanctity and from a great understanding of the laws that govern, and the labours that are given to, sanctity.[60]

The act of bearing a sin for another is closely related to, if not identical with, the conversion of energy described earlier in terms of Nancy and the storm.[61] The bearer makes of himself a way by which the sin can be taken into God: he assumes to himself the responsibility and the consequences of the sin, not in the pretense that he had committed it, and not because he is his brother's keeper or even because he is his brother's brother, but because he partakes of his brother's life. They co-inhere, each in the other, so that one can do what the other—for whatever reason—cannot, and so he does it.

With regard to the healing of the physical body by substituted love, Williams suggests that this can be done, but he adds, "The body is probably the last place where such interchange is possible."

In some states of romantic love it is felt that the power of healing exists, if only it could be brought into action, and on the basis of Romantic Theology it could so be brought into action. We habitually expect too little of ourselves. But it is not only in states of realization that the power exists. It is limited, peculiarly, by other duties. Most men are already so committed that they ought not, whatever their goodwill, to contemplate the carrying of the burden of paralysis or consumption or even lesser things. . . . Certainly it is reasonable to believe that the kind of burden might be transmuted into another equivalent kind, and in a full state of the kingdom upon earth such a transmutation would be agreeable and natural. It remains at present an achievement of which our "faith" is not yet capable. That is no reason why we should not practise faith, a faith in the interchange of the kingdom operating in matter as out of matter, because whatever distinction there may be between the two is only a distinction between modes of love.[62]

Especially, one should avoid making any such physical substitution a crucial experiment. Not all pain is a burden: it may be—as Pauline's grandmother (in *Descent into Hell*) found in dying—a necessary part of being born again, to be eagerly sought and endured. But there is no reason why one should not experiment here, as anywhere else, if he wishes to and if conditions allow it. Only he should be extremely careful in determining that such an act is called for, and in evaluating the results. "Do, and do not do": the latter, like the former, is an imperative.

This caution is the more necessary if it be true, as Williams evidently believed, that the energies employed in substitution are real natural and supernatural energies. What happens when they are misused is a major theme in *The Place of the Lion,* where Williams describes

those who desired the power of the Immortals, the virtue of the things that they sought, not for that virtue's sake, not even for the sake of fresh and greater experiences, but merely that their old experience might be more satisfactory to them. Foster wanted to be stronger than those with whom he came in contact; he had made himself a place for the lion and it seemed the lion was taking possession of its habitation; its roar echoing in the wilderness and the dry places of the soul.[63]

Even more bluntly: "It is this turning of the most sacred mysteries to the immediate security of the self that is the catastrophic thing."[64] Messias offered a perilous way and a terrible good: "blessed is he, whosoever shall find none occasion for stumbling in me," he said, as if he comprehended what man could do with his gifts. He warned of the narrow road and gate, and of the destruction that engulfs those who do not find them. It is the losing of life for *his* sake that brings eternal life.

But how can we know whether we are acting on the basis of direction from God, or from veiled self-desire? or whether we are like the man who was "inclined to call up his own spiritual reserves under . . . a quite honest pretence of invoking direction"?[65] We cannot be sure.

Christendom has demanded the closest examination of conscience to avoid that retrogression, but our motions slide down, one below the other, and the schism of intention is deeper than any other; where is certainty? who can be sure of any motive in any act? Yet the choice, the wish that may become the will, may be there, whatever our ignorance; to desire to follow the good is important, to desire to follow the good from the good is more important. Saint John eased the young Church: "if our hearts condemn us, God is greater than our hearts, and knoweth all things." Messias himself condescended to encouragement in the parable of the tares. "Sow good seed; but when good and evil spring up together, and all a mixed growth in the heart, do not fret, do not go hunting among motives for blades of wheat here and blades of tares there. I will separate all, I will save these and annihilate those; be at peace, be glad, leave decision to me. Only sow; work while it is yet day." In all communicated joy there is the sense of three great sayings. The first is the joyous mockery of Messias: "O fools and slow of heart to believe . . ." The second is his definition: "I am Alpha and Omega, the beginning and the end, the first and the last." The third is the threat which must inevitably accompany the coming of the heavenly thing on to earth: "Blessed is he whosoever shall not be offended at me."[66]

The practice of substituted love is a type of "what might be called 'loving from within.' One no longer merely loves an object; one has a sense of loving precisely from the great web in which the object and we are both combined. There is, if only transitorily, a flicker of living within the beloved."[67] Another name for loving from within is compassion—suffering with—which, Williams writes, "is a very great word; it is perhaps the most awful, absolute, and significant of all the names of God in relation to men . . . [and] the most intense name for the unity of men and women."[68] God has shown compassion in the strictest sense of that word:

He has substituted His Manhood for ours in the secrets of the Incarnation and Atonement. The principle of the Passion is that He gave His life "for"—that is, instead of and on behalf of—ours. In that sense He lives in us and we in Him, He and we co-inhere. "I live; yet not I but Christ liveth in me" said St. Paul, and defined the web of universal power towards substitution.[69]

We are continually borne by others. Therefore, willingly or un-
willingly we are perpetually in debt to God and to the whole creation.
The situation enforces humility: "If our lives are so carried by others
and so depend upon others, it becomes impossible to think very highly
of them."[70] But the situation also tends to generate resentment against
the implicit obligation thereby imposed upon us, which is one of the
reasons why, in the bearing of burdens, "The giver's part may be
harder than the taker's; that is why, here, it may be more blessed to
give than to receive, though in the equity of the kingdom there is little
difference."[71] The balance of exchange indeed requires that some return be made, and

it is natural that, in certain happy states (e.g., the Beatrician love),
there should be a desire to make any contract of the kind mutual, and
so it often may be. At the same time the tendency is sometimes for the
pattern not to return but to proceed. The old proverb said that there
was always one who kissed and one who took kisses; that too, accepted,
is in this sense a part of the pattern. The discovery that one cannot
well give back or be given back what one has given or been given in
the same place is sometimes as painful as the discovery that one is
being loved on principle and not from preference: a good deal of
conviction of the equality of all points in the web of the kingdom and
of the denial of the self is necessary to make it bearable.[72]

But the redeemed man has no desire to be free of obligation; gratitude
is the taproot of his existence. "The grateful mind would not lose the
debt it has already discharged; the debt is the means of its gratitude,
and its gratitude is the deliverance of its soul, its very way of life, and
the activity of its creation."[73] If circumstances provide for his giving
where he has received, all is most well. If not, some other will pay his
debt and he will pay another's. All is still most well, because the particular joy of mutuality has been replaced by the equal but different
joy of extending the pattern of interchange to include others. When
one gives to some other person, he may be repaid by a third, perhaps
in an entirely different coinage. The precise equity of the kingdom,
wherein all is gift, balances the accounts.

This equity cannot be equated with human justice, even at its best.
The latter is based on the principle that all shall be judged by the
same standard; the former specifies a sliding scale: "For with what

judgement ye judge, ye shall be judged." He who insists upon exact repayment in kind will have to account for every jot and tittle that he has received, for what the good earth and the air contributed to his being, for the order that sustained and the disorder that stimulated him. He who gives lavishly, without computing size of gift or of return, will receive with the same unmeasured prodigality.

Half a hundred brief comments, flung out to the mob of men's hearts, make it impossible for a child of the kingdom, for a Christian, to talk of justice or injustice so far as he personally is concerned; they make it impossible for him to *complain* of the unfairness of anything. They do not, presumably, stop him noticing what has happened, but it can never be a matter of protest. Judgement and measurement are always discouraged. You may have them if you will, but there is a sinister note in the promise that they shall be measured back to you in the same manner: "good measure, pressed down and running over shall men give into your bosoms." If you must have law, have it, "till thou hast paid the uttermost farthing."[74]

Messias told the parable of the workers who, hired at the eleventh hour, received the same wages as those who had worked all day. What does it matter, in infinite joy, whether one labored harder or longer than another, so long as all share in the End? Some enter at the last moment? What difference does it make, since they come? A guest, tardy in arriving at a banquet where there is more than enough for all, is encouraged by his fellow guests to catch up with them in eating and drinking and merriment. They commiserate with him over the impediment that delayed his pleasure in the celebration and their pleasure in his company. So, in the vineyard of heaven where the work is the feast of love, the latecomers are greeted by those who preceded them.

The necessary sacrifice: In the absolute sense, man cannot sacrifice—make holy—any more than he can save himself. It takes God to do that: "there's only one sacrifice, and the God of gods makes it, not you."[75] Man can only prepare to receive the one sacrifice and to co-inhere in it, offering his gift to be united with God's, and accepting all gifts as in union with his. Thus man "makes holy," and in no other way.

Sacrifice is the act by which evil is changed into good; he who, under

God, performs the act is sacrificed. Williams' clearest illustration of this
has already been described in terms of the conversion of energy:
Nancy's confrontation with the storm in *The Greater Trumps,* where
she draws upon herself the supernatural energy of the storm, and trans-
mutes its magical power into natural energy. She returns good for evil;
she sacrifices herself. This is the manner in which all salvation from
sin is achieved: the sin is not wiped out, but its energy is redirected.
Sinful man is not destroyed but changed—and changed by the introduction of another energy that counteracts the energy of original and
of actual sin. Therefore, without sacrifice there can be no salvation.

As always, nature repeats supernature. Without sacrifice there can
be no natural life. The herbivores depend for their physical existence
upon vegetable life; carnivores must destroy the flesh of other animals
in order to live. What responsibilities this imposes upon the so-called
lower animals, man does not know. He cannot judge of them; he can
only note the necessity. But it is worth remembering that if the lion
ever loses its appetite for lamb, it will either starve to death or its
identity as lion will be destroyed, and its paradisal lying-down with the
lamb may be the prelude to a sacrifice that is as natural and as willingly entered as when parents sacrifice their energies for their children,
teachers for their students, priests for their people, or anyone for the
work that he loves. It is conceivable that this sacrificial love may have
characterized Eden: there the arduous demands of sacrificing and
being sacrificed may have been welcomed as means of love. But here
and now, man must take life in order to live, and he cannot learn from
the lettuce or the steer whether it be willing to exchange its life for
his. He must either submit to the necessity for sacrificial giving and
receiving, as the tool and victim of necessity, or else curse God for
creating the necessity, and die.

Messias himself accepted the sacrifice of others, not only in the ways
that all men do by living, but also, more deeply, in preserving his own
life at its beginning. He owed his life to the Innocents of Bethlehem,
"those holy and adorable creatures whom the Church has canonized,
as it were, by universal acclamation and only because they suffered un-
knowingly in direct substitution for Christ."[76] The Innocents saved
another; themselves they could not save.

The law of the Hebrews prescribed an unblemished offering for the sacrifice: a flawed or weak creature could not carry the burden of sin that was laid upon it at the altar. Similarly, the new law brought by Messias specified a perfection, which was the more imperative because the new sacrifice was also the final one that covered all sins, "a full, perfect, and sufficient sacrifice, oblation, and satisfaction, for the sins of the whole world."[77] After this, "The disciple might not achieve perfection, but he must mean perfection, so only would Immanuel achieve perfection in him."[78] However, all later sacrifice was to be made indirectly, through Christ, the directness of earth giving way to the vicariousness of heaven.

Self-sacrifice thus is the lover's duty; that it may be his joy in no way changes its character as an exceedingly strenuous duty and a terrible joy. It remains easier to answer anger with anger than to alter anger into something else—as Williams remarked, "Malice was a much cosier thing than love"[79]—and the energy of anger or malice or injustice can be very great. The only difference between receiving evil impotently because one is unable to strike back, and receiving it redemptively because one refuses to let it rebound, lies in the presence or absence of personal protest. What is gained by deliberate and loving sacrifice is the conviction that somehow, sometime, good will ensue, and as anguish increases that assurance may dwindle to no more than a despairing hope. But no feeling, no awareness or lack of awareness, determines the nature of the operation. The one who is sacrificed continues to be the point at which energies are transformed and transmitted, and, in the divine justice, why should not he, rather than some other, act in this way? Why should he not become, in Williams' image, "the oxygen to the mountain-climber. No doubt, if one cylinder were not there, another would serve; there is nothing sacrosanct about oneself; anything might do as well. But if one is required to be oxygen, one had better be oxygen."[80]

The sacrifice of blood holds special significance in the Hebrew-Christian tradition. The Old Testament indicates that

for the serious moral offences there was little chance of personal "atonement." The sentence continually is death—death for idolatry, death for witchcraft, death for incest, death for adultery, death for murder. Other, and many, moral laws are laid down, but there are few definite penalties attached to them. It is, obscurely, the blood that is involved, the blood that is important; one might almost say that wherever the blood is involved the Lord is involved.[81]

This can be interpreted as referring to the principle of retaliation, and so, undoubtedly, it was sometimes understood. But even at its most crude and vindictive, the *lex talionis* foreshadowed the greater principle that the labor of converting evil into good must be proportionate to the magnitude of the evil. Only an eye needs to be given for an eye, but a life for a life.

When the rejection of the good is corrected by means of a second rejection, of evil, the doubling of the negative produces a positive. And because flesh and spirit are categories of the one identity, man, the negation of sin can be accomplished through the body and in some circumstances only through the body.

The blood belonged to the Lord throughout all animals and all men; it was the life of the flesh and it made atonement for the soul. It was sprinkled before God for the soul, instead of the soul; that is, as a substitution for the soul. The expiation for the sins of the soul (since sin was necessarily of the soul) was by the life of the flesh, either by the flesh that was in union with the soul that had sinned or by some other.[82]

To force another to sacrifice himself is an outrage, even when—as in obtaining food—it cannot be avoided. Equally, to shed blood in malice or carelessness is outrage: it no more constitutes sacrifice than martyrdom that lacks *caritas* is holy. Blood can be offered for sin only by the will of the victim, or by the mystery of its consecration by the Divine Compassion. The Innocents are canonized by the Church, but the Christian must choose before he can enter the process of sacrifice, either by willing to be sacrificed, or by asking the Mercy of God to consecrate the sacrifices by which he is sustained.

Williams emphasizes the high significance of the pouring out of the blood by giving two other examples: "surgical blood-shedding . . . is, as the need for it is, a result of the Fall," and

there is also, of course, that other great natural bloodshed common to half the human race—menstruation. . . . it is not impossible that that is an image, naturally, of the great bloodshed on Calvary, and perhaps, supernaturally, in relation to it. Women share the victimization of the blood; it is why, being the sacrifice so, they cannot be the priests. They are mothers and, in that special sense, victims; witnesses, in the body, to the suffering of the body, and the method of Redemption.[83]

Whether the recurrent event be endured as a curse or presented as an oblation, it has meaning beyond itself.

Flesh knows what spirit knows,
but spirit knows it knows—categories of identity:
women's flesh lives the quest of the Grail
in the change from Camelot to Carbonek and from Carbonek to Sarras,
puberty to Carbonek, and the stanching, and Carbonek to death.
Blessed is she who gives herself to the journey.[84]

Forgiveness: Not all sacrifice requires the shedding of blood, though it does require the giving of life. Williams describes forgiveness as

the operation of "offering oneself for another" . . . for there can be only two attitudes towards the sin of another towards oneself; one is to entertain a grudge, the other is not to entertain a grudge. To entertain it is precisely to prefer the selfhood to that other, that is precisely not to offer oneself; and in consequence (what is certainly as important), to prevent one properly apprehending how another is offered instead of oneself. It is as necessary to accept this sacrifice as to make it, and as necessary to live from it.[85]

The forgiveness of sins "is the great fundamental covenant not only between man and man but between man and God."[86] "Forgiveness, if it is at all a principle of that interchanged life, is certainly the deepest of all; if it is not, then the whole principle of interchange is false."[87]

Much of the discussion of forgiveness is impeded by the common belief that forgiveness implies, or results in, forgetting the sin. The difficulty with this view lies partly in the virtual impossibility of willing forgetfulness, and partly in the nature of the offense considered simply as an event: what has happened has happened, and in mere honesty it ought not to be pushed out of the mind. Another difficulty arises from the Christian doctrine of eternity, which precludes forgetting: "forgetfulness implies a temporal state; there can be no eternal oblivion of an act of which there is an eternal awareness, and the very nature of eternity is awareness of all: 'the perfect and simultaneous possession of everlasting life.' "[88]

Things are but themselves; . . . There must then be nothing excluded; and the willingness to exclude nothing must itself exclude only the will to exclude. Such a result means something which, in our ordinary speech, may be called forgiveness; though the thing itself . . . is too swift, too tender, too lovely for a name which—to most of us—is a rather heavy and solemn determination.[89]

But if forgiveness fails to nullify, and excludes forgetting, the sin, what can it mean? A restoration of love? How can love be restored when neither the act nor the knowledge of the act has been obliterated?

All Hallows' Eve contains a description of forgiveness in terms that make remembering the sin essential to the act. Lester, tormented by the memory of her sins against Betty, asks for pardon. Betty, however, does not recall anything between them that needs forgiveness.

Lester realized that this was going to be worse than she had supposed. She had prepared herself to ask for forgiveness, but that, it seemed, was not enough. She must herself bring the truth to Betty's reluctant mind; nothing else than the truth would be any good. . . . She said—it was the most bitter thing she had ever done; she seemed to taste on her tongue the hard and bitter substance of that moment; she said: "Try and remember."[90]

By recollecting, Betty bore again the burden of her earlier sorrow, and again—but this time willingly and therefore sacrificially—became the victim of her persecutor. Meanwhile Lester subdued herself to the fact of her sin, and became the victim of her victim. She confronted her past fully, and fully repudiated it.

Within the scope of the novel, the sin and the forgiveness are not again referred to. Betty and Lester seem to have forgotten the acts of forgiving and being forgiven as they take up their new duties. On the further side of forgiveness, this is permissible.

There are two methods of reconciliation: that which remembers the injury in love and that which forgets the injury in love. . . . Either may be desirable here and now, though there can, of course, be no question which is finally desirable and even necessary to the existence of the Blessed City. There (its architect told us and all its architecture maintains) all things are to be known. We had better not forget it; but even so, "he that believeth shall not make haste." Oblivion—say, perfect seclusion of the injury in God—is often here a safer means. It is often likely that to remember the injury would lead only to some opposite injury.[91]

Williams points out elsewhere that after the first five minutes of pure intention and knowledge, both become corrupted.[92] A sense of superiority intervenes ("How noble of me to forgive!"), or a devious recollection that the sin was a fact and should be remembered, so that almost at the moment of forgiving one withdraws from it into a false appeal to honesty. Self-deception always attends man in these matters; nothing except vigilance can save him from delusion. If he does succumb to it, the Lord has warned: " 'I also will choose their delusions'— one of the more appalling phrases of the Bible."[93] Intelligence is as necessary here as in any other exchange.

The act of forgiveness, like all the exchanges, can take place only between equals. There can be no sense of superiority in forgiving, because the pardoner needs also to be pardoned. It is

the guilty who forgives and not the innocent; not perhaps the guilty in that one act, but guilty of how much else, of how much that led up to that act, guilty even in the very act of mutual pardon—that is, of mutual reconciled love—of how much of weakness, folly, reluctance, pride, or greed. The guilty repents; the as greatly guilty forgives; there is therefore but one maxim for both: "make haste."[94]

Likewise, the Christian's "awful consciousness (in any serious matter) that he [the pardoner] is necessarily exercising, in his proper degree, the conceded prerogative of Christ, prevents pride, prevents anything but shame."[95] Only God forgives; only God makes forgiveness possible between men; and human pardon is vicarious, he in us and we in him. Recognition of this prevents that travesty upon forgiveness wherein pardon is made to depend upon repentance or reformation.

. . . there is a profound difference between any such reidentification of love between heaven and earth and between earth and earth. What may be justly required in the one case must not be required in the other. It is all very well for the Divine Thing of heaven to require some kind of intention of good, not exactly as a condition of pardon but as a means of the existence of its perfection. Men were never meant to be as gods or to know as gods, and for men to make any such intention a part of their pardon is precisely to try to behave as gods. It is the renewal of the first and most dreadful error, the desire to know as gods; the reversal of the Incarnation, by which God knew as Man, the heresy of thought and action denounced in the Athanasian Creed— it is precisely the attempt to convert the Godhead into flesh and not the taking of the manhood into God. The intention to do differently may be passionately offered; it must never be required—not in the most secret recesses of that self which can only blush with shame to find itself pardoning and with delight at the infinite laughter of the universe at a created being forgiving another created being. The ancient cry of "Don't do it again" is never a part of pardon. It is conceivable that Saint Peter reidentified love between himself and his brother four hundred and ninety times in a day; it is inconceivable that each time he made it a condition of love that it shouldn't happen again—it would be a slur on intelligence as well as love. To consent to know evil as good only on condition that the evil never happens again is silly; it is conditioning one's knowledge—as if one consented to know that the Antipodes existed only on condition that no one ever mentioned the Antipodes. All limitation of pardon must come, if at all, from the side of the sinner, in the frequent cry of "I won't do it again," in the more frequent cry of "I won't, but I shall. . . ." Heaven has had to explain to us not only itself but ourselves; it has had to create for us not only pardon but the nature of the desire for pardon. It has therefore defined the cry of the sinner, but it has not suggested that other sinners should take upon themselves to demand the cry before they submit, with their brothers, to its single glorious existence in both.[96]

Forgiveness that is not absolute is not forgiveness; it excludes something, and thus leaves the reconciliation incomplete. On earth, such failure may be tolerable, but it is completely incompatible with eternity —not with eternal bliss or eternal love, but with the essential nature of eternal life.

Finally, there are things that do not need to be forgiven, and things than cannot be forgiven. In *Many Dimensions,* Lord Arglay refers to a clerical error that his secretary has made through inattention, and she asks if he has not forgiven her. He replies, "No, I do not think you are *forgiven*."[97] Elsewhere, Williams confirms the implication in more general terms: "Love, we have been told, is slow to anger; it is, as a result, slow to forgive, for it will not be in a hurry to assume that there is anything to forgive; and if there is, it will not be in a hurry to make a business of forgiving."[98]

With respect to sins that cannot be forgiven:

You cannot forgive a madman for you cannot be in proper rational relation with him. You can, I suppose, love him by such an act of goodwill as one might exercise towards a cat or an angel. But his life (as Wordsworth said) "is hid with Christ in God"; it is alien from us. There can be no mutuality.[99]

Neither can one forgive sins from which he has not suffered: he then stands outside the situation and can have no active relationship with it unless one of the participants asks his help. But a person who desires to forgive, and cannot, can

entreat anyone who loved him to make an effort in that direction on his behalf. Much may be done by a vicarious virtue, so only that the original desire remains sincere and industrious. A man may begin to be generous or devout or even chaste in and through another, so long as his own efforts to join himself with that virtue do not fail. . . . But such a vicarious beauty of achievement in forgiveness is a very different thing from the lamentable folly to those who hurry, unharmed, to forgive or not to forgive harm done to others. It is the direct purpose of the injured alone that matters.[100]

Apart from those situations where forgiveness is not needed or is impossible, lie all the other offenses, great and small. Which may be forgiven? which must be forgiven? All of them, without exception.

Forgiveness of all injuries is demanded of the Christian because of the nature of our Lord, and it is demanded entirely. The phrase "things that cannot be forgiven" is therefore to him intellectually meaningless. But it may in fact mean a good deal all the same. It is true that few of us are, fortunately, in a position to understand that meaning; no injuries of which the forgiveness seems unbelievable have ever been done us. But probably there are at the present moment more persons alive in Europe than for many generations to whom such injuries have been done. . . . In the ruined houses of Rotterdam—or indeed of England—among the oppressed thousands of Poland, there are those to whom the phrase "things that cannot be forgiven" has a fearful meaning. Must they nevertheless be forgiven? they must.[101]

"Heroic sanctity is required perhaps to forgive, but *not* to forgive is ordinary sin."[102] There remains, however, another factor to be considered: forgiveness is a mutual act, and without mutuality it cannot be accomplished. If the offender refuses to ask or to accept forgiveness, he cannot be forgiven, and this entails a horror: he is not released from his sin against us, so that we cannot be released either. We are bound into the pattern of unreconciled sin, of evil that has not been converted into good.

He who refuses to forgive or to be forgiven has cut himself off from the co-inherence. It is one of the options. We can hold toward such a person a steady good will; we can dispose ourselves toward forgiving him or being forgiven by him. "The mutual act of forgiveness is a holy thing; the proper dispositions towards it, accepted or not accepted, remain holy."[103] As for our relationships with him:

Whoever refuses . . . it is difficult to see what else can be done except to leave him alone. If he shuts himself out of the mortal co-inherence, or we; if he shuts himself out of the act in which, more than any other, the mortal co-inheres with the divine, or we; then that solitude is the answer. If it is he who refuses, and we have been sincere in our good-will, then at least we are innocent there—if we have not supposed ourselves to be innocent in anything else.[104]

It sounds harsh; it is harsh. But the universe "has not our kindness or our decency; if it is good, its goodness is of another kind than ours."[105] Even Incarnate Love has no other alternative to leaving him alone, unless it overrides his freedom. The burden of unreconciled sin can only be given to the Lord, that he may give us the release that that other has denied.

THE END AND THE RECONCILING

For the Christian romantic, the critical problem of life is the reconciliation of great opposites: the Beatrician moment of lucidity and the moment of outrage at her death; freedom and necessity; love and sin. His feeling intellect convinces him that these all are parts of a single pattern, or else there is no pattern at all, anywhere, but only the dark wood where Dante's beasts prowl. The romantic cannot escape that all-or-nothing commitment; the Christian cannot evade defining it in terms of God.

The central point at issue here is not the contradiction between good and evil, but the contradiction within the good.

Certainly our sins and faults destroy the good. But our efforts after the good also destroy it. The very pursuit of goodness becomes a hunt; that which was to be our lord becomes a victim. It is necessary to behave well here? We do. What is the result? The destruction of some equal good. There is no more significant or more terrible tale in the New Testament than that which surrounded the young Incarnacy with the dying Innocents: the chastisement of His peace was upon them.[106]

This is not sin: this is necessity. We cannot live, even physically, without taking life. We cannot choose between two alternatives, both of which contain good, without destroying one of them. We cannot act, in any important matter, without committing outrage. Williams' image for this is a strange and awesome one: Galahad, close to death with agony of the spirit, kneeling before the Castle of the Grail to implore forgiveness of his father Lancelot and of the fellowship of the Round Table. Bors, speaking for all, asks him:

> "What should we forgive?"
> "Forgive Us," the High Prince said, "for Our existence;
> forgive the means of grace and the hope of glory . . ."[107]

Grace itself betrays the good. Evil produced evil when the unfaithfulness that resulted in Galahad's conception flung Lancelot into madness. Evil produced good when Galahad was born of that adultery. But Galahad's achievement of the Grail is to inaugurate the breaking up of the Round Table: the good annihilates the good. True, this achievement constitutes a more exalted good than anything that the Table could bring to man: the end is gain. But also at the end "the death of a brave beauty is mutual everywhere."[108] Although the limited good of the Table had been truly good, the assault of holiness will eradicate not merely its admixture of evil, but its entire existence, evil and good together. Galahad grieves for the loss of the company and for the part that he plays in destroying it. The Quest of the Grail cannot be made compatible with the Company of Arthur, any more than eternity's

infinite contemporaniety is compatible with the temporal succession of
nature. Christ the Sword divides the good from the good. He creates it
and he destroys it.

>   . . . each loss of each image
> is single and full, a thing unrequited,
> plighted in presence to no recompense, no
> purchase of paradise; eyes see no future:
> when the Son of Man comes, he brings no faith in a future.[109]

Such is the last irony and the last horror. It recurs through Williams'
work in the figures of the Flame, the Skeleton, the Accuser, Prester
John, the Fool, the Invisible Knight, Satan (another Satan from
Milton's), the Third King, the Impossibility.[110] They are all destroyers,
"the total Birth intending the total Death."[111] Cranmer prays: "God,
without whom nothing is strong—" and the Skeleton answers:

> I respected you, Thomas; I heard; I am here.
> Do not fear; I am the nothing you meant.
> I am sent to gather you into that nothing.[112]

Let the rational intellect deny if it will that "nothingness" can be a
positive and powerful thing. The spirit and the flesh of man know that
absence as a presence that utterly kills. Or worse, that does not kill.
And it calls itself "Love."

Christianity itself, claiming to save man, betrays him into "that
state which is—almost adequately—called 'death-in-life.' "[113] It offers
in return the declaration that its Lord entered this nothingness and
himself became nothing, so that when we confront the nothingness, we
confront him. The Skeleton cries to Cranmer:

> You shall see Christ,
> see his back first—I am his back.

>   .   .   .   .
> I am Christ's back; I without face or breath,
> life in death, death in life,
> each a strife with, each a socket for, each,
> in the twisted rear of good will, backward-running speech,
> the derision that issues from doctrines of grace

>   .   .   .   .
> I am the thing that lives in the midst of the bones,
> that (seems it) thrives upon moans, the thing with no face

that spins through the brain on the edge of a spectral voice.
Rejoice, son of man, rejoice:
this is the body of Christ which is given for you;
feed on it in your heart by faith with thanksgiving.[114]

In Williams' Arthurian saga, the Invisible Slayer, Garlon, stands between Arthur and Lancelot as a close friend to both,[115] and as "a certain similitude to the figure of the Holy Ghost, as It exercises Its
operations in the world."[116] In *The House of the Octopus,* "The character of the Flame, or the *Lingua Coeli,* is meant to be exactly what
he says: that energy which went to the creation and was at Pentecost
(as it were) re-delivered in the manner of its own august covenant to
the Christian Church."[117] The "personal" name of the Holy Spirit is
Gift;[118] he is present in all the gifts of God, operating directly (after
the manner of nature) in the Incarnation, and indirectly (after the
manner of heaven) in all other acts of God's giving.

The Spirit's gift of nothingness unites the Way of the Affirmation of
Images with the Way of their Rejection. In affirming Beatrice's death,
Dante passionately reaffirms her reality. "Catch as catch can; but
absence is a catch of the presence."[119] This is true, however, only if the
loss is real because, as C. S. Lewis says,

if we deny the image we are losing, then clearly there is no loss to be
accepted. (Muddle-headed characters in Elizabethan plays sometimes
nobly reconcile themselves to death on the ground that life has never
been worth having: but if so, there is no nobility in dying and nothing
to be reconciled to.) . . . Whatever the last word about all sacrifice
and all the recurrent wrongs of history is going to be, it is not going to
be Stoical. The sacrificed goods and the goods that perished were real
goods: and God, so far from agreeing with Job's comforters, restored
to Job just such "images" as he had lost . . .[120]

But God did not return to Job the same things that he had lost. The
new flocks, the new sons and daughters, no doubt were as good as, or
better than, the old, but they were not the same ones, so that his enjoyment of the new necessarily included the memory of the lost and
of the desolation of losing them.

It is this which has distinguished the doctrines of Christendom; nothing
is to be lost or forgotten; all things are to be known. They can be

known as good, however evil, for they can be known as occasions of love. But known they must and shall be . . . [121]

If we cannot bring ourselves to love them, we can at least allow God to love them through us.

Part of love's duty toward the necessary destruction of the good is defined in Galahad's last words to his friends before he enters the Hallows: "salute me to my lord Sir Lancelot my father,"[122] where "Joy remembered joylessness."[123] At the other extreme, when the nadir of nothingness swept over the Archdeacon, joylessness remembered joy:

now, as he faced his enemies, he felt the interior loss which had attacked him at other stages of his pilgrimage grow into a final overwhelming desolation. He said to himself again, as he so often said, "This also is Thou," for desolation as well as abundance was but a means of knowing That which was All.[124]

These are acts of reconciliation, and "The Parousia is the appointed time of this . . . for the restoration is the perfect reconciliation of everything except that which will not be reconciled."[125]

"That which will not be reconciled." Man's reconciliation with God, with nature and life, with himself, depends upon what he wills. He can will to love that necessity which is natural and supernatural love, or he can will to hate it. Men are

free to recognize that opposite of freedom, free to make themselves servants. The only freedom is a freedom to choose obedience. It is true that obedience, in our happiest moments, is a thing so light, so rich, so rewarding, that it is hardly felt as obedience. As when we do not interrupt our friends' part in the conversation. But it is a chosen obedience, an accepted limitation, all the same.[126]

And the conditions of the choice are strict: we can obey love or obey its opposite, but we are not free to avoid obedience to something.

Choosing to submit ourselves to love, we deny our own wills. That rejection, however, must be supplemented with an affirmation lest seven devils rush in to replace the one that was purged. The Christian's rejection of his own will does not mean abandonment of all will, but a substituted will: "for my sake," "Christ liveth in me," "Lord, be it unto me according to thy word," "not my will, but thine, be done." Becoming nothing, man becomes capable of receiving life from its source. In that source, obedience to love is identical with freedom in love. There, necessity and freedom are two names for a single reality.

The alteration of necessity into freedom is paralleled by a change in the mode of loving.

The stress of love in man has altered. There is only one reason why anything should be loved on this earth—because God loves it. Beatrice (whoever and whatever Beatrice may be) is no longer to be loved for the gratification of the lover, in however pure or passionate a sense. She is no longer to be loved for herself alone; that is perhaps the height of ordinary inventions of literature, and it was much as is generally suggested. Beatrice anyhow is generally, and naturally, satisfied with that. But the kingdom of heaven is not satisfied. Beatrice is to be loved "for my sake." It sounds simple, and is difficult. It is the change in the laying down of the love and the life, hinted at by those masters of the spiritual way who speak of the soul abandoning the love of created things before she can find God. It is precisely *her* love—her own love of created things—that she abandons, and her own consciousness of love; and she may then, not improperly, when they say to her, "thy mother and thy brethren," look at all things round her and answer, "Behold my mother and my brethren."[127]

Man is not capable of loving of or from himself except in isolated moments. The life of love, where "all parts of [the] circumference move equally about that central Love of which his first love was the image and the promise,"[128] comes into being when he ceases to love and permits Love to do its own loving.

It needs to be remembered that, according to this thesis, God loves us in the same way and for the same reasons that he loves others. Therefore we are to know ourselves as occasions for love; we are to love ourselves in the same way and for the same reasons that we love our neighbors: for his sake, who created us as well as them. "Love your enemies," Messias declared. We are our own worst enemies? The command does not change, nor the significance of his stating it as a command. In this, as elsewhere, the emotion of affection may or may not follow, but charity will, the pure, undeviating *caritas* that is love-in-heaven, where the vagaries of natural passion are replaced by the flame of adoring and enduring joy.

The question of practicality remains. "Say, Do not do; and add,

And then do. The supernatural is the birth of action in the death of action."[129] To repeat, what is being considered here is not the abrogation of will but the exchange of wills. These occur in nature, when one submits to the authority of another person or to a statute or to a natural principle, and often this natural exchange is good. But in nature, the command "do not do" is likely to produce apathy, lack of initiative, and irresponsibility, whereas in the Christian substitution of wills, one of the parties to the transaction is beyond nature, so that natural law does not apply. It will be remembered that Williams wrote of the supernatural that it functions according to "laws greater than, if not in opposition to," the laws manifested in nature.[130] So when man exchanges God's will for his own, the death of action generates action. With volition as with knowledge, "After the affirmations we may have to discover the rejections, but we must still believe that after the rejections the greater affirmations are to return."[131] The lover affirms love and wills to become love; his choice impels the rejection of his own will, and after that death comes the resurrection of the will—and of love and of all things, the familiar things transformed into forms so fresh that they may not be recognized when they appear on any of the roads to Emmaus.

The Christian who is adult in love thus does not will to become or do or feel anything, but only to obey love:

There is an offensive cheerfulness encouraged by some Christians which is very trying to any person of moderate sensibility. We are to be bright; we are to smile at strangers; we are (last horror of daily life!) to get into conversation with strangers. It is some comfort to reflect that Messias was against our being bright as he was against our being gloomy. He was against our being anything at all. He indicated continually that it was our wish to do or be something by ourselves, even to be saved by ourselves, that was the root of the trouble. It is at least possible for some of us easily to deny ourselves any tendency towards a communal cheerfulness.[132]

This counsel sustains man in the long periods of monotony that characterize the life of Christian romanticism.

The assurance that Christianity is or ought to be thrilling, whether as an adventure or a catastrophe, is in danger perhaps of being a little overdone. Christianity, like all religions, is, frequently, almost un-mitigated boredom or even a slow misery, in which the command to rejoice always is the most difficult of all.[133]

Here Williams speaks both to the romantic in his periods of dryness, and to the non-romantic who does not experience the romantic ex-tremes. What he says of the theology of crisis is equally applicable to romantic theology: "Its danger is that it tends to demand catastrophic experience of every man, and to hint that lives not so called must be ignorant of grace. . . . It is the mystics as well as the priests who insist on us being converted in their way and not ours. And which is God's—!"[134]

The very richness of romanticism carries special dangers, because

the rich, while they remain rich, are practically incapable of salvation, at which all the Apostles were exceedingly astonished. Their astonish-ment is exceedingly funny to our vicariously generous minds. But if riches are not supposed to be confined to money, the astonishment be-comes more general. There are many who feel that while God might damn Rothschild he could hardly damn Rembrandt. Are the riches of Catullus and Carnegie so unequal, though so different? Sooner or later, nearly everyone is surprised at some kind of rich man being damned. The Divine Thing, for once, was tender to us; he restored a faint hope: "with God all things are possible." But the preliminary step is always assumed: "sell all that thou hast and give it to the poor"—and then we will talk. Then we will talk of that other thing without which even giving to the poor is useless, the thing for which at another time the precious ointment was reserved from the poor, the thing that is necessary to correct and qualify even good deeds, the thing that is formulated in the words "for my sake and the gospel's" or "in my name." Good deeds are not enough; even love is not enough unless it is love of a particular kind.[135]

Rightly then the young Pope Deodatus prays: "Rich in sorrow, rich in heart's heaviness, / blessed are we, bearing soul's wealth now . . . send not, send not, the rich empty away."[136]

"To love is to die and live again; to live from a new root."[137] To submit to love is to be free and to find that the contraries are recon-ciled. Herein love is like that figure among the Greater Trumps of the Tarot which "is called the Fool, because mankind finds it folly till it is known. It is sovereign or it is nothing, and if it is nothing then man was born dead."[138] It may be that man was and is born dead. Or it may be that Williams is right when he declares that love is sovereign, and when he defines love in terms of co-inherence, and loving in terms of forgiveness and sacrifice and the bearing of burdens. How can we tell which is true? "It is, as our Lord told us long ago, only the compulsion of the soul that leads to a true knowledge of the doctrine."[139] We have been promised that if we ask, we shall be given. What we shall be given, we cannot know until we have intelligently and diligently asked.

9

THE CITY OF LOVE

Politics are, or should be, a part of caritas; *they are the matter to which the form of* caritas *must be applied.*
— RELIGION AND LOVE IN DANTE, 14–15

The life of romantic love begins, proceeds, and ends within a community which, like the Beatrice of the lover's passion, has a double nature. As she is at once a natural being and a God-bearing image, so societies both exist in themselves and image the eternal web of the co-inherent glory. Williams gives to that web the names "the Empire," "the Kingdom," "the Republic," and most often "the City." He sees all natural human groups, from families to the community of nations, as imaging that eternal City more or less adequately, from those "directed, at any rate in theory, by a metaphysical idea," to those which are "directed, both in theory and practice, by nothing but the continual pressure of events."[1] Natural societies vary in the content of the metaphysical ideas to which they adhere—the "American Dream" is not and should not be the same as the British or the Russian or the French Dream. But the principle of the City of Love is single, definite, and immutable: "it is the doctrine that no man lives to himself or indeed *from* himself. This is the doctrine common to nature and grace,"[2] the doctrine that unites all earthly societies with each other and with their eternal archetype.

The City has its own existence in eternity, separate from nature and yet entering and informing nature, so that "If, to use terms of space, we ascend towards it, it is still that which descends out of heaven, and is the cause and course of our ascent."[3] For the sake of brevity, the discussion that follows will be couched in terms of the relationship between the City and the State, with State here implying not only

177

national structures and governments, but also (with appropriate modifications) societies of every kind except those that carry a supernatural reference, such as the Church and the Christian family, which will be considered separately.

THE CITY AND THE STATE

It is Williams' thesis that the State images the City; the two therefore have identity with each other, yet are profoundly different. "The natural mass is not the supernatural web—not even when it calls itself Christendom."[4] What distinguishes the mass from the web is primarily the absence or the presence of choice. Nationality, race, and the natural capacities which direct and circumscribe individual activities, are determined by birth—if you will, by holy luck. But man belongs to the City by virtue of his decision to accept its principle of ordered exchange.

It is true that, historically, the City has often been as much a matter of birth as has the Nation. But the sense of deliberate action remains in our imagination; . . . Bestowal of citizenship is not quite the same thing as the issue of naturalization papers. We can deliberately found the City; the nation can, at best, only appear.[5]

One may be ignorant of the existence of the eternal City, but so long as he chooses to live by the principle of exchange, he is a citizen of it. No accident of time or place, of heritage or opportunity, excludes from full citizenship anyone who desires it, or releases anyone from the necessity of choosing for himself whether to enter or to leave it. It is a *res publica,* a public thing, a Republic, including all who live by derivation and substitution and sacrificial love. It does not select its members; they select themselves, or better, they find themselves in communion.

In his Arthurian poems, Williams portrays such a fellowship within Logres—Arthur's Britain—in the form of Taliessin's household, which had

    . . . no decision, no vote or admission,
    but for the single note that any soul

took of its own election of the Way; . . .
What says the creed of the Trinity? *quicunque vult* . . .[6]

The members of this company did not set themselves apart from
natural societies by founding separate institutions or by making public
profession of their commitment, and this is characteristic of the citizens of that City.

There is nothing to distinguish them from people outside the company
[writes C. S. Lewis] except the fact that they do consciously and joyously, and therefore excellently, what everyone save parasites has to do
in some fashion. From one point of view they are merely good slaves,
good soldiers, good clergy, good counsellors and the like. But their
goodness in each vocation springs from the fact that they have taken
into their hearts the doctrine of Exchange, have made "singular and
mutual confession" of "the mansion and session of each in each."[7]

The mutuality here specified does not need to be that of direct acquaintance: neighborhood in space and time is a means to community,
not a limitation upon it. A person can actively co-inhere in those who
have no awareness of either the principle or the act of co-inhering;
and he may be isolated from others of like mind by many years and
miles, yet share with them the processes of interchange.

The nature of the City can best be described in terms of certain of
the ways in which its life is visible in the State: (1) by examining the
State's exchanges by means of money and the division of labor; (2) by
explaining the hierarchy of the Republic; and (3) by contrasting the
attitudes toward history of the so-called Christian and non-Christian
states.

(1) The City functions by substituted love; its parallel in natural
societies is called the division of labor. One sows and another reaps; one
tends the farm or the shop while others attend to transportation or
justice or the home. They bear each other's burdens; they give and
receive in substitution. Small groups can make such interchanges
directly by bartering goods and labor, but larger, more complex
affiliations require more flexible modes of exchange.

The medium of that exchange, with us, is money. . . . Our social system exists by an unformed agreement that one person shall do one job

while another does another. Money is the means by which those jobs
are brought into relation. It is, usually, the medium in which particular
contracts are formed. And contract, or agreement, is the social fact of
"living by each other."[8]

Buying groceries, paying taxes, receiving payment for work, are matters
of expressing and extending participation in the lives of one's fellow
citizens and therefore are means of love.

Economic exchange can, of course, be corrupted. It is subject to
the same sins as the other images and acts of love: to the heretical
belief that money is a personal and permanent possession or that it is
sufficient in itself; to the failures of intellect in financial affairs; to the
separation of giving from receiving; to the incestuous breeding of
money with itself. One of Williams' poems[9] contains the summary of a
debate in King Arthur's Council on the question of coinage, the principal spokesmen being Sir Kay, Taliessin, and the Archbishop—
steward, poet, and priest, those whose vocations require them to be
specialists in the use of imagery. To Sir Kay, the steward, coins are *the*
medium of exchange. To Taliessin, they are "little loosed dragons,"
images of labor and of products, but so easily divided from that which
they image that they are often cut off from their imaging function and
acquire a damning autonomy. To the Archbishop coinage is *a* medium
of exchange, as subject to misuse as any other image, but equally necessary if communication is to widen beyond the face-to-face contacts of
barter.

(2) Exchange characterizes the State because the conditions of
natural existence impose such activity. In contrast, the City's exchanges
follow from love's determination to interchange with others, and from
love's delighted recognition of individual identity. Within the City,
"everything and everyone is unique and is the subject of due adoration
so, and yet, all being unique, 'none is afore or after other, none is
greater or less than another.' "[10] Each single thing contributes its
specific radiance to the general glory, and fulfills a function that no
other can perform in the same style. Therefore the City is a democracy.
"The Mother of God was not an apostle, yet the apostles were—only
apostles. Do you suppose she and they wrangled over equality?"[11] Or
did each joyously abase himself before the other? Where each is

unique, all must be humble, but also, all meet as equals and so fulfill
the prerequisite for love. Because "one cannot love downwards, *de haut
en bas*. That is reserved to God. One cannot love when one thinks oneself superior—even if one is superior. Human love is always between
equals,"[12] in the City and in cities alike.

This fact of uniqueness establishes not only the democracy of the
City, but also its hierarchical structure. Every citizen accepts and obeys
the authority of others with respect to their unique functions, and each
rightly claims and exercises authority with respect to his own. Now
one, now another, will be ascendant as the City's life requires the exercise of one or another function. Everywhere higher and lower degrees
of ability, skill, maturity, sanctity, status, are in evidence, but

the degrees continually change. He who is a good master of his craft
in music may do ill enough in the theatre, and the Prime Minister must
be docile to an expert scullion. Degree is the inbreathing and out-
breathing of joy, but with every breath the joy changes. If every living
creature is unique, it must necessarily be so.[13]

The sovereign is above his subjects. But they have bestowed his sovereignty upon him, by suffrage or by accepting hereditary rulership, and
because they make him what he is, they are above him. In C. S. Lewis'
words, "As willed necessity is freedom, so willed hierarchy becomes
equality . . . Each is mother and child, confessor and penitent,
teacher and pupil, lord and slave to the other. Each is his neighbour's
priest—and victim."[14] In this manner the City incarnates the co-
inherence of the Holy Trinity, wherein the Persons are equal with
respect to their Godhead, yet the Son is "inferior to the Father as
touching his Manhood."[15] Likewise, the Son is equal with man respect-
ing his manhood and superior to man in being God. The equality between Father and Son on the basis of their Godhood, and between
Jesus and man on the basis of their manhood, provides the meeting-
ground for interchange. Because of the hierarchy among these beings,
each has something to give and something to receive: love in its several
kinds, creating, redeeming, adoring.

An individual's position in the hierarchy depends upon his function,
but the function does not belong to the holder of it. The worker belongs to his work, although it is in his care, and he may adorn or

denigrate it, serve or betray it. "Our functions are not in existence for the sake even of our immortal beings, but our immortal beings for the sake of our functions."[16] Any specific vocation is no more than a means for expressing the general vocation of co-inhering in love that has been given to all men.

(3) All societies exhibit exchange; any society may be at once hierarchic and republican. But societies which claim to be in some sense Christian have one potentiality for action which is closed to all others. The "great humanitarian champions"[17] leave history behind them. They grant that the past has determined the nature of the present, and revere or revile it in token thereof, but for them it continues to exist only indirectly, as it creates the present. "The lack in their vision of union is that they cannot include the dead; the past, for them, is indeed past, and its agonies remain for ever unatoned."[18] In contrast, the Christian states can at least envision the redemption of the past. "History cannot redeem us; it is we who must, under God, redeem history."[19] That is, it is conceivable that a Christian state might recognize that the lives and deaths of its past victims do not merely extend into the present by the natural effect of past upon present, but that they continue to live in us and we in them. Therefore, we can determine whether their sufferings shall or shall not be made holy, as we accept or refuse their sacrifices, and as we accept or refuse the impact of the past evil and convert it into good. Charles Williams did not live to see the motions toward such an alteration, in the reconstruction measures taken after World War II by the victorious nations. The roots of these activities have largely lain in natural impulses; there has been little enough humility in the givers, little enough sharing of guilt, little enough love. The recipients have often resented the manner of giving and their need to receive. But however inadequate the motivations and the acts, natural states have made movements toward restoration; they are groping toward better methods and a wider scope for expressing their interdependence, in a direction that may someday express the co-inherence of the City, and approach the redemption of history.

> Man is one
> in sin from beginning to end, nor otherwise within

> sin's consummation, sin's opposite, the work of Man's Son,
> God's Son, Christ of the double Nature . . .[20]

While even a Christian state cannot eradicate sin, it offers the chance
of redemption to all—redemption in time for those of its citizens who
now live, or will live, under its law, and redemption of the past by
affirming the co-inherence of all times in eternity, and therefore in the
present.

THE INFAMY

The opposite to the City is the Infamy, which repudiates the co-
inherence, and "there is, in the end, no compromise between the two;
there is only choice."[21] Either the City's principle of exchange applies
universally, or it does not. The City declares that "the glory of God is
in facts. The almost incredible nature of things is that there is no fact
which is not in His glory. This is the great inclusion which makes the
City."[22] The Infamy

denies inclusion. It denies it first by definition; that is, it makes definition an implicit and immediate exclusion from its own limits. Definition, of course, is necessary. To say "he is a German" or "she is a
Christian" means that, and only that. It means the absence of certain
characteristics and the presence of other characteristics. It may imply
human arrangements. But it must not imply outrage. It must not, that
is, exclude from the exchanges of nature, or indeed (in whatever sense)
from the exchanges of supernature. All it can do is to order those exchanges in one particular way instead of another particular way. It can
make, as it were, "traffic regulations" for the convenience of traffic
among men. It can clear our heads but it was never meant to petrify
our hearts. Having defined, the Infamy proceeds to exclude, and then,
so far as it can, to enslave or to annihilate.[23]

Do we, as individuals, protect ourselves from intrusion, or refuse to acknowledge facts that we dislike or disapprove of? Do we, as states, protect ourselves by restricting trade with tariffs, or immigration with
quotas, or ideas with censorship? Then we are infamous. "To be, or to
desire to be, free from being hurt by others, is to be, or to desire to be,
free from the co-inherence of all human souls, which it was the express
intention of Christ to redeem."[24] Yet states have duties not only to

their eternal fulfillment but also to those of their citizens who neither know nor care about its perfected form. As the individual cannot—since the Fall—escape sin, so the state cannot escape outrage. It can usually avoid destroying its opponents in order to maintain itself, but it necessarily circumscribes freedom. It cannot grant unlimited self-direction to its individual citizens, or to other societies within or beyond its borders, without betraying its own proper life and function. Some degree of holy freedom and holy individuality must be sacrificed for the life of the state.

But the Infamy destroys freedom and individuality on principle. C. S. Lewis strikes at the root in saying:

When race is separated from race "and grace prized in schism," when all our pleasure is to be *inside* some partial and arbitrary group, then of course, we must have "outsiders" to despise and denounce—Jews, Capitalists, Papists, the Bourgeoisie, what-not—or it is no fun.[25]

We declare our unqualified superiority and their unqualified inferiority with respect to some factor that we consider essential: race, nationality, religion, possessions, skills, intelligence, or whatever, and decline equality with them except in so far as we condescend to grant it. Exchange with them takes place on the terms of our authority and their submission.

This is totalitarianism, "the subjection of all to one authority; the denial of all authorities but one."[26] The "one" can be an individual, a class, a council of state, or a "democracy intoxicated with itself"[27] that repudiates all authorities other than that of the greatest number. Whatever the style of government, the Infamy desires and produces uniformity rather than unity, coherence rather than co-inherence, by requiring every other authority to refer itself to the one for its right to exist and for its standards of behavior. It demands that art be dogmatic, that intellect be subservient to the state's ends, that love stop at its boundaries, in a process that swiftly intensifies homogeneity until art and intellect cease to have identity, and as to love—Hell's officer, in *The House of the Octopus,* describes the Infamy's attitude with sufficient clarity:

Your girl, now,
well—there she is. But if by a small scare

> or a small lure, she could have been brought to endure
> —and then to enjoy—first the thought of the soldier,
> and then the soldier, and then any soldier,
> and then . . . men! You see?[28]

Few, if any, states would push their authority this far, but it is a logical consequence of the doctrine pursued by the Infamy.

In opposition to the totalitarian state stands that which offers

> a multiplication of authorities; or at least, say, the giving free play to all authorities. This is the free State—a State which uses its power as much as possible towards the protection and preservation of other powers. It must positively encourage all other honourable authorities continued within it; its business indeed is precisely and only that.
> But if this is the nature of the authority of the State, is it also the nature of any authority? Surely, yes; surely this is precisely the very nature and life of authority. Where the family exists, for what else is the parents' authority meant? The child is to grow up to recognize exactly those other persons or things which make a proper demand on him—at school, in business, in love, in logic, in personal and intellectual relationships. . . . It is so among all proper academic chairs; the student is there encouraged to research, to the discovery of fresh facts; those fresh facts may overthrow the doctrine of his teacher; every right teacher knows it and encourages his pupil none the less for that.[29]

Such an organization of authorities leaves no place for rivalry. Taking Williams' example of the authority of poetry: "poetry is absolute in its own place, and even Beatrice cannot command it,"[30] but its own place is not making laws or repairing automobiles or administering the sacraments. A particular person might with equal proficiency create poetry and perform any of these other functions, as another person might divide his time between teaching and gardening. But "religion itself cannot order poetry about,"[31] and similarly, poetry has no authority over religion, the state, or mechanics, nor religion over any of the others, even though each of these authorities can appropriately, if indirectly, influence and be influenced by the others.

Though such multiplication of authorities in the eternal City of Love produces only joy, in cities and states it frequently generates the several opposites to joy. Williams plainly states the general difficulty in a dis-

cussion of the ancient protest of individuals against their governments
for involving them in war.

We are always in the condition that we are because of others.

This is all so elementary as to sound stupid. Yet to accept this profoundly is difficult. To be in a distressing and painful condition because
of others is a thing we all naturally resent. It is often the cause of
hatred towards those others, whether in public or private things. Yet
until we are willing to accept the mere fact without resentment we can
hardly be said to admit that other people exist. We may reject, we may
rebuke, we may contend against their action. But the very first condition
of admitting that their existence is as real as our own is to allow that
they have, as individuals, as much right to act in the way that they
decide as we have. They may be wicked and we good or vice versa;
that is a question of moral judgement, and therefore another question.
The main fact is that we are compelled to admit their decision, and to
admit that our lives, and often our deaths, depend on that.[32]

The network of exchange involves us all in other lives; it involves the
State in the "awful and devastating union" of sin, so that "the murders
in Poland are, in that sense, our sin. . . . it is not only Hitler but we
who are in Poland."[33] Because of what we did or left undone? No
doubt. But more profoundly:

If the Germans think the Jews—or if we once thought Thugs—enemies
of the public good, must not they or we suppress or banish them? To
deny it is to deny the nature of the Republic, the existence of the Public
Thing. Persecution, in that sense, always has been and always will be
a necessity of the Republic. The prohibition of totalitarian governments in all the liberated states of Europe now [1945] is a clear example. "You may have what government you will, *so long as—*" But
without the abolition of that "so long as" there can be no full freedom.[34]

The free State confesses that full freedom is impossible within societies on earth. The Infamy abhors such freedom, on earth and in
eternity. It refuses, in theory and practice, the doctrine that it co-
inheres in those whom it rejects, that it lives in them and they in it,
and that it lives for and from them.

Hostility begins to exist, surely, whenever and wherever we forget that we are nourished by, that we live from—whomever; when we think that we can *choose* by whom we shall be nourished. If *anthropos* has any meaning, if the web of humanity is in any sense one, if the City exists in our blood as well as in our desires, then we precisely must live from, and be nourished by, those whom we most wholly dislike and disapprove. . . . There is but one dichotomy: that between those who acknowledge that they live from the life of others, including their "enemies," and those who do not. It is in this sense, indeed, that we must "forgive" our enemies. And the moment the dichotomy is admitted, it immediately becomes a temptation. Whoever does not admit it is regarded as an "enemy," and we deny that we can possibly live and be nourished by *him*. *He* at least is alien? No. Terrible humility! we derive from those we denounce; "though they slay me, yet will I trust in them."[35]

Williams described World War II as "partly a war for natural compassion, for the mere right of any human being to 'sympathize' with or in any other human being."[36] It may be said that no agency external to man can in fact prevent his sympathy from extending where it will, and this, Williams says, is true:

No one can, in fact, prevent a man thinking, or interfere with the motions the soul has in itself; what he can do is to prevent utterance. He can prevent the tongue speaking or the ears hearing; the other may or may not follow. All these things are worked out in terms of flesh, and must be; our Lord Himself deigned to work out the conclusion of the whole matter in terms of flesh.[37]

Our physical bodies are images and incarnations of his; thus the murders, the mutilations, the concentration camps, are modes of repudiating the Incarnation. "To defend compassion by bombs and submarines is the hideous paradox to which we are reduced; to defend the body by destroying bodies."[38] It is either that, or abandoning the Infamy's victims to whatever fate the Infamy chooses to inflict upon them, to destroy them by permitting others to destroy them. We could perhaps save them by warring against the Infamy; that is, by killing; that is, by sinning against the Infamy in the same manner that it sins against its victims; that is, by ourselves becoming infamous. To such an intolerable impasse the Infamy brings us. We sin whatever we do. But: "To refuse the ancient heritage of guilt is to cut ourselves off from mankind as certainly as to refuse the new principle [of co-inherence].

It is necessary to submit to the one as freely as to the other."[39] Others
we save; ourselves we cannot save.

"It is a lame conclusion? a very lame conclusion. Mortal ones are
apt to be; only divine conclusions conclude."[40] We are left to perform
sacrifices of blood, and to repent both the sacrifices and their inevitability. We affirm our co-inherence in our enemy—while we bomb
his cities. We eradicate one of the sources from which we derive our
own lives. We pluck out our eye and we cut off our hand. We die with
the Infamy whom we kill, in the hope that he may ultimately discover
that in fact he lives in us and we in him. "There may be a just war;
there cannot be a holy war. As, I suppose, there may be a just execution; there can hardly be a 'holy' execution. But a holy man might take
part in either a war or an execution."[41]

The State does not, as a rule, go beyond natural co-inherence; it
may be that it cannot co-inhere supernaturally, because its citizenry
includes those who reject the eternal love predicated by Christianity,
either from ignorance of its true nature, or from intelligent conviction.
Even so, for a State to extend its understanding of its function so as to
co-inhere fully on the natural level would be to accomplish much. As a
preliminary, that State would need to recall—or to discern—that without individual difference among nations, there can be no interchange.
Again to quote C. S. Lewis:

if one is thinking simply of goodness in the abstract, one soon reaches
the fatal idea of something standardised—some common kind of life
to which all nations ought to progress. Of course, there are universal
rules to which all goodness must conform. But that's only the grammar
of virtue. It's not there that the sap is. He doesn't make two blades of
grass the same: how much less two saints, two nations . . . When
Logres really dominates Britain, when the goddess Reason, the divine
clearness, is really enthroned in France, when the order of Heaven is
really followed in China—why, then it will be spring.[42]

However, the flowering of national individuality would leave the
State with two major problems, one a matter of tolerance, and the
other of pardon. "To tolerate strange beliefs in others is barely possible; to tolerate strange tastes is impossible."[43] Conversely, to realize
consistently that one's own beliefs and tastes are not shared or perhaps
even respected, but are tolerated, is appallingly difficult. Yet it pre-

pares for the depth of forgiveness which consists in the willingness to be forgiven. Take what example you will, near or far—say, the Roman's destruction of Jerusalem in the first century A.D. It is conceivable that the Jews as a people should forgive Rome. But can Rome endure to be forgiven? Or will Rome point to the safety of the Empire, or to this or that, explaining the genuinely sound reasons for her action, anything to escape the intolerable burden of accepting her victim's pardon? Can the victor bear forgiveness from the vanquished? or the vanquished from the victor? Can peoples whose natural genius impels them to think in terms of yes *or* no pardon those whose genius leads them to a yes *and* no? Can either, in the conviction of his own rightness, bear to be pardoned by the other?[44]

To forgive, to tolerate, is arduous enough, but to consent to be tolerated and forgiven . . . this we cannot do except by the plenary grace of God. But it must be done. Among nations, as among individuals, "the Glory is always to be observed in others,"[45] and one of the functions of a free state is to protect and encourage the uniqueness of other states.

While the analogy between individual and social behavior presents points of illumination, care must be taken not to press it further than the nature of the analogues warrants. Writing of the difficulties of forgiveness between states, Williams notes: "The reason why a thing possible between men and women individually is almost impossible communally is, obviously, that communities are not individuals; the analogy fails."[46] States can bear one another's burdens on the level of nature, by international trade, loans, investments, relief; likewise they can sacrifice and pardon, though only within the relatively narrow limits of nature. A society that is consciously supernatural—the Church or the Christian family—can bear others' burdens and can sacrifice and pardon unto death, dying and rising again supernaturally, but no State—at least no modern free State—can do so without failing in its responsibilities. The State is not the Church, and the State sometimes (as in declaring war) must do what the Church is explicitly forbidden to do. But discussion of this problem cannot proceed until the nature of the Church has been defined, and that in turn must wait upon a more explicit definition of Christianity than has heretofore been possible.

THE FAITH AND THE CHURCH

Christianity differs from all other religions in asserting "that something *absolutely* new has happened";[47] its name is Reconciliation. This is not a matter of morality: the Christian ethic is not, and does not claim to be, unique. Some Christian formulations—substituted love, for example—are fresh, but that is another matter. Nor does the Christian Faith base its claim to uniqueness upon any special system of thought or manner of knowing:[48] for instance, the doctrine of co-inherence is not peculiar to Christianity, and is so universal in its manifestations as to be available to anyone who will take the trouble to look around him. Nor are supernaturalism, and the belief in universal and omnipotent love, distinctive of Christianity. Some Christian apologists have offered the historical basis of the Faith as the ground for its uniqueness, but this cannot be made decisive: "Christianity had to be historic because it is true; at least as much as it is true because it is historic."[49] And finally, Christianity does not maintain that it is grounded in greater rationality than any other religion. It insists that its propositions can never be irrefutably demonstrated, because such proof would make freedom impossible.

What is absolutely new, according to Christianity, is the event whereby God in Christ reconciled the world with himself, and reconciled life with life, the act by which the Incarnation redeemed the co-inherence. Christian ethics, Christian doctrine, Christian history, are all effects of that one cause, which is temporal and eternal at once, and is temporal because it is eternal, just as "the visible beginning of the Church is at Pentecost, but that is only a result of its actual beginning—and ending—in heaven."[50] The Christian Faith declares that human salvation, everywhere and under all conditions, consists of the reconciliation of man with very life by "the power of the Reconciler, and the nature of the Reconciler was of eternity as of time, of heaven as of earth, of absolute God as of essential Man."[51] Apart from his work, there is no salvation.

It may be objected that such operations [as reconciliation], in many and many a relationship of love, are purely "natural"; . . . So; but then the great goods do operate naturally. *Where there is love, there is Christ; where there is human reconciliation, there is the Church.* To say so is not in any way to weaken the supernatural: where the consciousness of that exists, the power of the operation ought in every way to pierce deeper, to last longer, to live stronger, than in the natural. The invocation of Immanuel is at the root of all, and where the invocation is conscious the consciousness of love should be greater. . . . indeed for many of us it is the natural passion of love rather than the supernatural principle which directs and encourages us. This is well enough; it is more than well; so long as we intend to pursue the natural into the more-than-natural of which it is a part.[52]

Thus the primary function of Christians and of the Church is to coinhere in God's reconciliation of all things unto himself.

And pagans? Christ "became the new thing. But that did not prevent Him from being the foundation of the old thing. He was, is, and is to be, the light that lighteneth every man."[53] It may be remembered that in *Descent into Hell,* when Stanhope was explaining to Pauline the doctrine of substituted love, he remarked that "there's no need to introduce Christ, unless you wish."[54] To insist that salvation depends upon knowledge of Christ or of Christian doctrines, or upon membership in a Christian church, is implicitly to deny that God is in, and reveals himself through, all nature, and thus to refuse the Incarnation, which was (and is) the perfect image and instance of the universal principle that "nature and grace are categories of one Identity."[55] "The great doctrines [of Christianity] are the only explanation and the only hope. But even the great doctrines are only the statement of something as wide as the universe and as deep as the human heart."[56] This does not make pagans Christian, in this life or any other, which is why Dante placed the great pagan philosophers in hell.

How could Plato, who in the famous close of the *Symposium* left all matter behind in his own plotted Way, be taken into the matter of the Christian Paradise? No; we could only save their personal souls by making nonsense of their personal work; this Dante refused to do. We have more tenderness for them, but Dante had more honour.[57]

Is Plato then damned? Williams offers as an alternative the situation of the nameless suicide in *Descent into Hell,* wandering in a kind of limbo after his death. "Because he had never had an opportunity to choose love, nor effectively heard the intolerable gospel proclaimed, he was to be offered it again, and now as salvation."[58] They only are damned who, confronting the true options, prefer their own will to the facts of the universe. In this life, Plato could not know what Christ was to bring; therefore, on Williams' hypothesis he cannot ultimately be damned for his beliefs. If he were wrong, and if after death he discovered he was wrong but clung to his philosophy none the less, then he would enter hell. And if he were right, and clung to his convictions merely because they were his, gloating over his correctness—"I told you so" can be another gate to hell. A "saved" Plato, however, may not be a Christian Plato: to be reconciled is one thing; to adhere to the Christian form and formulas of reconciliation is another, and the City may include many such forms. Or it may not.

Reconciliation within Christianity differs from reconciliation outside the Faith in three ways that are important here. First: the Christian, unlike the pagan, knows the full potentialities of reconciliation: that it reaches effectively into past and future, and that it comprehends nature and supernature alike. Implementing this, Christianity teaches the full range of techniques available to man: the bearing of burdens, the conversion of evil into good, forgiveness, sacrifice; and it encourages both the Way of the Negation and the Way of the Affirmation of Images, as equally valid ways of the soul.

Second: Christianity supports the Christian with a community that co-operates with his personal efforts, and provides him with a companionship independent of time and place. Although a Christian may occasionally feel, with St. Athanasius, that he stands against the world, he knows that he stands with the universe. The Christian Church is the community of reconciliation, the specific, deliberate, self-conscious incarnation of the City, and it is the only institution upon earth to be so. As Beatrice is the God-bearer to Dante, so the Church is the bearer of the eternal City to the world.

Third: the relationship between the Christian and God, and between the Church and God, is covenanted: they are joined by a contract. The contract may or may not bestow a higher or more intense grace than is available outside the contract in paganism or the Beatrician moment. It is not that which is the issue here, but rather the difference in kind between the relationships, because the contract involves its participants in singular rights and responsibilities.

The real distinction between Christians and non-Christians is here, as always, something very like the risk of hell. He who professes a supernatural validity for his virtuous acts must follow them out into that whole validity. He who professes only nature may be rewarded with the best of nature, perhaps with more than nature; he who professes more than nature, if he does not practise it, may be left with neither.[59]

It is plainly not true that all ways lead to the one God, but equally it is not true that he has provided only one way to himself. He offers man a contract, but he does not restrict himself, or man, to that sole type of relationship with him.

The contrast between covenanted and uncovenanted grace appears both with respect to Christianity and paganism, and also within Christianity, in the opposition—often the conflict—between the institutional churches and individual Christians who have claimed to be directly inspired by God, and whose inspiration has led them to attack the institution which, they believed, was failing in its work of reconciliation. That churches have failed, frequently and profoundly, cannot be denied. Neither can it be denied that some of these prophets, mystics, and reformers, were right. However:

It has not pleased God to build either the congregation of Israel or the fellowship of the Church on prophets. They are the warning, the correction, the voice in the wilderness. Occasionally they occur in the ranks of the priesthood—Augustine is an example. It is often true that they recall the attention of the faithful to certain facts which are becoming blurred or forgotten. They trouble the customary ritual with a new sound. They are loved and hated at once, and both by good men. They pronounce, generally, the need of man to repent and be turned. . . . "It is iniquity; even the solemn meeting."[60]

Yet to abandon or to destroy the solemn meeting would be to lose universality in the transmission of the word of reconciliation. "Without the Institution, the communication depends on personal genius."[61] Personal genius, however, seems to arise rarely and erratically; it cannot be commanded, and it cannot be adequately disciplined except by its peers. Therefore the prophet needs the institution in order to "correct the inevitable prejudice of single minds by association of judgement."[62] And the institution needs the prophets, the mystics, the reformers, to remind it constantly that it is reconciliation, not organization, that unites men with God and each other. "Neither mode of religion is, it seems, entirely adequate without the other; neither can remain at its best without the help of the other. There must be something all but automatic, as there must be something anything but automatic."[63] The methods co-inhere, and each ought to acknowledge the other's authority in its kind and degree, while maintaining its own sovereignty and limitations.

The exchange of powers between church and prophet is often handicapped by "the natural tendency of any organization to rival the fact which it is supposed to be organizing."[64] The Church has accepted its contract with its Lord—"where two or three are gathered together in my name," "whatsoever thou shalt bind on earth"—and on that basis it has ordered its procedures. But at various times it has employed the indispensable order as a basis for exclusion: it has become infamous. Williams gives to Cranmer the lament:

. . . salvation's way was lost, which Christ restored
in means of communion; now are means of communion adored
yet dyked from approach; untrod, unexplored,
is the road; instead of God are God's marvels displayed,
rivals to Christ are Christ's bounties made . . .[65]

Historically, churches have identified themselves with hierarchies, valid orders, rituals, sacraments, creeds, ethical codes, forms of government, particular leaders—true means of communion, all of them, but all distinct from the one Act of Reconciliation, and none of them essential to its communication. These means are God-bearing images, but being images they do not and cannot represent their basis perfectly or fully, and since any basis can be exhibited in many images, none can uphold a claim to exclusive validity. The rule that should govern the relationship of all these images is that of courtesy, which neither deprecates any, nor forgets at each moment that the Christian gospel of reconciliation has its basis in the reconciling work of Christ. It conveys his life, not its own.

The extent of permissible variation within Christianity can be illustrated by the Ways of the Affirmation and Rejection of Images.

Our sacred Lord, in his earthly existence, deigned to use both

methods. The miracle of Cana and all the miracles of healing are
works of the affirmation of images; the counsel to pluck out the eye is a
counsel of the rejection of images. It is said that he so rejected them
for himself that he had nowhere to lay his head, and that he so affirmed
them by his conduct that he was called a glutton and a wine-bibber.
He commanded his disciples to abandon all images but himself and
promised them, in terms of the same images, a hundred times what
they had abandoned. The Crucifixion and the Death are rejection and
affirmation at once, for they affirm death only to reject death; the
intensity of that death is the opportunity of its own dissolution; and
beyond that physical rejection of earth lies the re-affirmation of earth
which is called the Resurrection.[66]

His followers, individuals and institutions alike, have tended to empha-
size one or the other of these ways, rather than their exact balance.
The extremes within Protestantism are especially vivid in the contrast
between the Church of England, which follows primarily the Way of
Affirmation, and the Society of Friends, which has given institutional
form to the Way of Rejection. The Quakers, in their worship, reject all
images except the meeting together which images their unity with each
other in Christ; even the spoken word, which is permitted, is not required. The Anglicans stress imagery, "the spirit waiting for the letter,
without which it cannot perfectly be."[67] Both these institutions, while
they accentuate one way, contain and honor the other way. Quakerism
declares the Way of Affirmation in its concern for the freedom and
nourishment of all men, since all bear the Inner Light. The Church of
England confesses the Way of Rejection in its insistence that its hierarchy and sacraments are separate from the ultimate realities which
they represent and convey.

"Messias seems to have indicated that in the Church, as well as in
daily life, the Blessed One will conform his actions—at least, to a
degree—to the decisions of his creatures."[68] Men and organizations
may select either the Affirmative or the Negative Way as their primary
approach, and the Lord will respect that decision. Each way has its
danger, the temptation to neglect or to repudiate the other. "Images
can be as disciplinary as their lack; their rejection itself can be a
temptation."[69] But he who is three Persons in one Person is the ground
for the division between the ways, as well as for their union, and he is
Lord of all ways.

The Church is the knowledge of the mystical substance of man spirit-ually—in corruption and in redemption, and in neither can men be separated from each other until the heavenly division between tares and wheat, goats and sheep. But the wheat and the sheep were never encouraged by Christ to do the dividing.[70]

No visible church has achieved the full and final state of perfection for which it was made. "The Kingdom—or, apocalyptically, the City—is the state into which Christendom is called; but, except in vision, she is not yet the City. The City is the state which the Church is to be-come."[71] Ignorant and fallible though the Church be on earth, it has from its inception based itself on "the hypothesis . . . that there was operative within the Church the sacred and eternal reconciliation of all things, which the Church did not and could not deserve . . . it carried within it an energy not its own,"[72] that of the Holy Spirit. Everywhere and at all times the Church names its Lord and is known by that in-vocation, even when it lapses into the sin described by Williams in the lines, "God has only us to defend his glory, / and what will happen to that if we leave off killing?"[73] Or when "the hungry sheep look up for metaphysics, the profound metaphysics of the awful and redeeming body, and are given morals."[74] The Church depends, in all its activities, upon the Holy Ghost from whom it is derived, and

The activities of the Holy Ghost depend on nothing but Itself. But the success of the activities of the Holy Ghost (within the Church) does depend on a something beside Itself—it depends on the honesty of Christians. The honesty of Christians is a very desirable and also a very difficult thing. There can be few Christians alive who have not been aware, in themselves or in each other, of that great temptation—"to lie on the Lord's behalf" . . . [One] is apt to *pretend*—to pretend that intellectual arguments are valid when it should be clear that they are fallacious, that moral iniquity exists where there is no proof of it, and so on. An extremely distinguished dignitary of the Church once printed the statement that the proportion of happiness to unhappiness in a man's life was as nine to one—an absolutely unjustified statement. (I do not say it was false: the whole point is that one ought not to make that sort of generalization at all; it is unprovable.) This kind of thing is still too common. Accuracy, accuracy, and again accuracy! accuracy of mind and accuracy of emotion. If the Church is to look forward to a wholesome mental life her members must discipline themselves to honesty. The indulgence of any prejudice must be regarded as sinful, and an intellectual sin is as bad as a physical.[75]

Accuracy implies both precise thought and adequate information. Christians need to know, far more exactly than is usually the case, what the Church has been and what it is, especially with respect to the meaning of its hierarchy, its rituals, and its sacraments.

There are sound practical reasons why the Church should develop a hierarchical structure; also, there is a sound theological reason for hierarchies: they express and protect the institution's democratic character. At every level, from layman to prince of the Church, the individual member of the hierarchy derives his function and authority from his office, and not from his personal abilities or achievements. No human being is *worthy* of his membership in the Church. No human being is *worthy* of administering the sacraments, nor does ordination make him so when it assigns to him the priestly office. The Church's hierarchies are stable, but the stability is

rather of honourable function than of individual merit. The ancient monarchy of the English is one such. The anointed figure of the King does not "deserve" to be royal, and this is so clear that it saves us from the claims of merit which oligarchies and aristocracies are apt to set up.[76]

The geniuses and the saints of the Church constitute, as it were, a House of Peers—and let none withhold from them the reverence that is their due. Like the reformers, they "are found in all ages, and in all places, from the gutter to the Holy See; they are an absolute necessity to the Church, and it is perhaps only by their virtue that the gates of hell shall not prevail."[77] But the Church is "of the commons and the whole manner of love,"[78] the republic of the Faith.

By means of ritual, the Church ensures that reconciliation shall be continuously communicated: the offering and acceptance of the contract and of the sustaining act are made independent of the transitory moods of priest and people. "They might, contentedly and simply, sleep, eat, or make love. But once a week or so those simple satisfactions had the opportunity—and the duty—of seeing themselves illuminated by the Love that co-inhered in them."[79] In addition, even among Christians, the great experiences are often over-simplified, and the words *love* or *forgiveness* are thought to be sufficient. Obscurely resenting the theological disputes of the past, and not at all obscurely evading our moral duties in the future, we ask only that we shall act once and be done with it. The Church was wiser; it provides for a monotony of pardon. It used to be blamed for compelling its members ritually to declare themselves "miserable sinners" day by day, but it knew very well that if they did not do it ritually they would not do it at all, and it very well knew what in fact they were.[80]

Even with this reminder, man may forget what he is, but the Church, by calling it to his attention week after week, does all it can to save him from himself.

The ceremonies of the Church are not mere addenda, to be employed or dispensed with according to caprice. "For all things must be loved in order and after their proper kind and with (as one may say) the proper form—the manner and ceremony that belongs to it."[81] Ritual is an ordered means for adoring the ordered nature of love, and "one of the advantages of ceremony, rightly used, is that it gives a place to self-consciousness, and a means whereby self-consciousness may be lost in the consciousness of the office filled or the ritual carried out."[82] Specific rites vary in accordance with theological and cultural influences, and others less easy to name. For example, reverence can be expressed by covering the head, by uncovering it, or by denying the relevance of a covering. Elaboration and simplicity are equally valid expressions of the communal life of the spirit, but worship in community requires images of some sort, if only enough to affirm that these persons are so engaged. Without imagery, there is no communication at all among men.

Men must use their piety and intelligence to avoid idolatry; they could not and must not be saved by the Rejection of Images, except as their private vocations might dictate. But private vocations are not to lay down the law to Christendom; images—one may add, living images also—were to receive "proskunesis," particular honour.[83]

It is the function of ceremony to pay such honor by acts and utterances that are personal but not limited to the personal, that draw the individual worshiper into the vast procession of other men and into the universal processes of exchanged adoration and love.

The objection has sometimes been raised that these ceremonies set the rites themselves between individuals and God, but

why is it more "spiritual" to desire personal assurance than to receive that assurance through others? To desire that God shall communicate directly rather than indirectly? Men were one; they learnt from each other; they lived from each other: why is that web of souls less spiritual than one soul?[84]

The Church images the City, and it displays the communal order of the City not only by its members' mental and spiritual attitudes, but also by the participation of their bodies in song and silence, in the pageantry of vestments and the simple ceremony of bowing the head.

The sacraments are the Church's media of exchange. Like the King's coins, they "cover the years and the miles / and talk one style's dialects to London and Omsk."[85] They speak in one language to body and spirit, nature and supernature; they are the great images of identity, and the great covenanted means for establishing identity on earth as it is already established in heaven. A double reality is necessary for sacrament: the material image, whether affirmed or rejected, and its eternal basis. A double movement is necessary: "the lifting up of the manhood into God" and the descent of God to man. And a double act of choice is necessary: man's to receive and God's to give that joyous equality between himself and his creatures "which marks all happy human or celestial government, . . . that which has existed because first the Omnipotence withdrew its omnipotence, and decreed that submission should be by living will, or perhaps because in the Omnipotence itself there is an equality which subordinates itself."[86] When Christ became flesh, he submitted himself to men's decisions; so also "in the whole business of the sacraments which began when the Church began, the Lord deigned to commit himself to the hands of men, and to fulfil his agreement at their demand."[87] And as God in Christ was not merely inhabiting a human body but he *was* flesh, so in the sacraments spirit is not using matter any more than matter is using spirit: they co-inhere; they are categories of one identity.

Imagery itself is a way of exchange, and is used in the sacraments to effect other exchanges. In baptism, the water of earth represents the divine lucidity and the cleansing fire of heaven; by its administration the individual is naturalized as a citizen of the eternal City of super-natural love. From his physical conception he has partaken of natural co-inherence, but he can enter supernatural co-inherence only by a decision, either his own, as when an adult comes to be baptized, or by the decision of others who substitute their penitence, faith, and inten-tion for the infant's inevitable lack of these qualities. Whether or not the child later ratifies the choice that was made for him there, is an-other question, but until the time when he is prepared to confirm or to depart from it, he belongs both to nature and to supernature. By no will of his own, he had inherited natural existence; equally without his will he is naturalized into the City and made free of the supernatural glory. The rite establishes that the one who is baptized is sustained in the co-inherence by both worlds, and it informs the child (when he is of an age to receive the knowledge), his parents, the community, and the Church, of that fact.

It does not necessarily follow from this that the unbaptized are excluded from supernatural grace: "Flesh knows what spirit knows." But "spirit knows it knows":[88] the baptized are, and know themselves to be, under the contract. They may sometimes be the poorer for it: those outside the contract may perhaps press more determinedly toward God because they lack the assurance given by the rite. Perhaps the unbaptized more easily succumb to the nothingness of despair, that state "in which, humanly speaking, any gospel, even the Christian, is bound to be incapable of reception."[89] And perhaps they more easily fall prey to the delusion that they can, one way or another, save them-selves. On the other hand, the baptized are rich in knowledge and cer-tainty, but it was the rich who were specifically warned that they were in danger of being sent empty away.

The Eucharist is the central rite of Christianity, the continuation in time of Messias' Incarnation, and the supreme God-bearing image of that Incarnation. There "the co-inherence is fully in action: 'He in us and we in Him.' "[90] Notably, it is the sacrament that most directly in-volves the body: the communicant eats and drinks; the stomach digests the elements; the physical flesh is nourished and renewed. Man gave his flesh to Christ, and receives Christ's flesh back from him in a mystery of mutual exchange, so that the acts of exchange operate not only through minds, hearts, and wills, but also physically. "Repulsive materialism! But that was how the Divine Word talked."[91] Sacramental co-inherence, like all others, is a unity of separate things. Christ's body and ours do not coalesce: there is no confusion of substances in that union, no blurring of identities, but an interchange so profound as to constitute a physical union between separate lives and between strongly divergent modes of being.

This union-in-separation characterizes also the relationship between the physical body of Messias and the Eucharistic elements of bread and wine. The divine-human basis and the images are not one thing but two, yet the elements which image and transmit the basis share its essential nature: they are specific incarnations of the one Incarnation, types of the single Archetype, and are therefore both images and the very presence of that body. Similarly, when Beatrice becomes the God-bearer, she is not changed into God, nor combined with God; she is an image of him, existing in herself, deriving from something greater than herself, and in herself an instance of that being from whom she is derived. And so for the bread and the wine. The Eucharist is a God-bearer, *theotokos,* and it is *anthropotokos,* a bearer of man, uniting "all contraries in a mystery of exchange."[92]

That which physically nourishes the physical bodies of men also spiritually nourishes their spirits. However, so much has been said and written of the Eucharist as providing spiritual food that the theme does not need to be amplified here. Williams does not discuss at length that aspect of the rite: he knew his readers to be already informed on that score, as they were not on its materiality. But to assume, on that basis, that he underestimated the spiritual power and significance of the Eucharist, is to close the door upon understanding his interpretation of the Christian doctrines of matter and spirit, and of the sacraments.

By and large, the Church has been acutely aware of its duties and privileges with respect to the sacraments. Its failures have tended to develop from an unduly ponderous attitude toward these matters. The sacraments communicate the Lord; let us take them seriously. "This also is Thou." Their use calls for dignity and order, but not for pomposity or fussiness: "neither is this Thou." A certain lightness belongs

to Christian courtesy, even in the Holy of Holies, as an expression of
joy in reconciliation, and of humility because the informing act of
reconciliation is not the Church's nor the priest's, but God's.

And the Church's mind is not its own, but God's. Williams reminds
us that the "reluctance to define . . . has been one of the graces bestowed by God on the Church,"[93] and, in a contrary that is not a
contradiction:

> Will God dispute over words? no; but man
> must, if words mean anything, stand by words,
> since stand he must; and on earth protest to death
> against what at the same time is a jest in heaven.[94]

The creeds define the Christian faith; they state the terms of the
Christian contract. The Church provides a particular style of life
within the City; it does not build walls around it. "The invisible Church
moves in another manner than the visible; indeed the invisible must
include that earthly scepticism, opposition which the visible Church
so greatly needs and yet cannot formally include."[95] Were the churches
to affirm these proper limitations upon their function,

it might be possible now to praise the confessors of other obediences
without supposing that we compromised our own . . . It might be
possible to "exchange" our ignorance, even if our decisions and certi-
tudes must remain absolute. Those definitions apart, what is there
anywhere but ignorance, grace, and moral effort? Of our moral effort
the less said the better; grace is always itself alone, and demands only
our adoration; and therefore it is between our ignorances that our
courteous Lord might cause exchange to lie, till the exchange itself
became an invocation of the adorable Spirit who has so often deigned
to instruct and correct the Church by voices without as well as within
the Church.[96]

The exchange of ignorance is a mutual confession of sin, and a death.
But the outrage of death is supernaturally the door to newness of life
in Christ, and the Church must be willing to die—it must undergo
death with its Master and its members—before it can truly live.

The Church and the State are inextricably united by the bodies of
their people, but they may—they must—at times conflict in what they

demand of those people. Early in World War II, Williams stated the
problem in these terms:

Setting aside those who by vocation are pacifists at the present time,
what is the duty of church-folk as church-folk? Precisely the opposite
of their duty as nationals. Their duty as nationals involves separation
from and killing of German nationals. Their duty as church-folk
involves union with and spiritual dependence on Germans. Both duties
must be fulfilled. It is possible and probable that one duty should be
fulfilled more particularly by Christian soldiers and one more particularly by Christian priests. But neither can be separated from the other;
each exists co-inherently in the other.[97]

The body, however, cannot act in both ways at once. The whole man
can strike in grief and pity and compassion, but his arm strikes or it
does not. There is no middle ground for action.

Must we, for example, consent that men, other men, shall be killed and
maimed? The answer to that is simple—we must. We may do it by
ourselves inflicting death and torment on others (by bombs or however), or we may do it by abandoning others to death and torment (in
concentration camps or wherever), but one way or the other we have
to consent by our mere acts. To call the one war and the other peace
does not help. This—whichever it is—is certainly, in part, the result of
what we do. Is there any direction? Even to quote "Thou shalt not
kill" does not finally help, for we have been taught that consciously to
abandon men to death is, in fact, to kill. To hate is to kill; to kill is to
kill; and to leave to be killed is to kill; yes, though (like the lawyer in
the Gospel) we do not know who our neighbour is.[98]

The State and the Church cannot avoid war, poverty, ignorance, and
the conflict of interests: they inherit these outrages as individuals inherit original sin. Social sin there is; directly or indirectly all contribute to it, all pay for it. The Church cannot seclude its members
from involvement in the sins of society, and should not if it could, but
neither can it take over the State's functions. Historically "the Church
[has] both demanded and promised not the liberty of time and place
but the unconditional liberty of the co-inherent Kingdom which was
precisely free from time and place."[99] Yet at the same time, it is
responsible for the natural bodies and minds of those under its care:
it is *anthropotokos,* the bearer of men, as well as *theotokos,* the God-

bearer. Therefore, while "the great part of the Church . . . has not perhaps talked about our right to our opinions . . . it has talked with a noble rage in every generation about the right of the destitute to our food."[100] It must: "where the Church has forgotten, other ideologies do not bother to try and remember, and some certainly deny."[101]

The State has its own proper function, which is not that of the Church. Nature is not to be rejected in the name or power of super-nature, nor is nature to displace supernature. The natural State cannot be Christian without depriving its citizens of their freedom to live by something other than Christianity, but Christianity "cannot funda-mentally admit the right of an Opposition (to its dogmas) to exist; to refuse the Co-inherence is to separate oneself from the nature of things."[102] Conflict between Church and State is inevitable; none the less, both in their different ways incarnate the City. They co-inhere, and may yet discover a mode of co-inhering in love.

THE HOUSEHOLD OF LOVE

The theology of romantic love claims that marriage is one of the ways to final and complete reconciliation of body and soul with God. Because of the Incarnation,

Eros need not for ever be on his knees to Agape; he has a right to his delights; they are a part of the Way. *The division is not between the Eros of the flesh and the Agape of the soul; it is between the moment of love which sinks into hell and the moment which rises to the in-Godding.*[103]

In marriage, every issue arises which confronts the romantic: Beatrice's appearance as the God-bearer and her withdrawal, sin committed and endured, justice, redemption, the union of matter and spirit and of nature and eternity, freedom, authority, forgiveness, sacrifice, and all these in terms both of the individual and of society. Marriage indeed is a microcosm of the State—"in the family the problems which perplex the State have to be solved"[104]—and if the family be Christian, it is also a microcosm of the Church. To say this, however, does not imply that married life is the only vocation which concentrates the whole pattern of the romantic way, from falling in love to citizenship in the

Kingdom. The same difficulties and achievements appear in other forms for teachers, mystics, priests, politicians, poets, and anyone. But of the unnumbered vocations to which men and women are called, marriage is probably the most common. This does not mean that romantic love is, or ought to be, the necessary precondition for marriage, nor marriage a necessary consequence of romantic love, but only that "the clearest possibility of this Way, and perhaps the most difficult, may be in marriage, but the suggestion of it is defined wherever the suggestion of adoration is present."[105]

Neither the State nor—unfortunately—the Church usually concerns itself with the Beatrician vision that initiates the romantic way, except as it affects social behavior, until the time when the lovers wish to marry. Then both State and Church declare that this intention brings the lovers into direct relationship with the natural and supernatural communities. The State, to sustain its own principle of natural order, prescribes that its citizens fulfill various requirements of form and registration before they can marry. The Church demands of its members something more: it "has insisted that certain conditions are necessary for the carrying out of that great experiment of marriage: free choice, intention of fidelity, physical capacity."[106] First: the lovers, if they are Christian, must deliberately and thoughtfully choose to become love by the method of marriage, and no one shall enter this way with an unwilling companion. The experience of falling in love is not considered an adequate basis for the experiment: it must be reinforced with volition. Second: the lovers shall commit themselves to a limitation of the method: they shall work out the experiment to its end with the companion they have chosen.

The fidelity which the Church has declared to exist in marriage between Christians, and the finality in it which may be denied but cannot, this side of death, be destroyed, is of this nature, because there the nature of exchange has been accepted both in nature and in grace. The canonical conditions of marriage are rigorous for this reason; it is not proper that there should be any possibility of error. Accepted, they remain rigorous—an example of the truth that the vicarious and exchanged life which the Divine Spirit commands and communicates is not less but more inexorable than the individual and single, and that that also has its hierarchy and order of behaviour. In that life, as it moves in this life, the two shall be one; and the power which either draws on shall be double. This power may be for others besides them, but between them the opportunities of exchange are all to be thrown open.[107]

This is the basis upon which Williams makes his arresting comment: "Adultery is bad morals, but divorce is bad metaphysics."[108] Adulterers affirm the unity of husband and wife, although they behave antagonistically to it; but divorce of those who have united themselves before God pretends to dissolve a relationship that by its very nature is indissoluble except by death. The Church literally has no power to release the married from their marriage, and no authority to recognize a civil separation, because while the institution had witnessed and recorded the contract, the lovers' vows were made not to the Church but to the Person of Love, and "love does not belong to lovers, but they to it."[109] Since they do not belong to themselves, they cannot release themselves from their marital vows.

These first two criteria for Christian marriage, the choice of the method and the declaration of fidelity, are conjoined by the Church with a third: "the two shall be one flesh." No doubt this means sexual intercourse. But also it means something of which sexual relationships are an image, "that pattern of life itself which lies beneath sex"[110]—the pattern of physical exchange. Sex is one of the most obviously inclusive of the exchanges, often the most intense, sometimes the most difficult to perfect, but fundamentally different from other exchanges only in the restrictions placed upon its exercise by the laws of the State and by Christian doctrine. The reconciliation taught by Christianity does not mean the abolition of sex, but its redemption. "Spirit itself is not wholly effective—it is not therefore wholly itself—until it is one'd with matter. So, in spite of Keats, unheard melodies are not truly sweet till they are, one way or another, heard by instrumentation; therefore, not fully melodies."[111] A love which does not, in some manner include the body, is not fully love. Thus the Church permits second marriages when

the first experiment has been concluded by death, which is the intervention of Almighty God, though by that outrage which he himself endured . . . the very conditions of the great experiment are therefore removed. Marriage is, partly at least, a recovery of matter; where there is no matter there is no marriage.[112]

But the sovereign union of person with person does not have to be sexual. So far as we know, Messias did not marry; it does not follow from this either that his body was not involved with ours—both his birth and his death negate that lie—or that he regarded marriage as in itself an inferior way of the soul. It may well have been that he, like Galahad, "could not be preoccupied with women because he was preoccupied with something much more vital."[113] But he founded his Church upon Peter, who was married.

In any case, the Incarnation opened the way for men and women to know love by means of their bodies, and not primarily by means of their own bodies but by each other's. The disciplines of substitution apply to sexual, as much as to intellectual and spiritual, love. In actual experience, even natural enjoyment of sex depends upon enjoying the other rather than oneself, if only "because, sooner or later, there isn't anything to enjoy in oneself."[114] But the lover can delight entirely and freely in his mate's pleasure, being peripherally aware of his own response, centrally conscious of the other's, the joy of both perfected in each, and the double act engendering a double nature. The act is at once physical and spiritual: here as elsewhere "in our experiences sensuality and sanctity are so closely intertwined that our motives in some cases can hardly be separated until the tares are gathered out of the wheat by heavenly wit."[115]

"It is the business of all lovers to love each other's function."[116] Nowhere is this more apparent than in the radical exchange of faith and of burdens that takes place in the conception and bearing of children.

There is . . . a mutual willingness between the father and mother which results in the transference of seed. That it is so common does not lessen the trust implied; that one should abandon his seed to another, that one should receive the seed of another, is an exhibition of trust; it is almost the chief natural exhibition of that supernatural quality known as "faith"—a quality which has one of its own proper exhibitions in the interchange of the Eucharist . . .[117]

The new life of the child begins as does the new life of redemption, by an act—a physical act—of substitution between persons, one bearing and the other borne.

Within marriage, the fading of the Beatrician glory in the beloved creates no problems that are peculiar to that state; the appearance of a second image of love does, because the lover has sworn faithfulness to a primary image—the husband or wife. Williams discusses the "second image" in terms of Dante's "Lady of the Window," who may have been a woman or an allegorical figure of philosophy. The confusion has its own significance, since the second image may not be another man or woman; it may be the children of the marriage, or one's vocation or avocation or even an excessive piety, but the one principle applies to all. Following Williams' example, if after marriage one of the lovers falls in love with a third person, he may not discard the primary image—husband or wife—without treason to Love itself. Yet neither may he deny this new love, because to do that would be to flout accuracy. The alternative, which not even Dante found easy to follow, is to use the energy communicated by the second image for the heightening of the first. One continues to love the second image, which is as much a revelation as the first, but restricts the expression of that love and its position in the total structure of one's life.

The aim of the Romantic Way is "the two great ends of liberty and power" . . . To be free one must have power to accept or reject. Having thriven in one manner, we are offered the opportunity of thriving in another; we are offered the opportunity of being free in the glory. The second image is not to be denied; we are not to pretend it is not there, or indeed to diminish its worth; we are only asked to free ourselves from concupiscence in regard to it. . . . The first image was towards physical union; the second towards its separation. It repeats the first, in an opposite direction. But both movements are alike intense towards most noble Love: that is, towards the work of the primal Love in the creation.[118]

What is the other to do, that wife or husband whose function as primary image has been challenged by the second image? "There is but one permissible state to any who have seen love: *'una fiamma di caritade,'* 'a flame of love.' "[119] His or her task is to rejoice in every revelation that the other receives, whatever it be, because "he who hates the manifestation of the kingdom hates the kingdom; he is an apostate to the kingdom."[120] Jealousy will not serve, but then, neither will condoning of infidelity.

An awful truth lurks behind the comic figure of the complacent husband or wife; they are indecent, but the true decency is on the farther side. If it were possible to create in marriage a mutual adoration towards the second image, whenever and however it came, and also a mutual limitation of the method of it, I do not know what new liberties and powers might not be achieved. Meanwhile, so limiting the method, we must wholly practise passion without concupiscence wherever the principle of all the images appears.[121]

This general principle suggests how married lovers can respond in relationship to other images which have no direct sexual element, but which threaten the primary image. And as well, it carries implications beyond the individual and the marriage, into the structures of State and Church. The Church's primary image cannot be anything except the City of Love, through Christ who in his single person incarnates that City; styles of worship and organization are second images. In the State's hierarchy of images, such institutions as courts of law will stand higher than—say—the national anthem, and over all other images of the State rises the primary image of natural man in his blazing natural glory, exchanging with his fellows in freedom.

All second images provide ways for increasing the complexity and the inclusiveness of love. The primary image supplies order; it determines the emphasis to be given to all the others; it establishes proportion among them and a stability of method. Each of the second images is valued for its own sake and for its contribution to the whole, but is brought into coherent relationship with the whole by means of the first image. "For marriage itself is (among other things) an introduction to loves beyond itself, and if these loves are different in their nature, yet still every marriage has to encourage some sort of apparent rivalry to its uxoriousness if not to its uniqueness, and perhaps thrives the better so."[122] This establishment of proportion—if you will, of justice—among the images cannot be adequately described, because no analysis can hope to comprehend the delicacy of its adjustments. It does not operate by rules, but by the impulse that produces rules, that "passion acting in lucidity"[123] which is the equity of Grace.

The revelation which begins the romantic way implies its end in most holy Love, and its end in liberty and power fulfills the initiating vision. Love abandons man to freedom, in order that he may become love "not by the conversion of the Godhead into flesh, but by taking of the manhood into God." And the manhood means the entire man: the holy and glorious flesh with all that is other than flesh, the specifically human and all in the universe that is not man but to which man is, or will be, related. Nothing is to be lost or forgotten or ignored: "Proper Romanticism neither denies nor conceals, neither fears nor flies. It desires only accuracy; 'look, look; attend.' "[124] Therefore the ultimate reconciliation does no violence to man's integrity as man: he is not overthrown but liberated, not destroyed but re-created.

The nature of all love, human and divine alike, is exchange, at once separating and reconciling, the principle of order in the created world and in the One God who is Three Persons. The great themes of exchange—substitution, sacrifice, forgiveness, derivation—reverberate from the heart of the world to its ends, and repeat themselves in various modes from eternity to time and back again.

Messias . . . looked on the fields, he saw them white to harvest, he cried out of wages and fruit and eternal life, and at once of him that sowed and him that reaped and their common joy. And even as he said it, he flung his words into a wider circuit: "herein is that saying true, one soweth and another reapeth. I sent you to reap that whereon ye bestowed no labour; other men laboured and ye are entered into their labours." What! after self-sacrifice and crosses and giving up goods and life, the mind perplexed, the heart broken, the body wrecked—is there not a little success of our own, our own in him, of course, but at least his in us? None; "I sent you to reap that whereon ye bestowed no labour." The harvest is of others, as the beginning was in others, and the process was by others. . . . The first and final maxim in the present earth is *deny the self*, but—there or here—when the need for denial has passed, it may be possible to be astonished at the self as at everything else, when that which is God is known as the circle whose centre is everywhere and the circumference nowhere. "He saved others; himself he cannot save."[125]

From the beginning of time, the City of Love has been established upon earth, operating in accordance with this principle of interchange. It appears wherever individuals meditate upon and practice the arts of co-inherent love, where families and societies create social structures that are at once hierarchic and republican, where the Church communicates the reconciling love of God, and where a young boy and a young girl fall in love, and discover that all things are made new. "The new earth and the new heaven come like the two modes of knowledge, knowledge being the chief art of love, as love is the chief art of knowledge: earth a directness, heaven a substitution."[126] It is to this that the Christian romantic is called.

NOTES

Where no author is named in a note, the author is Charles Williams.

An asterisk following the title of an article indicates that it has been reprinted in Anne Ridler's anthology *The Image of the City and Other Essays* (see Bibliography for full reference), and that the citation refers to that book rather than to the original place of publication. Where Mrs. Ridler has altered the title of a piece, I have followed her, since anyone who desires to trace a quotation will probably find that volume more easily available to him than the various primary sources. However, the Bibliography gives the different titles and the full references, in all cases.

I have not thought it necessary to supply page numbers for quotations from reviews, articles, or poems that are only a page or two long as originally published.

Introduction
1. *He Came Down from Heaven.*
2. Maynard, *Our Best Poets,* 36.
3. *The Descent of the Dove.*
4. Sayers, Introduction to Williams' *James I,* ix.
5. Lewis, "William and the Arthuriad," 107.
6. These terms are fully defined in Chapter 1.
7. For example, among the principal sources for Williams' doctrine of the City are: "The Redeemed City,"* *All Hallows' Eve, Queen Elizabeth, He Came Down from Heaven, The Figure of Beatrice,* and "The Free Act."
8. "Autocriticisms."
9. *The English Poetic Mind,* vii.

Chapter 1. The Ways of the Images
1. Sayers, *Introductory Papers on Dante,* 8.
2. *Descent into Hell,* 50.
3. *Reason and Beauty in the Poetic Mind,* 54–55.
4. *Ibid.*

5. Lewis, *The Allegory of Love.*
6. *Rochester,* 155.
7. *Ibid.,* 51–52.
8. Sayers, *Further Papers on Dante,* 193.
9. *Bacon,* 145–146.
10. *The Region of the Summer Stars,* 31.
11. *Many Dimensions,* 56.
12. *The English Poetic Mind,* 101.
13. *The Figure of Beatrice,* 133.
14. "John Milton,"* 30.
15. *The House of the Octopus,* 79.
16. This definition is modified from that in *The Figure of Beatrice,* 7, where Williams is following Coleridge. But Coleridge's definition contains the form "derives from," instead of "points to" and "refers," thereby suggesting a metaphysical implication which I do not want to discuss here.
17. See Miss Sayers' comments on certain critics of Dante, in her *Introductory Papers on Dante,* xv.
18. *Taliessin through Logres,* 51.
19. Williams believed this to be a

213

quotation, but neither he nor—so far as I know—any of his students has ever been able to locate the source.

20. *The Forgiveness of Sins,* 135.
21. *The Descent of the Dove,* 197.
22. *The Forgiveness of Sins,* 141.
23. *Shadows of Ecstasy,* 36–37.
24. *The Figure of Beatrice,* 35.
25. *Bacon,* 106; see also *Witchcraft,* 76–77.
26. *The Place of the Lion,* 139.
27. Sayers, *Introductory Papers on Dante,* 122.
28. *The Figure of Beatrice,* 13.
29. *Ibid.,* 9–10.
30. *The Descent of the Dove,* 58.
31. *The Figure of Beatrice,* 114.
32. *Ibid.,* 134.
33. "A Dialogue on Hierarchy,"* 128.

Chapter 2. The Image of Beatrice
1. *The Figure of Beatrice,* 16.
2. *He Came Down from Heaven,* 66.
3. *The Figure of Beatrice,* 14.
4. *Ibid.,* 7.
5. *He Came Down from Heaven,* 69.
6. *Ibid.,* 68.
7. "Sensuality and Substance,"* 74.
8. *He Came Down from Heaven,* 65.
9. *Bacon.*
10. *The Figure of Beatrice,* 63.
11. "Blake and Wordsworth,"* 60.
12. *Descent into Hell,* 150.
13. *The English Poetic Mind,* 78.
14. *Religion and Love in Dante,* 8–10.
15. *The English Poetic Mind,* 59.
16. *The Figure of Beatrice,* 100.
17. "Patriotism."
18. "The Index of the Body,"* 81.
19. *He Came Down from Heaven,* 69.
20. *Ibid.,* 68.
21. *Taliessin through Logres,* 35–36.
22. Sayers, *Introductory Papers on Dante,* 123.
23. *He Came Down from Heaven,* 70.
24. *The Figure of Beatrice,* 28.
25. *He Came Down from Heaven,* 71.
26. *He Came Down from Heaven,* 78.
27. *Reason and Beauty in the Poetic Mind,* 55.

28. *The Figure of Beatrice,* 7–8.
29. *Ibid.,* 35.
30. *He Came Down from Heaven,* 74.
31. *The Place of the Lion,* 185.

Chapter 3. The Adam
1. "The Cross,"* 134.
2. "The Figure of Arthur," 80.
3. "A Verse Letter on Verse."
4. "Matter" and "spirit" are used here for convenience, in spite of the philosophical connotations and confusions attending them. Energy has many forms of organization; there are perceptible differences between heat, an idea, and a chunk of lead, and *some* words have to be used to indicate those differences.
5. *He Came Down from Heaven,* 77.
6. In *The Figure of Beatrice,* 92 n., Williams refers to the chapter on co-inherence in G. L. Prestige's *God in Patristic Theology* as "the clearest exposition I know of the theological definition of the Divine Life in this sense."
7. *The Descent of the Dove,* 234.
8. Williams comments in "The Way of Affirmation,"* 158, that "in the old legend Adam and Eve were, originally, one being." His use of "the Adam" points up the unity in their diversity before the Fall.
9. *He Came Down from Heaven,* 18.
10. *The Greater Trumps,* 153.
11. *He Came Down from Heaven,* 19.
12. *Ibid.,* 20.
13. *Reason and Beauty in the Poetic Mind,* 97.
14. *The Forgiveness of Sins,* 121.
15. *He Came Down from Heaven,* 20.
16. *Ibid.,* 21.
17. *The Forgiveness of Sins,* 183.
18. *He Came Down from Heaven,* 98–99. The concluding quotation is from Isaiah 45:7.
19. "Taliessin's Song of Logres," in *Three Plays,* 2–3.
20. "Natural Goodness,"* 76.

21. "The Index of the Body,"* 85.
22. *The Figure of Beatrice,* 48.
23. "The Cross,"* 138.
24. "Natural Goodness,"* 78.
25. *Descent into Hell,* 16.
26. *Ibid.,* 17.
27. *Ibid.,* 65.
28. *He Came Down from Heaven,* 22.
29. "The Cross,"* 132.
30. *Thomas Cranmer of Canterbury,* 9.
31. *He Came Down from Heaven,* 85.
32. *Ibid.,* 71.
33. *Ibid.,* 58–59.

Chapter 4. The Cross
 1. *He Came Down from Heaven,* 30–32.
 2. "The Cross,"* 131.
 3. *The Forgiveness of Sins,* 128.
 4. "The Cross,"* 135.
 5. *Ibid.,* 133.
 6. *The Forgiveness of Sins,* 130.
 7. "The Cross,"* 133–134.
 8. *Descent into Hell,* 149.
 9. *The Forgiveness of Sins,* 167.
10. *He Came Down from Heaven,* 59.
11. *The Forgiveness of Sins,* 131–132.
12. Here, and for the most part, Williams is using witchcraft as a conveniently dramatic, natural symbol for directed energy. It has particular value in his work for its power to suggest a range of possibilities of which we are not usually aware. See *Poetry at Present,* 63.
13. *The Greater Trumps,* 194–195.
14. "The Cross,"* 137.
15. *He Came Down from Heaven,* 83.
16. *Ibid.,* 86.
17. No part of Charles Williams' theology is more important, theoretically and practically, than his doctrine of substituted love, but it cannot be dealt with fully until certain other matters have been considered, notably the nature of time within eternity. For this reason, the principal discussion of substituted love has been placed

in Chapter 8; its full implications will be examined there and in Chapter 9.
18. *The Descent of the Dove,* 69–70.
19. "Natural Goodness,"* 78.
20. *He Came Down from Heaven,* 99.
21. "The Cross,"* 136.
22. *He Came Down from Heaven,* 12.
23. "Fathers and Heretics."
24. *The Forgiveness of Sins,* 119–120.
25. "Natural Goodness,"* 77.
26. *The Descent of the Dove,* 235.
27. *War in Heaven,* 56.
28. *The Descent of the Dove,* 59.
29. *Seed of Adam,* 11.
30. "The Figure of Arthur," 16.
31. *Rochester,* 251.
32. *The Descent of the Dove,* 138–139.
33. *Seed of Adam,* 12.
34. *Witchcraft,* 14. See also *Seed of Adam,* 27, 63.
35. "St. John,"* 88.
36. "The Figure of Arthur," 88.
37. *He Came Down from Heaven,* 46–47.
38. *Ibid.,* 78–79.
39. *The Figure of Beatrice,* 113.
40. Sayers, *Introductory Papers on Dante,* 64.
41. *Descent into Hell.*
42. *He Came Down from Heaven,* 63.
43. *Rochester,* 240.
44. *He Came Down from Heaven,* 95–96.

Chapter 5. Love in Three Persons
 1. *He Came Down from Heaven,* 15.
 2. *The Forgiveness of Sins,* 120–121.
 3. "John Milton,"* 35.
 4. *Reason and Beauty in the Poetic Mind,* 100.
 5. *The Figure of Beatrice,* 9.
 6. *The Descent of the Dove,* 122. Ellipses Williams'.
 7. "St. Anselm's Rabbit."
 8. *Many Dimensions,* 135.
 9. Bloy, quoted in "Eternal Purchase."
10. *He Came Down from Heaven,* 25.
11. *Ibid.,* 70.
12. *Ibid.,* 25.

13. *Descent into Hell*, 174.
14. *The Forgiveness of Sins*, 135.
15. *The Descent of the Dove*, 52.
16. Quoted in *The New Christian Year*, 141.
17. *The Figure of Beatrice*, 172.
18. Sayers, *Introductory Papers on Dante*, 48.
19. "The Redeemed City,"* 103.
20. *Ibid.*, 106.
21. "Notes on the Way" (E).
22. "Natural Goodness,"* 76.
23. *Quicunque vult.*
24. *He Came Down from Heaven*, 98, quoting the *Quicunque vult.*
25. *The Figure of Beatrice*, 197.
26. *The House of the Octopus*, 80.
27. *The Region of the Summer Stars*, 40.
28. *The Figure of Beatrice*, 197.
29. *The Descent of the Dove*, 39–40.
30. "St. Anselm's Rabbit."
31. *The Forgiveness of Sins*, 120.
32. *The Figure of Beatrice*, 136.
33. Lewis, "Williams and the Arthuriad," 105.
34. *He Came Down from Heaven*, 97.
35. *Ibid.*, 33. Note that this is also quoted as the heading for Part II.
36. *Taliessin through Logres*, 27–30; italics mine.
37. *Ibid.*, 6.
38. *He Came Down from Heaven*, 35.
39. *The Descent of the Dove*, 1.
40. See above, 79, quotation from *The Descent of the Dove*, 52.
41. *Descent into Hell*, 68–69.
42. *Many Dimensions*, 268, *passim.*
43. *The Place of the Lion*, 196.
44. *Descent into Hell*, 95.
45. "The Redeemed City,"* 110.
46. *The Descent of the Dove*, 89.
47. *Seed of Adam*, 59, *passim.*
48. Lewis, *Essays Presented to Charles Williams*, xii.
49. *He Came Down from Heaven*, 33.
50. *The Figure of Beatrice*, 38.
51. *He Came Down from Heaven*, 58.
52. *Ibid.*, 60.
53. Lewis, in *Essays Presented to Charles Williams*, xiii. See also *War in Heaven*, 165–166.

54. *The House of the Octopus*, 36.
55. *The Forgiveness of Sins*, 156.
56. *War in Heaven*, 251.
57. *Seed of Adam*, 11.
58. *The Region of the Summer Stars*, 41.
59. *Ibid.* See also Anne Ridler's quotation from Williams' commonplace book, in *The Image of the City*, lix: "Never decorate except in unimportant parts" as a possible principle of art.
60. *The Forgiveness of Sins*, 121.

Chapter 6. Nature and Supernature
1. Lewis, "Williams and the Arthuriad," 101.
2. *Witchcraft*, 14.
3. *The Region of the Summer Stars*, 8.
4. Lewis, "Williams and the Arthuriad," 100–101.
5. *Witchcraft*, 77–78.
6. *All Hallows' Eve*, 213.
7. Quoted in *The Figure of Beatrice*, 25.
8. *The Region of the Summer Stars*, 9.
9. From a note taken during conversation.
10. *The Descent of the Dove*, 14.
11. I cannot remember, or find, the source of this.
12. *He Came Down from Heaven*, 11.
13. *Descent into Hell*, 158.
14. *He Came Down from Heaven*, 92.
15. *Descent into Hell*, 107.
16. *The Descent of the Dove*, 69.
17. *Descent into Hell*, 102.
18. *Taliessin through Logres*, 31–32.
19. *Witchcraft*, 90.
20. *All Hallows' Eve*, 84–85.
21. Respectively: *Descent into Hell*, *War in Heaven*, *The Place of the Lion.*
22. *He Came Down from Heaven*, 101.
23. *The Descent of the Dove*, 59.
24. *The Forgiveness of Sins*, 170.
25. *Religion and Love in Dante*, 34.
26. *The Forgiveness of Sins*, 127–128.

27. *The Region of the Summer Stars,*
    26.
28. *Religion and Love in Dante,* 34.
29. *The Region of the Summer Stars,*
    1.
30. *The Greater Trumps,* 106.
31. *Descent into Hell,* 31.
32. "Sensuality and Substance,"* 75.
33. Lewis, "Williams and the Arthu-
    riad," 141.
34. Lewis, in *Essays Presented to
    Charles Williams,* 95.
35. *Witchcraft,* 301.
36. *War in Heaven,* 223–224.
37. *Witchcraft,* 298–299.
38. See *The Figure of Beatrice,* 107.
39. *Witchcraft,* 30–31.
40. *Descent into Hell,* 176.
41. *The Forgiveness of Sins,* 182.
42. "The Way of Exchange,"* 150.
43. "The Redeemed City,"* 109.
44. Quoted in Sayers, *Introductory
    Papers on Dante,* 121.
45. "Et in Sempiternum Pereant,"
    157.
46. "John Milton,"* 30.
47. *Descent into Hell,* 221–222.
48. *The Greater Trumps,* 134.
49. *The Figure of Beatrice,* 40.
50. Lewis, "Williams and the Arthu-
    riad," 135.
51. *War in Heaven,* 203.
52. Quoted in *The Figure of Beatrice,*
    24.
53. *Ibid.,* 36.

Chapter 7. The Perversion of Love
 1. *The Descent of the Dove,* 108.
 2. *Descent into Hell,* 188.
 3. *The House of the Octopus,* 104.
 4. *He Came Down from Heaven,* 23.
 5. *Ibid.,* 35–36.
 6. *Ibid.,* 78.
 7. "The Natural and the Rest."
 8. *He Came Down from Heaven,* 79.
 9. *The Figure of Beatrice,* 35.
10. *Rochester,* 84.
11. *Religion and Love in Dante,* 13–
    14.
12. *The Figure of Beatrice,* 36–37.
13. *The English Poetic Mind,* 142.
14. *The Figure of Beatrice,* 24.

15. *He Came Down from Heaven,* 79.
16. *Ibid.,* 80.
17. *Ibid.,* 80.
18. *Ibid.,* 83.
19. *Ibid.,* 25.
20. *The House of the Octopus,* 62.
21. *Ibid.,* 77–78.
22. *Judgement at Chelmsford,* 32.
23. *The Figure of Beatrice,* 124.
24. *He Came Down from Heaven,* 80.
25. *Religion and Love in Dante,* 21.
26. *The Figure of Beatrice,* 118–119.
27. *Descent into Hell,* 37.
28. *Rochester,* 185.
29. *The New Book of English Verse,*
    795.
30. *The House of the Octopus,* 49.
31. "The Index of the Body,"* 86.
32. "The Figure of Arthur," 78.
33. *Ibid.,* 85.
34. *He Came Down from Heaven,*
    56–57.
35. *War in Heaven,* 69.
36. *The House of the Octopus,* 107.
37. "The Figure of Arthur," 25.
38. "Transition and Decision."
39. "Lenten Meditation."
40. *He Came Down from Heaven,* 79.
41. *The Figure of Beatrice,* 47–48.
42. Pronunciation given in Index.
43. *Taliessin through Logres,* 34–35.
44. *Ibid.,* 36.
45. Lewis, "Williams and the Arthu-
    riad," 124.
46. Sayers, *The Mind of the Maker,*
    104–107.
47. *Religion and Love in Dante,* 22.
48. *The Figure of Beatrice,* 133.
49. *Ibid.,* 126.
50. *The Descent of the Dove,* 136.
51. "Ways of the Soul."
52. Attributed to Jesus by Paul, in
    Acts 20:35.
53. *Reason and Beauty in the Poetic
    Mind,* 111.
54. "John Milton,"* 31.
55. *The English Poetic Mind,* 122.
56. *Shadows of Ecstasy,* 135.
57. *Ibid.,* 136.
58. *Ibid.*
59. *Reason and Beauty in the Poetic
    Mind,* 112–113.

60. *The English Poetic Mind*, 123–124.
61. *All Hallows' Eve*, 109.
62. *Taliessin through Logres*, 40.
63. Lewis, "Williams and the Arthuriad," 130.
64. *Descent into Hell*, 174.
65. "Lilith," in *Heroes and Kings*, unpaged.
66. *Ibid.*
67. "The Image of Man,"* 145.
68. *Ibid.*
69. *Rochester*, 169.
70. *The House of the Octopus*, 79.
71. *Taliessin through Logres*, 60.
72. *The Figure of Beatrice*, 109.
73. *Reason and Beauty in the Poetic Mind*, 99.
74. *Poetry at Present*, 166.
75. *Shadows of Ecstasy*, 40.
76. *Ibid.*, 41.
77. *Ibid.*, 11.
78. *Ibid.*, 81.
79. *Ibid.*, 153, 154, 180.
80. *Ibid.*, 131.
81. *The New Christian Year*, 155.
82. "Letters to Peter—I."
83. *The House of the Octopus*, 106.
84. *He Came Down from Heaven*, 82–83.
85. Lewis, "Williams and the Arthuriad," 124–125.
86. *He Came Down from Heaven*, 25
87. *The Place of the Lion*, 203.
88. *Rochester*, 219–220.
89. Dante, *The Divine Comedy*, "Hell," III, 95–96; V, 23–24.
90. *All Hallows' Eve*, 99–100.
91. *Taliessin through Logres*, 44.
92. *Ibid.*
93. *He Came Down from Heaven*, 92
94. *All Hallows' Eve*, 44.
95. *Divorce*, 116.
96. *All Hallows' Eve*, 148.
97. *The Figure of Beatrice*, 138.

Chapter 8. The Way of Exchange
1. *Religion and Love in Dante*, 33.
2. *The Descent of the Dove*, 31.
3. *Ibid.*, 32.
4. "Deportment in Criticism."
5. *The Forgiveness of Sins*, 170.

6. *The Figure of Beatrice*, 59–60.
7. *He Came Down from Heaven*, 93–94.
8. *Judgement at Chelmsford*, 81.
9. *The Forgiveness of Sins*, 109.
10. "The Index of the Body,"* 87.
11. *Ibid.*, 85.
12. *Taliessin through Logres*, 72.
13. "The Making of *Taliessin*,"* 181.
14. *The Region of the Summer Stars*, 25.
15. *Taliessin through Logres*, 9; *The Region of the Summer Stars*, 61.
16. *Taliessin through Logres*, 12.
17. *The Greater Trumps*, 199–200.
18. *Review*, Murry's "The Betrayal of Christ by the Churches."
19. "The Redeemed City,"* 103.
20. *The Region of the Summer Stars*, 26.
21. *The Figure of Beatrice*, 37.
22. *All Hallows' Eve*, 189–190.
23. *Ibid.*, 211.
24. *The Region of the Summer Stars*, 26.
25. *The English Poetic Mind*, 205.
26. "The Image of the City in English Verse,"* 102.
27. "The Cross,"* 131.
28. "The Figure of Arthur," 58–59.
29. Lewis, "Williams and the Arthuriad," 169.
30. *The Place of the Lion*, 187.
31. *The Descent of the Dove*, 193.
32. *Ibid.*, 38.
33. *Rochester*, 239.
34. Quoted in *Witchcraft*, 281.
35. "Dr. Joad and Sin."
36. *Flecker of Dean Close*, 62.
37. *The Forgiveness of Sins*, 135.
38. *The Figure of Beatrice*, 67.
39. *The Descent of the Dove*, 25.
40. *War in Heaven*, 113.
41. *The Figure of Beatrice*, 36.
42. *Flecker of Dean Close*, 72.
43. *He Came Down from Heaven*, 97.
44. *Descent into Hell*, 100.
45. *Ibid.*, 105.
46. *Ibid.*, 98.
47. *Ibid.*, 99.
48. *He Came Down from Heaven*, 89.
49. *Descent into Hell*, 100–101.

50. *All Hallows' Eve,* 142.
51. *He Came Down from Heaven,* 88.
52. *Ibid.,* 89.
53. *Descent into Hell,* 99.
54. *Ibid.,* 108.
55. *Ibid.,* 172.
56. Lewis, "Williams and the Arthuriad," 123.
57. "The Way of Exchange,"* 154.
58. *He Came Down from Heaven,* 90.
59. *Bacon,* 255.
60. *The Letters of Evelyn Underhill,* 21.
61. Above, 62–63.
62. *He Came Down from Heaven,* 90–91.
63. *The Place of the Lion,* 148.
64. "The Figure of Arthur," 85.
65. Caithness, in *Shadows of Ecstasy,* 90.
66. *He Came Down from Heaven,* 103.
67. "The Way of Exchange,"* 153.
68. *Flecker of Dean Close,* 93.
69. "The Way of Exchange,"* 152.
70. *Ibid.,* 153.
71. *He Came Down from Heaven,* 89.
72. *Ibid.,* 91.
73. *Reason and Beauty in the Poetic Mind,* 111.
74. *He Came Down from Heaven,* 53.
75. *The Place of the Lion,* 145.
76. *Witchcraft,* 118.
77. *The Book of Common Prayer.*
78. *The Forgiveness of Sins,* 158.
79. *Descent into Hell,* 92.
80. *The Forgiveness of Sins,* 163.
81. *Ibid.,* 136.
82. *Ibid.,* 137.
83. *Ibid.,* 138.
84. *The Region of the Summer Stars,* 26–27. We may shrink from such a reference as this in the index of the body; cultural taboos and natural reticences encourage us to repudiate it. We are happy enough to grant that some parts of the body, and some physiological processes, have symbolic value— eyes, hands, the beating of the heart, breathing—but we are repelled by the similar use of other organs and activities. Yet if Williams is right in affirming the holiness of the entire body, then he is justified in using as images even those portions of the anatomy and specific functions to which, as a rule, we give less abundant honor.

   Whether menstruation *necessarily* has this association with sacrifice, and whether the sacrificial victim *necessarily* is disqualified from the priesthood, is another matter. Williams did interpret this image in this way. I am certain that he would have denied categorically that it *must* be so interpreted.
85. "Blake and Wordsworth,"* 66.
86. *Ibid.*
87. *The Forgiveness of Sins,* 108.
88. *He Came Down from Heaven,* 38.
89. *The English Poetic Mind,* 103.
90. *All Hallows' Eve,* 118.
91. *The Forgiveness of Sins,* 168.
92. *The Descent of the Dove,* 31; above, 139.
93. *The Forgivenes of Sins,* 143; Isaiah 66:4
94. *Ibid.,* 198.
95. *Ibid.,* 163–164.
96. *He Came Down from Heaven,* 60–61.
97. *Many Dimensions,* 231.
98. *The Forgiveness of Sins,* 161
99. *Ibid.,* 191.
100. *Ibid.,* 192.
101. *Ibid.,* 165.
102. *Ibid.,* 167.
103. *Ibid.,* 198.
104. *Ibid.,* 199.
105. *Descent into Hell,* 28.
106. "The Cross,"* 133.
107. *Taliessin through Logres,* 82.
108. *The Region of the Summer Stars,* 53.
109. *Ibid.,* 50–51.
110. Respectively: *The House of the Octopus, Thomas Cranmer of Canterbury, Judgement at Chelmsford, War in Heaven,*

The Greater Trumps, Arthurian poems, "The Rite of the Passion," *Seed of Adam,* "Introduction" to *The Letters of Evelyn Underhill.* See also "Scene from a Mystery."

111. *The Region of the Summer Stars,* 50.
112. *Thomas Cranmer of Canterbury,* 175.
113. *All Hallows' Eve,* 13.
114. *Thomas Cranmer of Canterbury,* 195–196.
115. *Taliessin through Logres,* 90.
116. "The Figure of Arthur," 86.
117. *The House of the Octopus,* 5.
118. "Soul and Body—and Both."
119. *Taliessin through Logres,* 67.
120. Lewis, "Williams and the Arthuriad," 181.
121. *He Came Down from Heaven,* 98.
122. "Malory and the Grail Legend,"* 194.
123. *Taliessin through Logres,* 81.
124. *War in Heaven,* 240.
125. *Review,* Langton's "Good and Evil Spirits," 234.
126. "The Free Act,"* 115.
127. *He Came Down from Heaven,* 100.
128. Sayers, *Introductory Papers on Dante,* 56.
129. *The Forgiveness of Sins,* 182–183.
130. *Witchcraft,* 14.
131. *The Figure of Beatrice,* 10–11.
132. *He Came Down from Heaven,* 96.
133. *Religion and Love in Dante,* 3.
134. "The Theology of Crisis."
135. *He Came Down from Heaven,* 54.
136. *The Region of the Summer Stars,* 52.
137. *He Came Down from Heaven,* 86.
138. *The Greater Trumps,* 196.
139. *The Forgiveness of Sins,* 108.

Chapter 9. The City of Love
1. *Queen Elizabeth,* 9.

2. "The Redeemed City,"* 104.
3. *Ibid.,* 110.
4. *The Descent of the Dove,* 87.
5. "The Image of the City,"* 92–93.
6. *The Region of the Summer Stars,* 36.
7. Lewis, "William and the Arthuriad," 142.
8. "The Way of Exchange,"* 149.
9. *Taliessin through Logres,* 42–45.
10. *He Came Down from Heaven,* 98.
11. "A Dialogue on Hierarchy,"* 129.
12. "Anti-Christ and the City's Laws,"* 120.
13. "A Dialogue on Hierarchy,"* 128.
14. Lewis, "Williams and the Arthuriad," 142–143.
15. *Quicunque vult.*
16. *The Figure of Beatrice,* 51.
17. "The Redeemed City,"* 102.
18. *Ibid.*
19. "Children of Light."
20. *Judgement at Chelmsford,* 41.
21. "The Redeemed City,"* 103.
22. *Ibid.,* 110.
23. *Ibid.,* 105–106.
24. *The Forgiveness of Sins,* 149.
25. Lewis, "Williams and the Arthuriad," 182.
26. "The Free Act,"* 113.
27. *The Figure of Beatrice,* 197.
28. *The House of the Octopus,* 47.
29. "The Free Act,"* 113–114.
30. *Religion and Love in Dante,* 18.
31. *The Figure of Beatrice,* 112.
32. "The Way of Exchange,"* 147–148.
33. "Church and State,"* 117.
34. "The Free Act,"* 114.
35. "Anthropotokos,"* 113.
36. "Notes on the Way" (C).
37. "The Redeemed City,"* 103.
38. "The War for Compassion."
39. *The Descent of the Dove,* 70.
40. *The Forgiveness of Sins,* 199–200.
41. "War and the Church."
42. Lewis, *That Hideous Strength,* 443–444.
43. "Dr. Inge's Mind."
44. The "yes-or-no, yes-and-no" illustration is from Williams' Byron lecture.

45. "The Redeemed City,"* 107.
46. *The Forgiveness of Sins,* 199.
47. "Leo the Great."
48. *The Descent of the Dove,* 7.
49. "Dr. Joad and Sin."
50. *The Descent of the Dove,* 1.
51. *He Came Down from Heaven,* 85.
52. *The Forgiveness of Sins,* 164; italics mine.
53. "Natural Goodness,"* 78.
54. *Descent into Hell,* 98; above, 149.
55. "Natural Goodness,"* 78.
56. *Ibid.,* 79.
57. *The Figure of Beatrice,* 117.
58. *Descent into Hell,* 118.
59. *The Forgiveness of Sins,* 164.
60. *Ibid.,* 139.
61. "Leo the Great."
62. *The New Book of English Verse,* 7.
63. *The Forgiveness of Sins,* 139.
64. *The Descent of the Dove,* 83.
65. *Thomas Cranmer of Canterbury,* 145.
66. *The Figure of Beatrice,* 10.
67. *The Forgiveness of Sins,* 166.
68. *The Descent of the Dove,* 30.
69. *Ibid.,* 59.
70. "Church and State,"* 116–117.
71. *The Descent of the Dove,* 15.
72. *He Came Down from Heaven,* 84–85.
73. *Thomas Cranmer of Canterbury,* 181.
74. "Sensuality and Substance,"* 75.
75. "The Way of Affirmation,"* 157.
76. "A Dialogue on Hierarchy,"* 128.
77. *Review,* Murry's "The Betrayal of Christ by the Churches."
78. *The Region of the Summer Stars,* 36.
79. *The Descent of the Dove,* 79.
80. "The Doctrine of Largesse,"* 140.
81. *The Figure of Beatrice,* 163.
82. *The English Poetic Mind,* 116–117.
83. *The Descent of the Dove,* 95.
84. *Review,* Murry's "The Betrayal of Christ by the Churches."
85. *Taliessin through Logres,* 44.
86. *All Hallows' Eve,* 149.
87. *The Descent of the Dove,* 33.
88. *The Region of the Summer Stars,* 26.
89. "The Way of Affirmation,"* 156.
90. "The Way of Exchange,"* 154.
91. "Sensuality and Substance,"* 75.
92. "The Figure of Arthur," 21.
93. *Witchcraft,* 82.
94. *The House of the Octopus,* 63.
95. *He Came Down from Heaven,* 87.
96. *The Descent of the Dove,* 232.
97. "Church and State,"* 116.
98. *The Forgiveness of Sins,* 172–173.
99. *The Descent of the Dove,* 218.
100. "More than Politics."
101. "Anthropotokos,"* 113.
102. *The Descent of the Dove,* 217.
103. *Religion and Love in Dante,* 40; italics mine.
104. "The Commonwealth in English Verse," 235.
105. *The Figure of Beatrice,* 15–16.
106. *Ibid.,* 49.
107. "The Redeemed City,"* 108.
108. *The Forgiveness of Sins,* 196.
109. *He Came Down from Heaven,* 80.
110. *Rochester,* 204.
111. "The Divine Realm."
112. *The Figure of Beatrice,* 51 n.
113. "The Making of *Taliessin,*"* 180.
114. *Descent into Hell,* 64.
115. *The Forgiveness of Sins,* 112.
116. *The Figure of Beatrice,* 195.
117. "The Redeemed City,"* 103.
118. *The Figure of Beatrice,* 49.
119. *He Came Down from Heaven,* 80.
120. *The Figure of Beatrice,* 50.
121. *Ibid.*
122. "The Free Act,"* 114.
123. *Many Dimensions,* 156.
124. *The Figure of Beatrice,* 35.
125. *He Came Down from Heaven,* 93–94.
126. *Ibid.,* 97–98.

BIBLIOGRAPHY

The following are the published writings of Charles Williams which I have consulted in preparing this book. In addition, Williams is known to have published a number of poems and book reviews, and an occasional article in a church paper, which I have not been able to locate.

Citations marked with an asterisk refer to material that has been reprinted in *The Image of the City and Other Essays* (Oxford University Press, 1958), an anthology of short pieces by Charles Williams, selected by Anne Ridler and with an excellent critical introduction by her.

Dates in parentheses refer to first publication.

For convenience of reference in the Notes, I have added letters (A, B, C, etc.) to identify the chronological sequence of the articles published in the *Time and Tide* departments "Men and Books" and "Notes on the Way."

*"Alexander Pope (1688–1744)." *Time and Tide,* Vol. 25, No. 22, May 27, 1944, pp. 466–468. Review of *The Twickenham Edition of the Poems of Alexander Pope,* Vols. II, IV, and V.

All Hallows' Eve. London: Faber & Faber Ltd., 1945. Novel.

*"Anthropotokos." See under "Men and Books" (A).

*"Anti-Christ and the City's Laws." See under "Notes on the Way" (A).

*"Apologue on the Parable of the Wedding Garment." *Time and Tide,* Vol. 21, No. 49, December 7, 1940, p. 1186. Poem.

*"Augustine and Athanasius." *Time and Tide,* Vol. 25, No. 26, June 24, 1944, p. 556. Review of *The Confessions of St. Augustine,* tr. F. J. Sheed, and *The Incarnation of the Word of God* by St. Athanasius, tr. by a Religious.

"The Authority of Christendom." *Time and Tide,* Vol. 21, No. 12, March 23, 1940, pp. 319–320. Review of *The Resurrection of Christendom* by J. H. Oldham; *Europe in Travail* by J. Middleton Murry; *Education and Social Change* by Fred Clarke; *The Message of the World-Wide Church* by W. Paton; and *Christianity and Justice* by O. C. Quick.

"Autocriticisms—9." *Week-End Review,* Vol. VIII, No. 193, November 18, 1933, p. 525. Illustrated with caricature by Coia. Review by Williams of his own *Reason and Beauty in the Poetic Mind.*

Bacon. London: Arthur Barker Ltd., 1933.

"Beauty Lately." English words by Charles Williams to music by George Frederick Handel. Arranged and edited by W. G. Whittaker. London: Oxford University Press, 1925.

"Biography 'Of Course.'" *Time and Tide,* Vol. 23, No. 38, September 19, 1942, pp. 743–744. Review of *A Life of Shakespeare* by Hesketh Pearson.

*"Blake and Wordsworth." *The Dublin Review,* Vol. 208, No. 417, April, 1941, pp. 175–186.

"Boars of Vau." *Time and Tide,* Vol. 24, No. 3, January 16, 1943, pp. 50 and 52. Review of *Stone Men of Malekula* by John Layard.

"Byron and Byronism." *Bulletin* of the British Institute of the University of Paris, 1938. Lecture.

"The Case of Harry Dobkin." *Time and Tide,* Vol. 25, No. 35, August 26, 1944, p. 748. Review of *The Trial of Harry Dobkin,* ed. by C. Bechofer Roberts.

*"The Chances and Changes of Myth." *Time and Tide,* Vol. 23, No. 29, July

18, 1942, pp. 581–582. Review of *La Grant Ystoire de Monsignor Tristan Li Bret,* ed. by F. C. Johnson.

*"Charles Williams on 'Taliessin through Logres.' " *The Poetry Review,* Vol. XXXII, March-April, 1941, pp. 77–81. [*"The Making of *Taliessin*"]

"Charles Williams's 'Notes on the Way.' " *Time and Tide,* Vol. 22, No. 39, September 27, 1941, p. 818. Letter, answering one printed the previous week.

"Children of Light." *Time and Tide,* Vol. 26, No. 18, May 5, 1945, p. 376. Review of *The Children of Light and the Children of Darkness* by Reinhold Niebuhr.

"Christ and Adam." *Time and Tide,* Vol. 21, No. 44, November 2, 1940, pp. 1067–1068. Review of *Regeneration* and *The Christ at Chartres* by Denis Saurat.

"Christianity and Judaism." *Time and Tide,* Vol. 25, No. 29, July 15, 1944, p. 624. Review of *Hated Servants* by H. F. Rubenstein.

*"Church and State." *Time and Tide,* Vol. XX, No. 42, October 21, 1939, pp. 1369–1370. Review of *Church and State* by Don Luigi Sturzo.

*"The Church Looks Forward." *St. Martin's Review,* No. 593, July, 1940. [*"The Way of Affirmation"]

*"Collects Composed for a Marriage." *The Image of the City,* p. 195.

"The Commonwealth in English Verse." *Contemporary Review,* Vol. CXXIV, No. 692, August, 1923, pp. 228–236.

"Criticism of Poetry." *Time and Tide,* Vol. 26, No. 3, January 20, 1945, p. 58. Review of *A Critical History of English Poetry* by H. J. Grierson and J. C. Smith.

*"The Cross." See *What the Cross Means to Me.* Essay.

"The Delphic Oracle." *Time and Tide,* Vol. 21, No. 14, April 6, 1940, pp. 369–370. Review of *The Delphic Oracle* by H. W. Parke.

"Deportment in Criticism." *The Poetry Review,* Vol. XXXII, No. 3, May-June, 1941, p. 188. Letter.

Descent into Hell. London: Faber & Faber Ltd., 1949. (1937) Novel.

The Descent of the Dove: A Short History of the Holy Spirit in the Church. London: Faber & Faber Ltd., 1950. (1939)

*"A Dialogue on Hierarchy." *Time and Tide,* Vol. 24, No. 40, October 2, 1943, p. 799.

"A Dialogue on Mr. Eliot's Poem." *The Dublin Review,* Vol. 212, No. 425, April, 1943, pp. 114–122.

"Dinadan's Song." *Time and Tide,* Vol. 22, No. 11, March 15, 1941, p. 210. Poem.

"The Divine Realm." *Time and Tide,* Vol. 25, No. 49, December 2, 1944, p. 1062. Review of *The Divine Realm* by E. Lampert.

"Divites Dimisit." *Theology,* Vol. XXXIX, No. 234, December, 1939, pp. 421–424. Poem, an early version of "The Prayers of the Pope."

Divorce. London: Oxford University Press, 1920. Poems.

"Dr. Inge's Mind." *Time and Tide,* Vol. 20, No. 50, December 16, 1939, p. 1617. Review of *A Pacifist in Trouble* by W. R. Inge.

"Dr. Joad and Sin." *Time and Tide,* Vol. 24, No. 11, March 13, 1943, pp. 211–212. Review of *God and Evil* by C. E. M. Joad.

*"The Doctrine of Largesse." *Time and Tide,* Vol. 22, No. 49, December 6, 1941, p. 1072. Review of *Forgiveness and Reconciliation* by Vincent Taylor.

"Earle Welby on Poetry." *Week-End Review,* Vol. VIII, No. 189, October 7, 1933, supplement, pp. 358–359. Review of *A Popular History of English Poetry* by T. Earle Welby.

"The Engine of Fascination." *Time and Tide,* Vol. 21, No. 50, December 14, 1940, pp. 1233–1234. Review of *Sacred and Profane Love* by Sacheverell Sitwell.

The English Poetic Mind. London: Oxford University Press, 1932. Literary criticism.

"The Epic Hero." *Time and Tide,* Vol. 26, No. 21, May 26, 1945, pp. 439–440. Review of *From Virgil to Milton* by C. M. Bowra.

"The Eternal Purchase." *Time and Tide,* Vol. 25, No. 44, October 28, 1944, pp. 946–947. Review of *We Have Been Friends Together* by Raïssa Maritain.

"Et in Sempiternum Pereant." *The London Mercury,* Vol. XXXIII, No. 194, December, 1935, pp. 151–158. Short story.

"The Exploration of Anonymity." *Week-End Review,* Vol. VIII, No. 183, September 9, 1933, p. 275. Review of *The English Galaxy,* ed. by Gerald Bullett.

*"Falstaff and Prince Henry." *Time and Tide,* Vol. 24, No. 43, October 23, 1943, pp. 869–870. Review of *The Fortunes of Falstaff* by John Dover Wilson. [*"Two Brief Essays on Shakesperian Topics: (2)"]

"Fathers and Heretics." *Time and Tide,* Vol. 21, No. 46, November 16, 1940, pp. 1122–1123. Review of *Fathers and Heretics* by G. L. Prestige.

"The Figure of Arthur." In *Arthurian Torso,* Containing the Posthumous Fragment of the Figure of Arthur by Charles Williams and a commentary on the Arthurian Poems of Charles Williams by C. S. Lewis. London: Oxford University Press, 1948.

The Figure of Beatrice: A Study in Dante. London: Faber & Faber Ltd., 1943.

"The First Dialectical Republic." *Time and Tide,* Vol. 24, No. 35, August 28, 1943, pp. 704–705. Review of *Time, the Refreshing River* by Joseph Needham.

Flecker of Dean Close. London: The Canterbury Press, 1946. Biography.

"For a Musician's Birthday Book." *Time and Tide,* Vol. 22, No. 48, November 29, 1941, p. 1038. Poem.

The Forgiveness of Sins. Printed with *He Came Down from Heaven,* q.v.

*"The Free Act." *Time and Tide,* Vol. 26, No. 12, March 24, 1945, pp. 253–254. Review of *The Rights of Man* by Jacques Maritain.

"Freedom and Poetry." *Time and Tide,* Vol. 21, No. 28, July 13, 1940, pp. 736–737. Review of *The Pattern of Freedom,* chosen by Bruce Richmond.

*"Gerard Hopkins." *Time and Tide,* Vol. 26, No. 5, February 3, 1945, pp. 102–103. Review of *Gerard Manley Hopkins* by W. H. Gardner, Vol. I.

"Gerard Hopkins and Milton." *The Poetry Review,* Vol. XXX, 1939, pp. 307–308. Letter.

"Gerard Manley Hopkins." *The Times Literary Supplement,* No. 1,509, January 1, 1931, p. 12. Letter.

"Good King Arthur." *Time and Tide,* Vol. 25, No. 38, September 16, 1944, p. 817. Review of *The Battle for Britain in the Fifth Century* by T. D. Reed.

The Greater Trumps. London: Faber & Faber Ltd., 1954. (1932) Novel.

"Hardy." *Time and Tide,* Vol. 24, No. 19, May 8, 1943, p. 380. Review of *Hardy the Novelist* by Lord David Cecil.

"The Headland of Perachora." *Time and Tide,* Vol. 24, No. 39, September 25, 1943, p. 786. Review of *The Traveller's Journey Is Done* by Dilys Powell.

He Came Down from Heaven and *The Forgiveness of Sins.* London: Faber & Faber Ltd., 1950. (1938 and 1942)

"Henry V." In *Shakespeare Criticism 1919–1935.* Selected and with an Introduction by Anne Ridler. London: Oxford University Press, 1936.

Henry VII. London: Arthur Barker Ltd., 1937. Biography.

Heroes and Kings. London: The Sylvan Press, 1930, privately printed. Poems.

"The Hero in English Verse." *The Contemporary Review,* Vol. CXVIII, No. 660, December, 1920, pp. 831–838.

"The History of Critical Music." *The Dominant,* Vol. I, No. 6, April, 1928, supplement, pp. iv–v.

"H.M.P." *The Lantern* (Oxford University Press), January, 1939, pp. 98–101. Unsigned article on Miss Helen M. Peacock.

"Homage to Mr. Belloc." *Time and Tide,* Vol. 23, No. 48, November 28, 1942, pp. 952 and 954. Review of *For Hilaire Belloc,* ed. by Douglas Woodruff.

The House of the Octopus. London: Edinburgh House Press, 1945.

"Il ben dell' Intelletto." *Time and Tide,* Vol. 23, No. 21, May 23, 1942, p. 436. Review of *Life and the Poet* by Stephen Spender; *Beyond the 'Isms* by Olaf Stapledon; and *Masters of Reality* by Una Ellis-Fermor.

**"The Image of Man." *Time and Tide,* Vol. 23, No. 7, February 14, 1942, pp. 136–137. Review of *The Nature and Destiny of Man: 1. Human Nature* by Reinhold Niebuhr.

**"The Image of the City in English Verse." *The Dublin Review,* Vol. 207, No. 414, July, 1940, pp. 39–51.

**"The Index of the Body." *The Dublin Review,* Vol. 211, No. 422, July, 1942, pp. 13–20.

Introductions and Editorial Work

    A Book of Longer Modern Verse. Selected and with an Introduction by Edward A. Parker, and Notes by Charles Williams. London: Oxford University Press, 1926.

    *A Book of Victorian Narrative Verse. Chosen by Charles Williams. London: Oxford University Press, 1927. [**"Victorian Narrative Verse"]

    The New Book of English Verse. Edited and with an Introduction by Charles Williams. London: Victor Gollancz, 1935.

    Poems of Home and Overseas. Compiled by Charles Williams and V. H. Collins. London: Oxford University Press, 1921.

    Dickens, Charles. *The Mystery of Edwin Drood.* With a Supplementary Note by Charles Williams. London: Oxford University Press, The World's Classics Series, 1924.

    Gibson, W. W. *Solway Ford and Other Poems.* A Selection made by Charles Williams. London: Faber & Faber, 1945.

    Hopkins, Gerard Manley. *Poems of Gerard Manley Hopkins.* Edited with Notes by Robert Bridges. Second edition with a critical Introduction by Charles Williams. London: Oxford University Press, 1930.

Kierkegaard, Søren. *The Present Age*. With Introduction by Charles Williams. London: Oxford University Press, 1940.

*Landor, Walter Savage. *Imaginary Conversations*. Selected by T. Earle Welby; Introduction by Charles Williams. London: Oxford University Press, 1934. [*"Landor"]

*Milton, John. *The English Poems of John Milton*. With an Introduction by Charles Williams. London: Oxford University Press, The World's Classics Series, 1940.

Underhill, Evelyn. *The Letters of Evelyn Underhill*. Edited and with an Introduction by Charles Williams. London: Longmans, Green and Co., 1943.

Webster, John. *The Duchess of Malfi*. With introductory essays by George Rylands and Charles Williams. London: Sylvan Press, 1945.

"I Saw Eternity . . ." *Time and Tide*, Vol. 24, No. 33, August 14, 1943, p. 668. Review of *Human Destiny* by Reinhold Niebuhr.

James I. London: Arthur Barker Ltd., 1951. (1934)

*"The Jews." *Time and Tide*, Vol. 24, No. 52, December 25, 1943, p. 1066. Review of *Redeeming the Time* by Jacques Maritain.

"The Jews and Jacques Maritain." *Time and Tide*, Vol. 25, No. 2, January 8, 1944, p. 25. Letter.

*"John Calvin." *Time and Tide*, Vol. 22, No. 13, March 29, 1941, pp. 271–272. Review of *Calvinism* by A. Dakin.

*"John Milton." See under *Introductions and Editorial Work*.

Judgement at Chelmsford. London: Oxford University Press, 1939. Play.

*"Landor." See under *Introductions and Editorial Work*.

*"The Last of the Kings." *Time and Tide*, Vol. 21, No. 8, February 24, 1940, p. 198. Review of *The Last Rally: A Study of Charles II* by Hilaire Belloc.

"Lenten Meditation." *Time and Tide*, Vol. 25, No. 9, February 26, 1944, p. 180. Review of *Prophets for a Day of Judgment* by A. E. Baker.

"Leo the Great." *Time and Tide*, Vol. 22, No. 38, September 20, 1941, pp. 802–803. Review of *Life and Times of St. Leo the Great* by Trevor Jalland.

"A Letter from Charles Williams." *Time and Tide*, Vol. 22, No. 21, May 24, 1941, pp. 442–443. Review of *A Treasury of the World's Great Letters* by M. Lincoln Schuster.

"Letters in Hell." *Time and Tide*, Vol. 23, No. 12, March 21, 1942, pp. 245–246. Review of *The Screwtape Letters* by C. S. Lewis.

"Letters to Peter—I." *G. K.'s Weekly*, Vol. XXII, No. 573, March 5, 1936, pp. 382–383. Review of *Victoria of England* by Edith Sitwell.

"Letters to Peter—II." *G. K.'s Weekly*, Vol. XXIII, No. 577, April 2, 1936, pp. 52–53. Review of *Home University Library*.

"Letters to Peter—III." *G. K.'s Weekly*, Vol. XXIII, No. 581, April 30, 1936, pp. 114–115. Review of William Hayley's biography of himself.

"Letters to Peter—IV." *G. K.'s Weekly*, Vol. XXIII, No. 585, May 28, 1936, pp. 178–179. Review of *Trent's Own Case* by E. C. Bentley and H. Warner Allen.

"Letters to Peter—V." *G. K.'s Weekly*, Vol. XXIII, No. 588, June 18, 1936, pp. 229–230. Review of *An Essay on the Restoration of Property* by Hilaire Belloc.

"Letters to Peter—VI." *G. K.'s Weekly*, Vol. XXIII, No. 593, July 23, 1936, pp. 306–307. Review of *Murder off Miami* by Dennis Wheatley and J. G. Hinks.

"The Literary Epic." *Britain Today,* No. 112, August, 1945, pp. 40–41. Review of *From Virgil to Milton* by C. M. Bowra.

*"The Liturgy." *Time and Tide,* Vol. 22, No. 52, December 27, 1941, p. 1146. Review of *The High Church Tradition* by G. W. O. Addleshaw.

"The Living Milton." *The Spectator,* No. 6060, August 18, 1944, p. 154. Review of *Milton, Man and Thinker* by Denis Saurat.

*"Lord Macaulay." In *Six Short Biographies,* edited by R. C. and N. Goffin. London: Oxford University Press, 1933.

"Maid and Measure." *Time and Tide,* Vol. 25, No. 19, May 6, 1944, pp. 400–401. Review of *The English Bible* by Sir Herbert Grierson, and *The Bible: Its Letter and Spirit* by W. C. Dick.

*"The Making of *Taliessin.*" See under "Charles Williams on 'Taliessin through Logres.'"

*"Malory and the Grail Legend." *The Dublin Review,* Vol. 214, No. 429, April, 1944, pp. 144–153.

Many Dimensions. London: Faber & Faber Ltd., 1947. (1931) Novel.

The Masque of Perusal. London: Henderson and Spalding Ltd., 1929. Play, privately printed.

The Masque of the Manuscript. London: Henderson and Spalding Ltd., 1927. Play, privately printed.

*"Men and Books." (A) *Time and Tide,* Vol. XIX, No. 43, October 22, 1938, pp. 1463–1464. Review of *True Humanism* by Jacques Maritain, and *Solitude and Society* by Nicolas Berdyaev. [*"Anthropotokos"]

*"Men and Books." (B) *Time and Tide,* Vol. XX, No. 11, March 18, 1939, pp. 344 and 346. Review of *Rejoice in the Lamb* by Christopher Smart, ed. by W. Force Stead. [*"Rejoice in the Lamb"]

"Men and Books." (C) *Time and Tide,* Vol. XX, No. 25, June 24, 1939, p. 833. Review of Dante's *The Divine Comedy: Hell and Purgatory,* tr. by John D. Sinclair.

"Men and Books." (D) *Time and Tide,* Vol. 20, No. 38, September 23, 1939, p. 1256. Review of *Torquemada: Scourge of the Jews* by Thomas Hope.

"Michael Drayton." *Time and Tide,* Vol. 22, No. 44, November 1, 1941, p. 940. Review of *Michael Drayton and His Circle* by Bernard H. Newdigate.

"Mr. Graves and Mary Powell." *Time and Tide,* Vol. 24, No. 9, February 27, 1943, p. 168. Review of *Wife to Mr. Milton* by Robert Graves.

"Moments' Monuments." *Week-End Review,* Vol. VIII, No. 181, August 26, 1933, pp. 213–214. Review of *Poems, 1912–1932* by Edward Shanks.

"The Moon." A Cantata prepared . . . from the airs of Henry Purcell by W. Gillies Whittaker, the words by Charles Williams. London: Oxford University Press, 1923.

"More Power to Mr. Belloc." *Time and Tide,* Vol. 23, No. 19, May 9, 1942, p. 390. Review of *Elizabethan Commentary* by Hilaire Belloc.

"More than Politics." *Time and Tide,* Vol. XX, No. 16, April 22, 1939, p. 512. Review of *Beyond Politics* by Christopher Dawson; *The Poor and Ourselves* by Daniel-Rops; and *Christianity and Economics* by Lord Stamp.

"Mortal Strife." *The New English Weekly and The New Age,* Vol. XXI, No. 21, September 10, 1942, pp. 169–170. Review of *Mortal Strife* by John Cowper Powys.

"Moses When the Light Came On." *Time and Tide,* Vol. XX, No. 23, June 10, 1939, p. 758. Review of *Moses and Monotheism* by Sigmund Freud.

"Murder." *Time and Tide,* Vol. 26, No. 20, May 19, 1945, p. 421. Review of *The Trial of R. S. Buckfield,* ed. by C. W. Beckhofer Roberts.

A Myth of Shakespeare. London: Oxford University Press, 1928. Play.

"The Natural and the Rest." *Time and Tide,* Vol. 23, No. 41, October 10, 1942, pp. 804–805. Review of *Catholic Art and Culture* by E. J. Watkin; *The Mind of a Poet* by Raymond Dexter Havens; and *An Anthology of Religious Verse,* ed. by Norman Nicholson.

*"Natural Goodness." *Theology,* Vol. XLIII, No. 256, October, 1941, pp. 211–216.

"Nature and the Poets." *Time and Tide,* Vol. 22, No. 27, July 5, 1941, pp. 564–565. Review of *An Anthology of Nature Poetry,* ed. by Viola Meynell.

"The Nature of Charity." *Time and Tide,* Vol. XX, No. 8, February 25, 1939, pp. 244–245. Review of *A Popular History of the Church* by Philip Hughes, and *History of the Dogma of the Trinity* by Jules Lebreton.

The New Christian Year. London: Oxford University Press, 1941. Anthology.

*"The New Milton." *The London Mercury,* Vol. XXXVI, No. 213, July, 1937, pp. 255–261.

"Notes on Religious Drama." *Chelmsford Diocesan Chronicle,* Vol. 23, No. 5, May, 1937, pp. 75–76.

*"Notes on the Arthurian Myth." *The Image of the City,* pp. 175–179.

*"Notes on the Way." (A) *Time and Tide,* Vol. XIX, No. 35, August 27, 1938, pp. 1195–1197. [*"Anti-Christ and the City's Laws"]

*"Notes on the Way," (B) *Time and Tide,* Vol. XIX, No. 36, September 3, 1938, pp. 1218–1220. [*"Sound and Variations"]

"Notes on the Way." (C) *Time and Tide,* Vol. 22, No. 37, September 13, 1941, p. 769.

"Notes on the Way." (D) *Time and Tide,* Vol. 23, No. 9, February 28, 1942, pp. 170–171.

"Notes on the Way." (E) *Time and Tide,* Vol. 23, No. 10, March 7, 1942, pp. 194–195.

"Occupation." *Time and Tide,* Vol. 24, No. 50, December 11, 1943, pp. 1024 and 1026. Review of *Greek Fire* by Andre Michalopoulos; *Miracle in Hellas* by Betty Wason; and *Greece Fights On* by Symmachos.

"The One-Eared Man." *The Dominant,* Vol. I, No. 2, December, 1927, pp. 11–12.

*"One Way of Love." *Time and Tide,* Vol. 21, No. 15, April 13, 1940, p. 394. Review of *Passion and Society* by Denis de Rougemont.

"On the Sanctissimum: With an Epilogue." *Theology,* Vol. XLIII, No. 255, September, 1941, pp. 141–144. Poems.

"Our Protestant Past." *The Spectator,* No. 5969, November 20, 1942, p. 486. Review of *Catholicism and English Literature* by Edward Hutton.

*"The Parable of the Wedding Garment." See under "Apologue on the Parable . . ."

"Paracelsus (Died 24 September 1541)." *Time and Tide,* Vol. 22, No. 39, September 27, 1941, pp. 820–821.

The Passion of Christ. Being the Gospel and Narrative of the Passion, with short passages taken from the saints and doctors of the Church. London: Oxford University Press, 1939. Anthology.

"Patriotism." *Time and Tide,* Vol. 23, No. 5, January 31, 1942, p. 100. Review of *The Moral Blitz* by Bernard Causton.

"Percivale's Song." In *New English Poems,* collected by Lascelles Abercrombie. London: Victor Gollancz, Ltd., 1931.

"The Periodical." *The Periodical,* Vol. 24, No. 200, July, 1939, p. 77. Poem.

"Personalism?" *Time and Tide,* Vol. 24, No. 48, November 27, 1943, p. 971. Letter.

"Petrarch and the Middle Ages." *Time and Tide,* Vol. 24, No. 45, November 6, 1943, pp. 907–908. Review of *Petrarch and the Renascence* by J. H. Whitfield.

The Place of the Lion. London: Faber & Faber Ltd., 1952. (1931) Novel.

Poems of Conformity. London: Oxford University Press, 1917.

"Poetry and Other Things." *Time and Tide,* Vol. 22, No. 18, May 3, 1941, pp. 365–366. Review of *Noble Castle* by Christopher Hollis; *Poetry and the Modern World* by David Daiches; and *The Faith in England* by A. Herbert Rees.

Poetry at Present. London: Oxford University Press, 1930. Literary criticism.

"The Poetry of Health." *Time and Tide,* Vol. 21, No. 40, October 5, 1940. p. 990. Review of *East Coker* by T. S. Eliot.

"A Poet's Notebook." *Time and Tide,* Vol. 24, No. 26, June 26, 1943, pp. 524–525. Review of *A Poet's Notebook* by Edith Sitwell.

"A Poet's Papers." *Time and Tide,* Vol. XVIII, No. 8, February 20, 1937, p. 238. Letter.

"The Productions of Time." *Time and Tide,* Vol. 22, No. 4, January 25, 1941, pp. 72–73. Review of theological works by Dom Bernard Clements, F. R. Barry, Leslie D. Weatherhead, A. A. David, C. A. Alington, and J. V. Langmead Casserley.

"The Prophetic Vision." *Time and Tide,* Vol. 23, No. 14, April 4, 1942, p. 294. Review of *Poetry and Prophecy* by N. K. Chadwick, and *Nostradamus: Or the Future Foretold* by James Laver.

Queen Elizabeth [I]. London: Duckworth, 1936. Biography.

"Queen Victoria." In *More Short Biographies,* ed. by R. C. Goffin. London: Oxford University Press, 1938.

Reason and Beauty in the Poetic Mind. London: Oxford University Press, 1933. Literary Criticism.

"The Recovery of Spiritual Initiative." *Christendom, A Journal of Christian Sociology,* Vol. X, No. 40, December, 1940, pp. 238–249.

*"The Redeemed City." *The Dublin Review,* Vol. 209, No. 419, October, 1941, pp. 120–128.

The Region of the Summer Stars. London: Oxford University Press, 1944.

*"Rejoice in the Lamb." See under "Men and Books" (B).

Religion and Love in Dante. London: The Dacre Press: A. and C. Black Ltd., 1941. Pamphlet.

*"Religious Drama." *Good Speech* (Quarterly Review of the Speech Fellowship), April, 1938.

"Renovations of Intelligence." *Time and Tide,* Vol. 22, No. 33, August 16, 1941, pp. 689–690. Review of *The Mind of the Maker* by Dorothy L. Sayers, and *The Recovery of the West* by Michael Roberts.

"Reunion." *Time and Tide,* Vol. XX, No. 14, April 8, 1939, pp. 450–451. Review of *The Family Reunion* by T. S. Eliot.

Reviews, untitled, of:

Auden, W. H. *New Year Letter. The Dublin Review,* Vol. 209, No. 418, July, 1941, pp. 99–101.

Barrett, Helen M. *Boethius. The Dublin Review,* Vol. 207, No. 415, October, 1940, pp. 252–253.

Brittain, Vera. *The Testament of Friendship. Theology,* Vol. XL, No. 238, April, 1940, p. 319.

de la Mare, Walter. *Collected Poems. The Dublin Review,* Vol. 211, No. 423, October, 1942, pp. 185–186.

Every, George S.S.M. *Christian Discrimination. Theology.* Vol. XLII, No. 249, March, 1941, pp. 182–183.

Ford, Ford Madox. *The March of Literature. Theology,* Vol. XL, No. 238, April, 1940, pp. 311–313.

Kipling, Rudyard. *A Choice of Kipling's Verse.* Made by T. S. Eliot. *The Dublin Review,* Vol. 210, No. 421, April, 1942, pp. 207–208.

Langton, Edward. *Good and Evil Spirits. Theology,* Vol. XLV, No. 269, November, 1942, pp. 232–234.

Lewis, C. S. *The Problem of Pain. Theology,* Vol. XLII, No. 247, January, 1941, pp. 62–63.

Lewis, C. S. *The Screwtape Letters. The Dublin Review,* Vol. 211, No. 423, October, 1942, pp. 170–171.

Messner, The Very Rev. Monsignor J. *Man's Suffering and God's Love. The Dublin Review,* Vol. 210, No. 420, January, 1942, pp. 73–74.

Murry, J. Middleton. *The Betrayal of Christ by the Churches. The Dublin Review,* Vol. 208, No. 416, January, 1941, pp. 127–129.

The New Testament in Basic English. Theology, Vol. XLIII, No. 254, August, 1941, pp. 117–118.

Nicodemus. *Renascence. The Dublin Review,* Vol. 213, No. 427, October, 1943, pp. 192–193.

Richey, M. F. *Essays on the Medieval German Love Lyrics. The Dublin Review,* Vol. 213, No. 426, July, 1943, pp. 94–96.

Rodgers, W. R. *Awake! The Dublin Review,* Vol. 209, No. 419, October, 1941, p. 216.

Rowse, A. L. *Poems of a Decade. The Dublin Review,* Vol. 210, No. 420, January, 1942, p. 95.

Sampson, Ashley. *The Ghost of Mr. Brown. Theology,* Vol. XLIII, No. 256, October, 1941, p. 256.

Sitwell, Edith. *Edith Sitwell's Anthology. Life and Letters Today,* Vol. 25, No. 33, May, 1940, pp. 211–213.

Sitwell, Edith. *Street Songs. The Dublin Review,* Vol. 210, No. 421, April, 1942, pp. 208–209.

Thomas, Dylan. *The Map of Love. Life and Letters Today,* Vol. 23, No. 27, November, 1939, pp. 237–239.

Tillotson, Geoffrey. *Essays in Criticism and Research. The Dublin Review,* Vol. 210, No. 421, April, 1942, pp. 202–203.

Tillyard, E. M. W. *The Miltonic Setting: Past and Present. The Criterion,* Vol. XVII, No. LXIX, July, 1938, pp. 738–740.

Woodruff, Douglas, ed. *For Hilaire Belloc. The Dublin Review,* Vol. 212, No. 424, January, 1943, pp. 85–87.

"Rimbaud and the Poetic Change." *Time and Tide,* Vol. XIX, No. 24, June 11, 1938, p. 832. Review of *Arthur Rimbaud* by Enid Starkie.

Rochester. London: Arthur Barker Ltd., 1935. Biography.

"The Romantic Imagination." *The New English Weekly and The New Age,* Vol. XXVII, No. 4, May 10, 1945, pp. 33–34. Review of *Romanticism Comes of Age* by Owen Barfield.

"Romanticism." *Time and Tide,* Vol. 23, No. 52, December 26, 1942, pp. 1045–1046. Review of *The Romantics: An Anthology* chosen by Geoffrey Grigson.

"The Romantic Need." *Time and Tide,* Vol. 21, No. 5, February 3, 1940, pp. 113–114. Review of *Tradition and Romanticism* by B. Ifor Evans.

"St. Anselm's Rabbit." *Time and Tide,* Vol. 24, No. 41, October 9, 1943, p. 828. Review of *He Who Is* by E. L. Mascall.

*"St. John." See under "St. John and Dr. Singer."

*"St. John and Dr. Singer." *Time and Tide,* Vol. 24, No. 30, July 24, 1943, pp. 614–615. Review of *Christianity According to St. John* by W. F. Howard, and *The Christian Failure* by Charles Singer.

"St. John of the Cross: 1542–91." *Time and Tide,* Vol. 23, No. 26, June 27, 1942, p. 522.

"Scene from a Mystery." *The New Witness,* Vol. XV, No. 371, December 12, 1919, pp. 70–73. Play.

Seed of Adam and Other Plays. With an Introduction by Anne Ridler. London: Oxford University Press, 1948. Containing "Seed of Adam," "The Death of Good Fortune," "The House by the Stable," and "Grab and Grace."

*"Sensuality and Substance." *Theology,* Vol. XXXVIII, No. 227, May, 1939, pp. 352–360.

Shadows of Ecstasy. London: Faber & Faber Ltd., 1948. (1933) Novel.

*"Shakespeare." *Time and Tide,* Vol. 25, No. 28, July 8, 1944, p. 598. Review of *Shakespeare and the Popular Dramatic Tradition* by S. L. Bethell.

"Shakespeare's History." *Time and Tide,* Vol. 26, No. 15, April 14, 1945, p. 314. Review of *Shakespeare's History Plays* by E. M. W. Tillyard.

A Short Life of Shakespeare. Abridged by Charles Williams from Sir William Chambers's *William Shakespeare: A Study of Facts and Problems.* London: Oxford University Press, 1933.

The Silver Stair. London: Herbert and Daniel, 1912. Poems.

*"The Society of Jesus." *Time and Tide,* Vol. 22, No. 9, March 1, 1941, pp. 176–177. Review of *The Origin of the Jesuits* by James Brodrick, S.J.

"Soul and Body—and Both." *Time and Tide,* Vol. 21, No. 37, September 14, 1940, p. 927. Review of *The Idea of the Soul in Western Philosophy and Science* by William Ellis.

*"Sound and Variations." See under "Notes on the Way" (B).

"Stabat Mater Dolorosa." Set to music by George Olroyd, English translation by Charles Williams. London: Oxford University Press, 1926.

" 'Staring at Miracle.' " *Time and Tide,* Vol. XVIII, No. 49, December 4, 1937, pp. 1674 and 1676. Review of *A Vision* by W. B. Yeats.

Stories of Great Names. London: Oxford University Press, 1937.

Stories Retold by Charles Williams
  The Ring and the Book by Robert Browning. Story retold by Charles Williams. Bombay: Oxford University Press, 1934.
  The Story of the Aeneid. Retold by Charles Williams. Bombay: Oxford University Press, 1936.

"Taliessin in the Rose-Garden." *The Dublin Review,* Vol. 208, No. 416, January, 1941, pp. 82–86. Poem. [Somewhat different from the version in *The Region of the Summer Stars.*]

"Taliessin's Song of Lancelot's Mass." In *New English Poems: . . .* Collection made by Lascelles Abercrombie. London: Victor Gollancz Ltd., 1931. Poem. [Somewhat different from the version in *Taliessin through Logres.*]

Taliessin through Logres. London: Oxford University Press, 1938. [The first four of the poems herein were printed, in an earlier version, in *Christendom, A Journal of Christian Sociology,* Vol. VIII, No. 29, March, 1938, pp. 19–30.]

"Tasso." *Time and Tide,* Vol. 25, No. 11, March 11, 1944, p. 216.

"Taste in Literature." *The Listener,* Vol. XXIV, No. 624, 26 December 1940, pp. 913–914. Transcript of discussion.

"The Theology of Crisis." *Time and Tide,* Vol. 21, No. 24, June 15, 1940, pp. 644–645. Review of *The Terrible Crystal* by M. Chaning-Pearce; *The Fate of Modern Culture* by J. V. Langmead Casserley; *God the Living and the True* by D. M. MacKinnon; and *Man, His Origin and Destiny* by E. L. Mascall.

"They Will Examine." *Time and Tide,* Vol. 24, No. 15, April 10, 1943, p. 299. Review of *Spirit of Flame* by E. Allison Peers, and *Donne: A Spirit in Conflict* by Evelyn Hardy.

Thomas Cranmer of Canterbury. In *Four Modern Verse Plays,* ed. by E. Martin Browne. Penguin Books, 1957. (1936)

Three Plays. London: Oxford University Press, 1931. Containing "The Witch," "The Chaste Wanton," and "The Rite of the Passion."

"To Music." *The Dominant,* Vol. I, No. 8, June, 1928, p. 40. Poem.

"Transition and Decision." *Time and Tide,* Vol. 21, No. 10, March 9, 1940, pp. 254–255. Review of *The Novel and the Modern World* by David Daiches.

"Trial by Symbols." *Week-End Review,* Vol. VIII, No. 179, August 12, 1933, pp. 168–169. Review of *Trial by Virgins* by David Larg.

" 'Troilus and Cressida' and 'Hamlet.' " In *Shakespeare Criticism 1919–1935.* Selected and with an Introduction by Anne Ridler. London: Oxford University Press, 1936.

"The Twenty-Fourth of May, 1738." *Time and Tide,* Vol. XIX, No. 21, May 21, 1938, pp. 722–723. Review of *Wesley's England* by J. H. Whiteley, and *England: Before and After Wesley* by J. Wesley Bready.

*"Two Brief Essays on Shakespearean Topics." See under "Shakespeare" and "Falstaff and Prince Henry."

"Uncommon Fairness." *Time and Tide,* Vol. 21, No. 52, December 28, 1940, pp. 1274–1275. Review of *Augustans and Romantics, 1689–1830* by H. P. W. Dyson and John Butt.

"An Urbanity." Poem, privately printed about 1927.

*"Vergil." *Time and Tide,* Vol. 25, No. 14, April 1, 1944, pp. 289–290. Review of *Roman Vergil* by W. Jackson Knight.

"A Verse Letter on Verse." *Time and Tide,* Vol. 24, No. 24, June 12, 1943, p. 484. Review of *Season and Festival* by Herbert Palmer; *Selected Poems* by John Hall, Keith Douglas, and Norman Nicholson; and *Selected Poems* by Herman Melville.

*"Victorian Narrative Verse." See under *Introductions and Editorial Work.*

"The Virgin Birth." *Time and Tide,* Vol. 24, No. 14, April 3, 1943, p. 276.

Review of *The Virgin Birth in History and Faith* by Douglas Edwards.
*"War and the Church." *Time and Tide*, Vol. 21, No. 36, September 7, 1940,
    pp. 910–911. Review of *The Early Christian Attitude to War* by C. St.
    John Cadoux, and *This War and Christian Ethics: A Symposium*.
"The War for Compassion." *The Sword of the Spirit*, May, 1941, p. 7.
War in Heaven. London: Faber & Faber Ltd., 1947. (1930) Novel.
*"The Way of Affirmation." See under "The Church Looks Forward."
The Way of Exchange. London: James Clarke and Company Ltd., 1941.
    Pamphlet.
"Ways of the Soul." *The New English Weekly and The New Age*, Vol. XX,
    No. 11, January 8, 1942, pp. 103–104. Review of *Grey Éminence* by
    Aldous Huxley.
[*Essay in] *What the Cross Means to Me: A Theological Symposium*. London:
    James Clarke and Company, Ltd., 1943. [*"The Cross"]
Windows of Night. London: Oxford University Press, 1924. Poems.
Witchcraft. London: Faber & Faber Ltd., 1941. History.
"Ximenez of Spain." *Time and Tide*, Vol. 21, No. 22, June 1, 1940, pp.
    587–588. Review of *Grand Inquisitor* by Walter Starkie.

                               OTHER WORKS CITED
Dante Alighieri. *The Comedy: Hell and Purgatory*. Translated by Dorothy L.
    Sayers. Penguin Books, 1949 and 1955.
Lewis, C. S. *The Allegory of Love*. London: Oxford University Press, 1953.
Lewis, C. S. *That Hideous Strength*. New York: Macmillan Company, 1946.
Lewis, C. S. "Williams and the Arthuriad." In *Arthurian Torso*, Containing
    the Posthumous Fragment of the Figure of Arthur by Charles Williams
    and a Commentary on the Arthurian Poems of Charles Williams by C. S.
    Lewis. London: Oxford University Press, 1948.
Lewis, C. S., editor. *Essays Presented to Charles Williams*. London: Oxford
    University Press, 1947.
Maynard, Theodore. *Our Best Poets*. New York: Henry Holt and Company,
    1922.
Ridler, Anne. *The Image of the City and Other Essays* [by Charles Williams],
    Selected by Anne Ridler with a Critical Introduction. London: Oxford
    University Press, 1958.
Sayers, Dorothy L. *Further Papers on Dante*. London: Methuen and Co.
    Ltd., 1957.
Sayers, Dorothy L. *Introductory Papers on Dante*. London: Methuen and Co.
    Ltd., 1954.
Sayers, Dorothy L. *The Mind of the Maker*. New York: Harcourt, Brace and
    Co., 1941.
Sayers, Dorothy L. Introduction to Williams' *James I*, q.v.

INDEX

Charles Williams' books are not indexed by name except where an extensive illustration was taken from his Arthurian poems or one of his novels, and where the discussion might directly illuminate the study of these specific works.

235